MICROCOMPUTERS AND MUSIC

Gary E. Wittlich
Indiana University

John W. Schaffer
Purdue University

Larry R. Babb
Control Data Corporation

Prentice-Hall   Englewood Cliffs, New Jersey 07632

Library of Congress Cataloging-in-Publication Data

Wittlich, Gary E., 1934–
  Microcomputers and music.

  Bibliography: p.
  Includes index.
    1. Computer composition.   2. Computer music—
Instruction and study.   I. Schaffer, John W.
II. Babb, Larry R.   III. Title.
MT56.W57 1986   781.6′1′0285416   85-19229
ISBN 0-13-580515-5

Editorial/production supervision and interior design: Lori L. Baronian
Cover Design: Whitman Studio, Inc.
Manufacturing buyer: Ray Keating

Printed in the United States of America

10 9 8 7 6 5 4 3 2 1

ISBN 0-13-580515-5   01

Prentice-Hall International (UK) Limited, *London*
Prentice-Hall of Australia Pty. Limited, *Sydney*
Editora Prentice-Hall do Brasil, Ltda., *Rio de Janeiro*
Prentice-Hall Canada Inc., *Toronto*
Prentice-Hall Hispanoamericana, S.A., *Mexico*
Prentice-Hall of India Private Limited, *New Delhi*
Prentice-Hall of Japan, Inc., *Tokyo*
Prentice-Hall of Southeast Asia Pte. Ltd., *Singapore*
Whitehall Books Limited, *Wellington, New Zealand*

CONTENTS

AND MANIPULATION   32
    Pitch Class and Letter Class   32
    Transposition and Inversion mod12 and mod7   32
    A MODulus Function   34
    Converting Letter Names to Letter Numbers   35
    Brinkman's Binomial Representation   36

3   DATA STRUCTURES
    FOR MUSIC APPLICATIONS   40

    SUBSCRIPTED VARIABLES: ARRAYS   40
        Arrays in One Dimension   40
        A Program to Sort Data: The Exchange Sort   42
        Finding the Largest
        (or Smallest) Number   44
        Finding the Interval Succession
        of a Collection of Pitches   44
        A Generalized Imbrication Program   45
        Indirect Referencing of Arrays   48
        Counting Each Pitch in a Melody   49
        Counting Pitches with Accidentals   50
        Using Parallel Arrays
        to Convert PC Letters to Numbers   51
        Creating a Set of Pitches:
        Eliminating Duplicates   52
    TWO-DIMENSIONAL ARRAYS   54
        An Array of Triads   55
        A Twelve-tone Matrix   58
        A Prime Form Routine   61
    LINKED LISTS   64
        Programming for Linked Lists in BASIC   67

4   STRUCTURED PROGRAMMING FOR COMPUTER-ASSISTED
    INSTRUCTION LESSONS   74

    INTRODUCTION   74
    DESIGN OF A CAI DRILL LESSON   76
        First Stage: The Lesson as a Whole   77
        Second Stage: Diagramming Program Flow   77
        Third Stage: Developing
        Specific Program Strategies   79
    SOME PRELIMINARY INFORMATION   82
    TITLE AND INITIALIZATION SUBROUTINES   82
    DIRECTIONS AND FINAL STATISTICS   83
    THE GET SUBROUTINE   85
    MAIN INDEX AND INPUT SUBROUTINES   85

PREFACE

With the proliferation of books on microcomputer hardware and software, it may seem impractical to contribute still another book on computing. Yet books that address microcomputer applications in music are virtually nonexistent. Examples of computer programs given in the many books on the market rarely include problems of relevance to musicians, with the exception of an occasional musical game or a utility program for generating sound. While this is not a particular problem in books intended for teaching fundamentals of a programming language, the absence of specific information about how the computer may be employed to solve music-related problems makes it extremely difficult to develop programs of any real significance without a considerable amount of prior computing experience. It is to remedy this lack of information that we have developed this book.

The primary aim of this book is to demonstrate how microcomputers can be used effectively in the solution of problems of interest to musicians. To this end we introduce a variety of programming techniques and algorithms and demonstrate their application in a variety of tasks. We do not deal with computer-aided composition, however, for several reasons. First, we have chosen to focus on microcomputers as they come "from the box," that is, without the addition of peripherals such as sound synthesis hardware and software. Second, computer-aided music composition typically makes use of existing commercially developed programs, many of which do a satisfactory job when used in conjunction with sound synthesis hardware interfaced with an appropriate microcomputer. Using these programs is more a matter of finding out what the software can do rather than learning about how the computer is programmed to do it.

This book focuses on fundamental concepts and programming in BASIC, which stands for *Beginner's All-Purpose Symbolic Instruction Code*. Even though there are more powerful languages available, our reasons for choosing BASIC are summarized by Arthur Luehrmann, a well-known writer on computer programming:

> More people know how to write programs in Basic than in any other computer language. Already, 10 million people own computers with Basic as the only built-in language. The number will double in the next year or two. Basic programming manuals will outnumber by a wide margin all the rest of the manuals put together.*

It seems illogical to ignore a language so many already know. As Luehrmann points out, people learn BASIC for the same reason that "people in Peoria learn English and people in Paris learn French. Quality is not a consideration. If the choice of a natural language depended on its quality, no one would learn English." So long as programs are logically designed and well-structured, then the choice of a language becomes much less of an issue.

A main concern of our writing is to impart good program design and programming habits as a basis for developing good software. For this reason, we have adopted "structured programming" as our approach to program development and coding. Such programming is based on "top-down" design which begins with an abstract, or general, idea and gradually refines the idea through a series of hierarchically organized modules, each more specific than the one above it in the hierarchy. A structured program is similarly modular and consists of a series of subprograms, or subroutines, each of which performs a specific task under the control of a main program that calls the subroutines into use. The importance of a well-structured approach underlying applications is to provide a solid foundation for programming so that the ideas introduced can be transferred to any computer with sufficient capabilities for realizing solutions to specific problems.

Our dicussion of programming concepts and applications is non-computer-specific for the first four chapters. However, because we provide chapters on microcomputer graphics and sound generation capabilities which differ significantly among computers, we have chosen three microcomputers for which we give specific implementations in later portions of the book. These are the Apple II family, the Commodore 64, and the IBM PC, three microcomputers that have captured a major share of the computing market at the time of this writing, especially for educational use. Other than requiring disk-based microcomputer systems, our programs require no hardware other than that provided

*See Arthur Luehrmann's Structured Programming in Basic, in *Creative Computing*, five issues (May–October), 1984.

with the basic computer system. For programs involving sound and graphics on the Commodore 64, we do require use of the enhanced BASIC package called "Simon's BASIC." This choice was made because graphics and sound programming using Commodore BASIC is difficult for inexperienced programmers. Simon's BASIC is widely available and inexpensive (about $29.95).

PREREQUISITES FOR USING THE BOOK

To make best use of this book, the reader should have an elementary understanding of BASIC programming commands and syntax. In particular the reader should understand the use of variables and constants, BASIC arithmetic, INPUT and PRINT commands, FOR-NEXT loops, and the GOTO and IF-THEN branching commands. The reader should also be generally familiar with the concept of a subprogram, or subroutine, and its associated GOSUB and RETURN commands. We suggest that these fundamental programming principles and commands can be mastered in a relatively few hours of self-study using one of the many BASIC manuals now available. Other BASIC language commands and concepts—for example, string functions, programmer-defined functions, and arrays—are defined and given illustrations prior to being used in applications. To aid the reader, we provide a Guide to BASIC summarizing BASIC commands and syntax in Appendix A.

ORGANIZATION AND CONTENT

The book is organized into seven chapters. The first is devoted to an introduction of the concepts of top-down design and structured programming. In this chapter, we introduce fundamental program processes that underlie computer programming and outline a systematic procedure for developing well-structured programs. Included also are the use of pseudo-code and flowcharting as program development aids.

The second chapter introduces alphanumeric and numeric data representations and manipulation. Included are several different music codes and procedures for "parsing" them, along with a number of subroutines that may be used for various music applications.

Chapter 3 is devoted to computer data structures, that is, to ways of organizing data to enable its manipulation. Arrays in one and two dimensions and linked list structures are defined and illustrated. In addition, a number of useful program utilities are introduced.

The fourth chapter deals with computer-assisted instruction design principles and programming concepts. In this chapter we outline a musical interval drill program and work through a number of the subroutines needed to implement it. Also introduced are two powerful algorithms for generating intervals and chords.

Chapters 5 and 6 deal, in turn, with microcomputer graphics and sound generation. In Chapter 5 we introduce general principles of microcomputer graphics as well as specific BASIC programs for each of the microcomputers. A main inclusion of this chapter is the outline and partial implementation of a music editor program with which music may be written and displayed on the screen. The linked list data structure of Chapter 3 serves as the basis of this program, to which we return in the final chapter. In Chapter 6, we introduce basic principles of acoustics and computer sound synthesis and then give specific music applications and code for the three machines. The chapter concludes with a melody player program for each of the computers that draws in large part on programming procedures introduced in previous chapters.

In the seventh and final chapter, we present and explain the design and code specifics of three complete programs of use to musicians, with implementations for each of the Apple, Commodore, and IBM microcomputers. This chapter serves as the culmination of the book by drawing together a number of the programming concepts and subroutines introduced in earlier chapters.

USES OF THE BOOK

There are three uses that this book might serve. First, this book is about programming microcomputers to perform useful tasks for musicians. With the great emphasis being placed on educational computing and with the increasing availability of microcomputers in homes and in schools, the computer can be a powerful tool for learning. For noninstructional applications, microcomputers can be useful to musicians for such tasks as data management and analysis. But to develop appropriate software, especially to create individually tailored programs, requires computer expertise in addition to subject matter knowledge. Even for those who do not wish to develop their own programs, an understanding of efficient and effective program design will help greatly in developing a sensitivity to good program structure. This sensitivity, in turn, becomes very useful for evaluating published software.

A second use of the book is as a textbook. The approach to program organization and implementation and the exercises found in Chapters 2 through 6 have been used effectively in a course in computers and music given annually at Indiana University as well as in a variety of workshops. We have also used many of the design principles in the development of microcomputer software for both instructional and research use.

Finally, a third purpose for the book follows from our need to know. Ours is an information-oriented society and one in which the computer plays an ever more prominent role in our daily lives. Many people, whether professionally trained in music or musical amateurs, are interested in computers and music and in the combination of the two.

ABOUT THE AUTHORS

Gary E. Wittlich is Professor and Coordinator of Graduate Studies in Music Theory at Indiana University. Since 1969, he has taught an annual course in the use of the computer for music research and instruction, and since 1980, he has given workshops in computer-based music instruction. He has received support for computer research from the National Science Foundation, has published articles on computers and music in a variety of journals, has authored instructional lessons for a variety of computer systems, and has developed instructional materials for interactive videodisk delivery under support from the National Endowment for the Humanities.

John Wm. Schaffer teaches in the Division of Music at Purdue University. He has studied music at Wayne State University and at Indiana University. At Indiana, he has also studied computer science and has worked extensively with both mainframe computers and microcomputers. For the past several years he has been responsible for developing a computer-assisted music rudiments package for the Apple II in use at Indiana. With Wittlich he has helped teach courses and workshops on instructional uses of the computer for musicians.

Larry R. Babb has studied music and computer science at St. Olaf College and at Indiana University. He has experience both with mainframe computers and with microcomputers, as well as with a variety of both high- and low-level programming languages. He has also helped teach courses and workshops in computers and music and has recently completed a species counterpoint tutorial/drill lesson for the Apple II. He has served as a computing consultant for the St. Olaf College Academic Computing Center and for the School of Music at Indiana University. He is currently working in computer-aided design for Control Data Corporation.

1

INTRODUCTION TO TOP-DOWN DESIGN AND STRUCTURED PROGRAMMING

The purpose of this chapter is to introduce principles of effective program design and coding. These principles are important not only for initial design and implementation of a program, but also for modifying existing programs—especially those written by another programmer. The design and programming principles presented in this chapter will be used for programs and program segments throughout the book.

TOP-DOWN DESIGN

The term **top-down** refers to design that works from general to specific, or abstract to concrete. The idea is to start with a concept and gradually refine the concept to include all of its logically ordered details. For example, the concept "triad" suggests first of all a collection of three notes arranged in thirds, not a specific collection of pitches. Working from the general concept "triad" to more specific instances, we might come up with the following top-down ordering:

General   triad
            major triad
            major triad in root position
Specific   C major triad : C4, E4, G4

Taking a more complex example, suppose we were assigned the task of describing classical sonata form. We can use a **tree diagram** to represent the

1

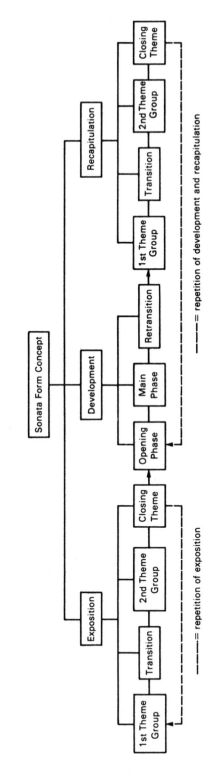

Figure 1.1

————— = repetition of exposition

————— = repetition of development and recapitulation

2

form parts in which each branch moving from top to bottom denotes an increase in specificity. For example, in Figure 1.1, the top box shows the sonata form concept, the point of departure for the subsequent branches. The next level of structure shows three branches representing the main sections: exposition, development, and recapitulation. Arrows pointing to the right illustrate the succession of the three sections. The following level shows the next main division: the theme groups of the outer sections and the main phases of the development section.

Beyond the detail shown in the diagram, we could break down the form further into the phrase structure of the theme sections, then the subphrase structure, followed by motive structure. Different persons might organize the structure somewhat differently according to individual views of normative classical sonata form, but the main point is that each subsequent level of branches brings in the next level of complexity so that the breakdown is systematic and thorough.

STRUCTURED PROGRAMMING

The term **structured programming** refers to a programming style using top-down design principles in which **modularity** is a primary concern. Developing the program as a series of modules, each of which performs a discrete task (or a series of closely related tasks), makes it easy to refine or revise the program after it is implemented and works properly.

To demonstrate the idea of structured programming as applied to a musical task, let's say we wanted to have the computer play a melody from Schumann's *Album for the Young*. (See Figure 1.2)

For the time being we'll leave aside the specifics of sound generation (which we cover later in Chapter 6). For now we'll assume that we have a command called PLAY (as in IBM BASICA) that plays a note or a string of notes as encoded; for example, PLAY "A" plays the note A, while PLAY "A,B,C+,D,E,F+,G+,A" plays the A major scale. Of course, to really encode the

Figure 1.2 Schumann, *Album for the Young*

melody we would have to provide octave specifications and durations, but to simplify matters for the moment we will deal only with note names.

To play the Schumann melody we could simply write a series of statements telling the computer to play each note in turn until all notes are played. For example:

```
10   PLAY "E"
20   PLAY "D"
30   PLAY "C"
     .

     .
etc.
     .

890  PLAY "C"
900  END
```

which would take 89 PLAY commands. This might be called the "brute force" solution!

Or, we could set up a loop and read in the notes one at a time as data until all notes were played:

```
10   READ N$
20   PLAY N$
30   GOTO 10
40   END
50   DATA E,D,C,D,E,F,G,...,C
```

This solution takes much less code than the previous one. (It also causes an OUT OF DATA IN LINE 10 error!) However, while the solution is more economical in terms of code, we suggest that there is a better, more systematic way to approach playing the melody by computer.

The solution we advocate is to organize the program to reflect the form of the melody. The form can be diagrammed by a letter scheme showing the relationship between major sections and the phrases of the sections:

A   B   A'

a b a b'   c d c'   a b a' b'

Here, as is usually the case in such diagrams, reuse of a letter means repetition of a phrase or section, and the prime sign denotes slight change in the repeated unit from its original pattern.

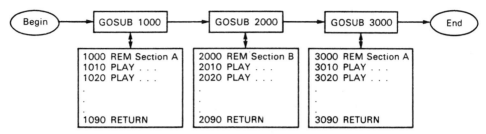

Figure 1.3

To reflect the structure of the melody, the program could utilize sub-routines by means of a GOSUB command to access a unique program module for each main section. The diagram in Figure 1.3 shows the flow of the program as "blocks" of code devoted to main and subroutine sections. The arrows pointing right show the succession of three subroutine calls, while the arrows pointing up and down show the flow from each GOSUB to its respective subroutine and the return from it.

In Example 1.1 we provide a sketch of the program divided into modules by subroutine calls. To document the code so that it is clear to the reader what the program does, we use the REMark statement for comment lines and the colon for spacing. Later we'll introduce other formatting conventions intended to help make the code readable. Note that we use lower case letters in comments and we indent code to aid in reading, even though some versions of BASIC (such as Applesoft) do not permit this.

Example 1.1

```
100     GOSUB 1000                        :REM play section A
110     GOSUB 2000                        :REM play section B
120     GOSUB 3000                        :REM play section A'
130     END                               :REM end of program
190     :
1000    REM section A
1010      PLAY "E,D,C,D,E,F,G"            :REM phrase a
1020      PLAY "F,G,E,F,D,F,C,D"          :REM phrase b
1030      PLAY "E,D,C,D,E,F,G"            :REM phrase a
1040      PLAY "F,G,E,F,D,C"              :REM phrase b'
1090    RETURN
1099    :
2000    REM section B
2010      PLAY "B,A,G,A,B,C,D"            :REM phrase c
2020      PLAY "C,D,B,C,A,C,G,A"          :REM phrase d
2030      PLAY "B,A,G,A,B,C,D,E"          :REM phrase c' in
```

```
2040    PLAY "C,D,B,C,A,G,B,C,D"              :REM two parts
2090    RETURN
2099    :
3000    REM section A'
3010      PLAY "E,D,C,D,E,F,G"                :REM phrase a
3020      PLAY "F,G,E,F,D,F,C,D"              :REM phrase b
3030      PLAY "E,D,C,D,E,F,G,A"              :REM phrase a'
3040      PLAY "F,G,E,F,D,C"                  :REM phrase b'
3090    RETURN
```

We can think of this program organization in terms of a **main** (or **calling**) **driver** portion of the program that calls the subroutines, each of which performs a discrete task, namely to play one phrase of the melody. We begin each subroutine with a comment line to give a brief description of its purpose, and each one of course ends with a RETURN that returns control of the program to the next statement after the one that called the subroutine in the main program. Compared with the solutions given above, the organization of this modular version is much clearer, both from the point of view of reading the code and for subsequent modifications.

You have probably already thought of another way of organizing the subroutines for the A and A' sections of Schumann's melody, namely to have the subroutines themselves call subroutines, each of which would be devoted to one phrase of the melody. A sketch of this solution appears in Example 1.2.

Example 1.2

```
100  GOSUB 1000            :REM play section A
110  GOSUB 2000            :REM play section B
120  GOSUB 3000            :REM play section A'
130  END                   :REM end of program
190  :
1000 REM section A
1010    GOSUB 4000         :REM play phrase a
1020    GOSUB 5000         :REM play phrase b
1030    GOSUB 4000         :REM repeat phrase a
1040    GOSUB 6000         :REM play phrase b'
1090 RETURN
1099 :
2000 REM section B
2010    GOSUB 7000         :REM play phrase c
2020    GOSUB 8000         :REM play phrase d
2030    GOSUB 9000         :REM play phrase c'
2090 RETURN
2099 :
3000 REM section A'
3010    GOSUB 4000         :REM repeat phrase a
3020    GOSUB 5000         :REM repeat phrase b
3030    GOSUB 10000        :REM play phrase a'
3040    GOSUB 6000         :REM repeat phrase b'
3090 RETURN
3099 :
4000 REM phrase a
4010    PLAY "E,D,C,D,E,F,G"
4090 RETURN
```

```
4099 :
5000 REM phrase b
5010    PLAY "F,G,E,F,D,F,C,D"
5090 RETURN
5099 :
6000 REM phrase b'
  .
  .
etc
  .
  .
```

The solution in Example 1.2 is logical; it reflects clearly the repeated phrases within the melody. Here we use subroutines that are called from more than one point within the program. These are called **global** subroutines. Those subroutines called from only one point are **local** subroutines. However, while the organization is clear and easy to read, it does lengthen the code considerably and does not add much if anything by way of clarity to the solution in Example 1.1. Thus, program structure can be seen to be a trade-off between logical design and simplicity. There are no hard and fast rules about program structure and subroutine length and organization. However, there are some structured program guidelines that we present shortly.

DEVELOPING A STRUCTURED PROGRAM

To introduce the steps to follow in planning and developing a structured program, we begin with an unstructured solution to a game by way of example. We will then solve the same programming problem in a structured program approach.

Our game is one in which the player enters the name of a composer in response to the title of a famous composition. Three guesses are permitted before the correct answer is given. There are ten titles to be guessed. Example 1.3 is an outline of the unstructured program in what may be called "pseudo-code," that is, statements similar to but not actual BASIC statements. We will use pseudo-code frequently to illustrate our discussions. Arrows show the flow of the program.

As you can see from the arrows, the flow is tangled, or as it is commonly said, is "spaghetti" code, since it seems analogous to a plate of spaghetti. Far from being an exception, this type of coding is common. It is characterized by too many GOTOs resulting in too many branches back and forth in the program. It is one of the objectives of structured programming to eliminate overuse of GOTOs and to make the flow of a program as straightforward as possible.

Example 1.3

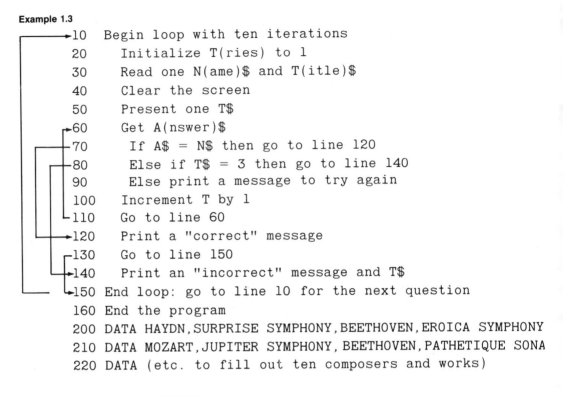

```
  10  Begin loop with ten iterations
  20      Initialize T(ries) to 1
  30      Read one N(ame)$ and T(itle)$
  40      Clear the screen
  50      Present one T$
  60      Get A(nswer)$
  70       If A$ = N$ then go to line 120
  80       Else if T$ = 3 then go to line 140
  90       Else print a message to try again
 100      Increment T by 1
 110      Go to line 60
 120      Print a "correct" message
 130      Go to line 150
 140      Print an "incorrect" message and T$
 150  End loop: go to line 10 for the next question
 160  End the program
 200  DATA HAYDN,SURPRISE SYMPHONY,BEETHOVEN,EROICA SYMPHONY
 210  DATA MOZART,JUPITER SYMPHONY,BEETHOVEN,PATHETIQUE SONA
 220  DATA (etc. to fill out ten composers and works)
```

STRUCTURED PROGRAM PROCESSES

The BASIC language has many commands, and programs can be organized in many ways. However, structured programs are organized in terms of three processes or **blocks** called **action, branch,** and **loop** blocks. All programming processes can be fit into one or another of these blocks, including nesting one block inside another.

Figures 1.4a–g demonstrate these three block types with flowcharts and short programs in pseudo-code to illustrate the processes. The flowchart symbols used in these illustrations and elsewhere within the book are shown and defined below.

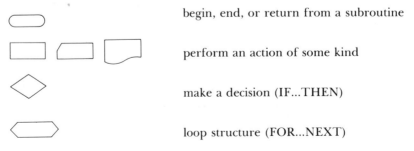

begin, end, or return from a subroutine

perform an action of some kind

make a decision (IF...THEN)

loop structure (FOR...NEXT)

Note that we give three action symbols, representing in turn a process (such as addition), data acquisition (such as INPUT or READ), and output (such as PRINT).

An **action** block is a statement or a series of statements that simply do something, that is, perform some action, for example, adding two numbers or printing something. It involves a straight-line sequence of events, as shown in Figure 1.4a.

A **branch** block always involves two paths from it based on the decision made to initiate the branch process. Branch blocks are characterized by the BASIC statement IF...THEN. Two groups of statements are involved, only one of which is to be performed. This is shown in Figure 1.4b.

Alternatively, one of the groups of statements may be null, that is, it may involve no statement. This is shown in Figure 1.4c.

Finally, a **loop** block involves doing something more than once. The shortest and simplest form of loop is the FOR...NEXT type in which the loop is performed a set number of times before exit from it.

Frequently, however, it is not known how many times to perform the action(s) within the loop. Such loops may be characterized as **while** and **until** loops. The former type repeats a process while a condition exists, and the latter loop repeats a process until a condition exists. More elegant BASIC implementations (such as VAX-11 BASIC) have command structures that accommodate the different processes. However, in most implementations of BASIC, the programming will be essentially as shown in Figures 1.4e and f.

From the illustrations, one important point is to be observed: in each

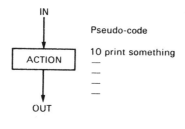

Figure 1.4a

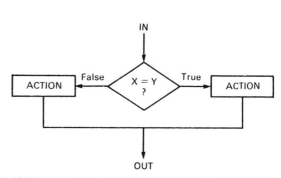

```
10 If X = Y then take true action and go to 30
20    else take false action
30 continue
```

Figure 1.4b

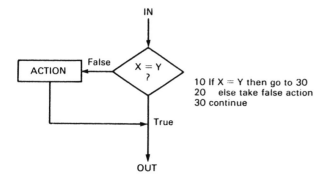

10 If X = Y then go to 30
20   else take false action
30 continue

Figure 1.4c

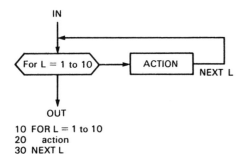

10 FOR L = 1 to 10
20   action
30 NEXT L

Figure 1.4d

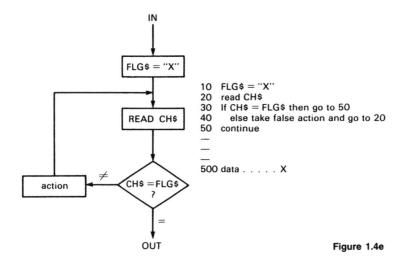

10   FLG$ = "X"
20   read CH$
30   If CH$ = FLG$ then go to 50
40   else take false action and go to 20
50   continue
—
—
—
500 data X

Figure 1.4e

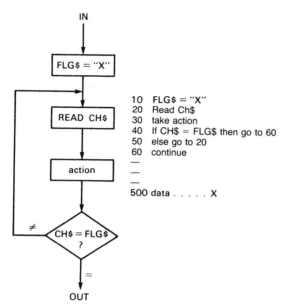

```
10  FLG$ = "X"
20  Read Ch$
30  take action
40  If CH$ = FLG$ then go to 60
50  else go to 20
60  continue
—
—
—
500 data . . . . . X
```

Figure 1.4f

block type, there is only **one** path into the block and **one** path out of the block, even in nested branch blocks as shown in Figure 1.4g.

The goal of structured programming is to organize programs as straight-line sequences of blocks, each of which performs an action, a branch, or a loop, or nested combinations of these.

Guidelines for Structured Programs

We suggest the following guidelines be used to organize a structured program.

1. As much as possible, flow of the program should be downward.
2. If programs must flow backwards (that is, upward), they should do so only under the direct control of a defined loop structure (such as those shown in Figures 1.4e–f).
3. There should be but one path into and one path out of a program block.
4. Each subroutine within a program should perform but one function (such as, reading data, printing data, playing a melody phrase).
5. If within any subroutine you are having to branch to several points both forward and backward, chances are the subroutine is too complex and you should divide it into one or more simpler subroutines. As a rule of thumb, limit subroutines to one screen of code (about 24 lines).
6. The subroutines that perform the operations of the program should be called from a main program, and the main program's chief function should be to issue these calls. Subroutines may, of course, call other subroutines.
7. Try to make subroutines "universal" by using variables instead of constants where possible. This achieves generality and improves speed.

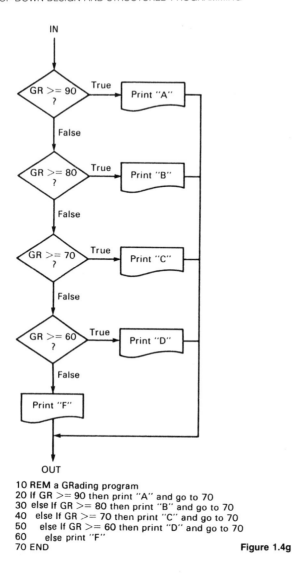

```
10 REM a GRading program
20 If GR >= 90 then print "A" and go to 70
30 else If GR >= 80 then print "B" and go to 70
40   else If GR >= 70 then print "C" and go to 70
50     else If GR >= 60 then print "D" and go to 70
60       else print "F"
70 END
```

Figure 1.4g

Steps in Developing
a Structured Program

Just as musical composition is an individual matter in which each composer has his or her own way of approaching a work, so programming is an individual matter. Nevertheless, we suggest the following set of steps in developing a structured program. As you become more proficient as a programmer, some of the steps can be bypassed, although even experienced programmers generally advocate taking a systematic approach to developing programs—particularly long ones.

1. Start with the main program and describe in simple English sentences what it does. Avoid details at this stage; they will be added in later steps.
2. Translate the sentences into pseudo-code statements or into block diagrams with arrows showing the desired flow. If more than a few lines of code are needed for each statement, chances are GOSUBs should be inserted referring to sub-routines where the detail will be included.
3. Follow the same two steps above for the subroutines.
4. Translate the pseudo-code into BASIC code for the main program section. For subroutines, all that is needed at this stage are print statements (called *echo-checks*) to serve as feedback to indicate flow of the program and RETURNs.
5. Complete the program code and run the program to test whether it operates as planned. You may find that more subroutines are needed. If so, design them following the steps above.
6. Refine or modify the program as desired.

You'll find that following this set of steps will make such program changes very straightforward.

Let us now use this development procedure to cast the unstructured program of Example 1.3 in a structured form.

Main routine: Step 1 (description)

Display a famous title
Allow three guesses to name the composer
Do ten times

Main routine: Step 2 (pseudo-code)

```
10 Begin loop with ten iterations
20    GOSUB 500              :REM name, title, question
30    GOSUB 600              :REM answer, evaluate, message
40 End loop
90 END
```

The main program is a simple loop within which there are two actions taken, namely calling the two subroutines that do the work of the program.

Subroutines: Step 1 (description)

Subroutine 500
    Read the composer's name and associated title
    Display the title as a question
    Return to the calling program
Subroutine 600
    Get player's response
    Compare it with the correct answer
        If answered in three tries then judge correct
        Else judge wrong

Print appropriate messages
Return to the calling program

*Subroutines: Step 2
(pseudo-code and diagram)*

```
500 REM subroutine name, title, question
510    Clear the screen
520    Read a N(ame)$ and a T(itle)$
530    Print a question and T$
590 RETURN
599 :
600 REM subroutine answer, evaluate, message
610    Initialize T(ries) to 1
620    Get an A(nswer)$
630     If A$ = N$ then print 'correct' message: Goto 670
640     Else if T 3 then print 'incorrect' message
              : Goto 670
650     Else increment T
660    GOTO 620
670    pause before continuing
690 RETURN
```

Subroutine 500 is very simple: it consists of only three actions. Subroutine 600, however, is more complex: it consists of a loop, within which are nested actions and branches. To help illustrate the block structure of this subroutine, Figure 1.5 provides a picture of the processes involved. Note that we have enclosed the loop and the branch blocks in dotted lines to help clarify the structure.

*Main and Subroutines:
Step 3 (skeleton BASIC code)*

```
10    REM main program
20      FOR  L = 1 TO 10                 :REM 10 questions
30        GOSUB 500                      :REM name, title, question
40        GOSUB 600                      :REM answer, evaluate, message
50      NEXT L
60      END
99    :
500   REM subroutine name, title, question
510     CLS                             :REM clear screen
```

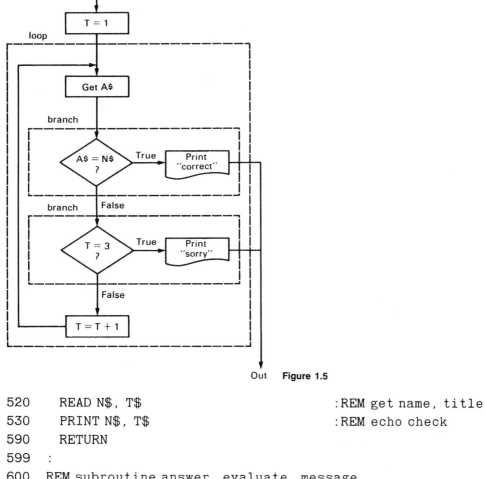

Out **Figure 1.5**

```
520    READ N$, T$                            :REM get name, title
530    PRINT N$, T$                           :REM echo check
590    RETURN
599    :
600  REM subroutine answer, evaluate, message
610    T = 1                                  :REM initialize T(ries)
620    INPUT A$                               :REM get answer
630     IF A$ = N$ THEN PRINT "OK":
                GOTO 670                       :REM evaluate and echo OK
640      IF T = 3 THEN PRINT "NO":
                GOTO 670                       :REM check T, echo NO
650    PRINT "TRY AGAIN"
660    T = T + 1: GOTO 620                    :REM bump T, try again
670    PRINT "PRESS RETURN TO                 :REM RETURN will allow
            CONTINUE"                               continuation
```

```
680      INPUT Q$
690      RETURN
699      :
900      DATA HAYDN,SURPRISE SYMPHONY,BEETHOVEN,EROICA SYMPHONY
910      DATA MOZART,JUPITER SYMPHONY,BEETHOVEN,PATHETIQUE SONATA
920      DATA (etc. to fill out ten composers and works)
```

At this point, the code should be entered and the program run to determine whether it works as intended. Try a variety of responses for input to determine whether the evaluation works as it should. The feedback from the echo-checks will provide the information you need. Once everything works in the skeletal form, you are ready to complete the BASIC code for the finished version of the program.

Main program and Subroutines:
Step 4 (completed BASIC code)

```
10    REM ##############
11    REM COMPOSER GAME
12    REM ##############
13    :
20    FOR  L = 1 TO 10              :REM 10 questions
30       GOSUB 500                  :REM name, title, question
40       GOSUB 600                  :REM answer, evaluate, message
50    NEXT L
89    :
90    END                          :REM end of program
99    :
500   REM ==============
501   REM subroutine name, title, question
502   REM ==============
503   :
510   CLS                          :REM clear the screen
520   READ N$,T$                   :REM get name, title
530   PRINT "WHO COMPOSED THE   ";T$   :REM show question
589   :
590   RETURN
599   :
600   REM ==============
601   REM subroutine answer, evaluate, message
```

```
602    REM ==============
603    :
610      T = 1                          :REM initialize T(ries)
620      INPUT A$                       :REM get answer
630       IF A$ = N$ THEN PRINT "CORRECT!":
                    GOTO 670            :REM evaluate and print
640       IF T = 3 THEN PRINT "SORRY, THE COMPOSER IS   ";N$:
                    GOTO 670            :REM appropriate messages
650      PRINT "TRY AGAIN"
660      T = T + 1: GOTO 620            :REM get another answer
670      PRINT "PRESS RETURN TO         :REM RETURN will allow
                 CONTINUE"                   continuation
680      INPUT Q$
689    :
690      RETURN
699    :
900      DATA HAYDN,SURPRISE SYMPHONY,BEETHOVEN,EROICA SYMPHONY
910      DATA MOZART,JUPITER SYMPHONY,BEETHOVEN,PATHETIQUE SONATA
920      DATA SCHUBERT,UNFINISHED SYMPHONY,BARTOK,MIKROKOSMOS
930      DATA LISZT,FAUST SYMPHONY,HANDEL,MESSIAH
940      DATA BACH,BRANDENBURG CONCERTI,STRAVINSKY,SYMPHONY OF PSALMS
```

The coded version above includes some conventions we will adopt throughout the book in our program code. First, we enclose main program and subroutine headings in REMark statements and in different symbols to set them off visually. For example, we will often set main headings in pound signs (#), global subroutines in equals signs (=), and local subroutines (of which there are none in this program) in dashes (–). Second, we indent code to help outline the block structure clearly. Code within FOR-NEXT loops is indented two spaces, and IF...THEN statements are indented one space within any level. We try to keep statements on the same hierarchical level aligned, such as successive PRINTs. As much as possible, we use line numbers ending in 90 for END and RETURN statements, and we set these off by preceding and following colons. Third, we use mnemonics (memory aids) where possible for variable and constant names so that they are easier to remember. Fourth, we include REMarks to document processes within program segments, although they are often not necessary in a well-structured design. And finally, we use CLS (as in line 510) to symbolize the command to CLear the Screen, though the actual command to do so will differ from machine to machine. We have found all of these aids helpful and recommend them to you to help you develop skill in creating structured programs.

We urge you to enter the program as shown and run it. We suggest that you then make some simple modifications to test your understanding. Among them might be changing the spacing on the screen for presenting the question; highlighting the question by inverse video (if your computer permits this); presenting final statistics in the form of the number of answers correct on the first try, the number missed after three tries, and so forth. Whatever changes you might wish to make, you'll find it immeasurably easier to make them in a structured program than in an unstructured version such as that shown in Example 1.3.

2

DATA REPRESENTATION
AND MANIPULATION

In this chapter we discuss and demonstrate ways to represent musical score symbols for microcomputer applications and how to manipulate that data. There are two sections to the chapter, one on alphanumeric, or character string representation, the other on numerical representation. Illustrations will include program segments and subroutines that can be included in music analysis utility programs or in instructional programs. The principles of data representation and manipulation introduced here will also find application in later chapters. Exercises for reinforcement appear throughout the chapter.

ALPHANUMERIC STRING REPRESENTATION
AND MANIPULATION

The 1960s marked a period when many musicians first became aware of the potential of the computer for music applications. During this time, several codes were developed for representing music in machine-readable form. The typical computer keyboard, of course, does not include music symbols, and thus music notation has to be symbolized with other than musical characters. Different codes were developed for different purposes, some for music printing, some to enable building music data bases, and some for music analysis. Often codes were developed only for specific applications without much thought given to their use by anyone other than the code's inventor. To give an idea of two of the more complete codes that have been used for a variety of music applications, especially for data base and retrieval purposes and for music analysis, we include brief introductions to both the **Digital-Alternate Representation of Musical Scores** (DARMS) and the **Music Translation** (MUSTRAN) codes.

THE DARMS CODE

The DARMS code was developed initially by Stefan Bauer-Mengelberg, a professional musician who works also in the area of computer science. DARMS, originally called Ford-Columbia code, after the foundation and university that sponsored its development, was designed to provide machine-readable representation of musical scores for use in music printing. For a variety of reasons, its original purpose has never been fully realized. However, DARMS has been used by a number of musicologists and music theorists who have found the code amenable to their needs for creating musical score data bases for research purposes.

DARMS is a complete code capable of representing nearly any musical symbol that might appear in a score notated in common music notation. For this reason and because it is an alternative musical notation, encoding in DARMS can be time-consuming and error prone. To aid the encoder, supporting software to check the encoded sample for syntax errors has been developed, along with a program called the Canonizer that translates the code into a form more easily processed by the computer.

In spite of the complexity of the code, subsets of the complete code can be used for research purposes, say for building data bases to be used for style analysis. Obviously, if analysis is to be performed on the encoded data, procedures for breaking down the code into its constituent elements (pitches, durations, etc.) have to be developed and implemented. We examine some typical procedures for this purpose later in this chapter. For now, we'll demonstrate how a simple melody might appear as encoded in DARMS.

As an example of DARMS code, study the encoded melody provided in the figure. The version of the code marked *1* is a full encoding of the melody, while the version marked *2* is a shorthand version.

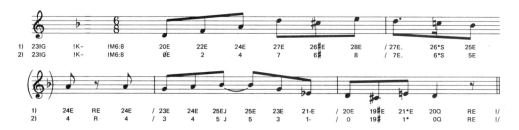

Figure 2.1 DARMS Code

Following is a brief description of the DARMS symbols used in the melody.

1. Pitches are encoded as **space** (or staff) codes. Reading from the bottom up, the lines are numbered 21, 23, 25, 27, and 29, or 1, 3, 5, 7, and 9 in the shorthand code. Spaces are 22, 24, 26, and 28 (or 2, 4, 6, and 8) starting with the bottom space. Spaces and leger lines above the staff run from 30 to 49, while spaces and lines below the staff run from 20 to 0. Shorthand versions would normally not be allowed for notes out of the staff to avoid confusion with the same integers used within.

If a second staff is needed within an instrumental part (e.g. piano, second oboe), then it is added beneath the given staff and 50 is added to 21 to denote its first line. Similarly, a third staff added below the second begins with line 121.

2. Accidentals are

= sharp
* = natural
— = flat

For double accidentals, double the ones given.

3. Duration codes are encoded with the following abbreviations for note values:

W = whole note
H = half note
Q = quarter note
E = eighth note
S = sixteenth note
T = thirty-second note
X = sixty-fourth note
Y = one hundred twenty-eighth note
Z = two hundred fifty-sixth note
. = dot

Groupettes are also provided for in the language. Ties are indicated by affixing the letter J to the first note of each tied pair. Rests are indicated by a letter R followed by the length of the rest, for example, RQ. Note in the shorthand version that immediately repeated durations (such as the eighth notes in Figure 2.1) are omitted.

4. Other symbols used in the encoded melody are the following:

a. Encoded items are separated by blanks (one or more).
b. Bar lines are encoded as virgules (/).

c. Clefs are symbolized by a number indicating the line on which they appear (e.g. 23 for G and 77 for F clefs) followed by an exclamation point (!) and the letter name of the clef.

d. Key signatures are symbolized !Knacc, where n = the number of and acc = the type of accidental, such as !K3#. When n = 1, n may be omitted, as in our example.

e. Meter signatures are !Mt:b, where t = the top number, b = the bottom number of the signature.

f. Double bars typical of endings of pieces are encoded as !/.

Study the code for its features. Note that the normal ordering of encoded notes is spacecode/accidental/duration/dot, with the tie being added before the dot.

For more information on DARMS code, see Raymond Erickson and Anthony B. Wolff, "The DARMS Project: implementation of an artificial language for the representation of music," in *Computers and Language Research*, Walter A. Sedelow, Jr. and Sally Yeates Sedelow (Eds.). New York: Mouton Publishers, 1983.

THE MUSTRAN CODE

MUSTRAN was developed by Jerome Wenker at Indiana University for use in ethnomusicological research, in particular for the analysis of folk melodies. Over the time since its initial development, MUSTRAN has been upgraded in response to user input, and it includes a software package called a "translator" that reads the encoded symbols, breaks them down into their constituents, and stores these in tables. The tables are then used as input to analysis routines written in the FORTRAN programming language. Like DARMS, MUSTRAN was developed for use on mainframe computers because it requires a good deal of internal computer memory. However, also like DARMS, subsets of its code may be used for applications on computers with more limited memory.

A MUSTRAN encoded version of the melody in Figure 2.1 is shown in Figure 2.2.

MUSTRAN's basic features are summarized below:

1. Duration codes are numbers:

    1 = whole note
    2 = half note
    4 = quarter note
    8 = eighth note
   16 = sixteenth note
    etc.
    . = dot

GS, K1$K, 6=8, 8D, 8F, 8A, 8D+, 8*C+, 8E+, /, 8D+., 16NC+, 8B, 8A, 8R, 8A, /,

8G, 8A, 8B, 8BJ, 8G 8$E, /, 8D, 8*C, 8NE, 4D, 8R, //, END

Figure 2.2 MUSTRAN Code

As in DARMS, provisions are made for groupettes, though not as extensively. Ties in MUSTRAN are indicated by affixing the letter J to the second note of each tied pair. Rests are symbolized by the letter R preceded by a duration, such as 8R.

2. Accidentals are:

* = sharp
N = natural
$ = flat

For double accidentals, double the given code for each type.

3. Pitch codes are letter names A through G, with a plus sign (+) added to the octave above middle C, two plus signs for the next octave higher, and so forth. Minus signs (−) are added similarly to indicate octaves below middle C.

4. Other symbols in the encoded melody are the following:
   a. Encoded items are separated by commas. Spaces immediately before or after a comma are disregarded.
   b. Bar lines are symbolized by virgules (/). Double bars double the virgules (//).
   c. Clefs are indicated as GS (for G Staff), FS (for F Staff), CS (for C Staff), with provisions for other than the standard clefs.
   d. Key signatures are enclosed by the letter K and indicate the number and type of accidentals in the signature, such as K1$K.
   e. Meter signatures are symbolized t=b, where t = the top, and b = the bottom number in the signature.
   f. Pieces end with the letters END as the last item.

The order of a MUSTRAN encoded pitch item is duration/accidental/pitch/dot, with ties (J) following the pitch name. Study the code and compare it with the DARMS version. Later we provide a short program to find sets of pitches in a Chopin melody using the DARMS code for pitch encoding.

For more information on MUSTRAN, see the following two articles, both authored by Jerome Wenker:

"A Computer-Oriented Music Notation Including Ethnomusicological Symbols," in *Musicology and the Computer,* Barry S. Brook (Ed.). New York: CUNY Press, 1970, pp. 91–129.

"MUSTRAN II: A Foundation for Computational Musicology," in *Computers in the Humanities,* J. L. Mitchell (Ed.). Edinburgh: The University Press, 1974, pp. 267–280.

A TYPICAL MICROCOMPUTER MUSIC CODE

Typically, those who work with microcomputers, either for computer-assisted instruction or for research purposes, do not need codes that represent all the features of a music score. Rather, there are four characteristics that are commonly represented, namely note letter names, accidentals, octave designations, and note lengths. To help remember the sequence, we use the mnemonics LTTR/ACC/OCT/LNTH. To encode the sequence, we use the following keys on the computer keyboard:

LTTR: C,D,E,F,G,A,B
ACC: + (sharp), ++ (double sharp)
      – (flat), –– (double flat)
OCT: the numbers 0 through 8 for octaves starting on the C's on the piano, with middle C = 4
LNTH: 48 = whole note
       32 = whole note triplet
       24 = half note
       16 = half note triplet
       12 = quarter note
       8 = quarter note triplet
       6 = eighth note
       4 = eighth note triplet
       3 = sixteenth note

Note that the LNTH values are proportional, for example, three triplet quarter notes equal one half note, that is 3 * 8 = 24. While this scheme does not cover all note values, it does cover the most commonly used values.

We will use the abbreviation LTTR/ACC/OCT/LNTH throughout the book to refer to this code.

STRING PARSING AND MANIPULATION

BASIC String Functions

For most programs, we need to break down the code into its parts, for example, to know how to orient music notation on a screen display (which we detail in Chapter 5). Isolating particular characters within a string is called **parsing.**

Assume that the variable CODE$ contains the LTTR/ACC/OCT sequence "G+4" for the following illustrations.

LEFT$()

To find characters on the left side of a string, we use the LEFT$() function. The parentheses following the function name are used to denote that an **argument,** that is, something for the function to operate on, must be supplied. For example, LEFT$(CODE$,1) will find the first character in the string CODE$, in this case the LTTR code, G. LEFT$(CODE$,2) would find the first two characters, G+. When characters are located by a string function, the function is said to **return** a value. One caution is that the function cannot find more characters than the string contains. Thus, LEFT$(CODE$,4) would produce an error in BASIC.

RIGHT$()

Similarly, RIGHT$(CODE$,1) will return the rightmost character in CODE$. RIGHT$(CODE$,2) will return the last two characters in CODE$, and so forth.

MID$()

The most powerful of three standard string functions is MID$(), for it can locate characters within a string starting at any position. For example, MID$(CODE$,2,1) will return the character "+", that is, one character starting at the second position within CODE$. Or MID$ can utilize only two arguments to return all the characters remaining in a string starting at any position. Thus MID$(CODE$,2) would return "+4".

Other Useful String Functions

LEN ()

In our discussion above, we noted that LEFT$(CODE$,4) would produce an error because there were only three characters in CODE$. One way to avoid looking for too many characters is to first determine how many characters the string contains, assign that value to a variable, then use the variable to control the maximum number of characters sought. The following code demonstrates one example using the LEN () function.

Example 2.1

```
10   NUM = LEN(CODE$)          :REM NUM = number of characters in CODE$
20   FOR C = 1 TO NUM
```

```
30      PRINT LEFT$(CODE$,C)    :REM print C characters in CODE$
40   NEXT C
50   END
```

Output will appear as

        G
        G+
        G+4

VAL()

By use of the VAL function, we can convert a character string representation of a number (e.g. "2") to its actual numerical value (2). For example, as we will find in later programs that call for user input of numbers, it is better to use alphanumeric data entry, that is, allow any character to be entered. This is because if a numerical data type is called for, entry of a nonnumerical type will cause an error. Once entered as alphanumeric variables, numbers (e.g. NUM$) can be converted to actual integers by using the VAL() function. For example, following the statement NUM$ = RIGHT$ (CODE$, 1), the statement NUM = VAL(NUM$) will convert "4" to 4 and store it in the variable NUM. Note that VAL() will convert to numbers everything up to the first nonnumeric character in a string, for example NUM = VAL("123ABC") will assign the number 123 to NUM.

STR$()

We can reverse the process described above in VAL() with STR$(), that is, ST$ = STR$(123) will assign "123" to ST$. While we will not use this function as much as VAL in this book, nevertheless STR$() can be quite valuable, as for example when joining together (concatenating) strings, which we discuss in the next section.

ASC()

Another useful function is ASC(). Each character recognized by the computer has a particular ASCII (American Standard Code for Information Interchange) code defined for it. The letter "A", for example, is ASCII 65, "B" is ASCII 66. In this way letters can be compared "alphabetically" just as numbers can be compared by using the inequality signs ($<$, $>$, etc.), for the computer "sees" them as numbers. We can determine intervals (differences) between letters by expressions such as X = ASC("C") $-$ ASC("A"); here X = 2, that is, X = 67 $-$ 65.

CHR$()

Finally, the function CHR$ can be used to convert the ASCII value to the character it represents. Given the integer 65, the statement PRINT CHR$(65) will print "A". We shall see particular uses for the ASC() and CHR$() functions in the next chapter.

As an example of string parsing, consider the subroutine given below. It is part of a longer program that we will return to when we discuss microcomputer graphics (Chapter 5), and we will refer to it later in this chapter when we talk about converting alphanumeric code to numeric code. The subroutine is used to get music code input from the user. The variable ANS$ (for ANSwer) contains a coded pitch, such as "G+4", entered in response to a question. The basic procedure is to examine the answer to determine if it is of the correct length, that is, if it has enough and not too many characters. If it is of acceptable length, then the string is parsed for each part of the code, namely the note name, the accidental type, and the octave designation. If any errors are encountered, then a "flag" (ER for ERror) is set, that is, assigned the value 1. After parsing CODE$, the flag value is tested, and if it is "on" (=1), then a branch back to the beginning of the procedure is made to reenter the code. If no errors are encountered, or if the user has elected to quit, then the subroutine returns to the calling program. (The symbol "Ø" is to distinguish zero from the letter O.)

Example 2.2

```
2000 REM ****************
2001 REM * Input ANS$
2002 REM ****************
2003 :
2010     ER = Ø: N$ = "" : O$ = "" : A$ = "" : ANS$ = ""
2020     INPUT ANS$ : IF ANS$ = "" THEN 2Ø2Ø
2030      IF LEN(ANS$) > 4 THEN ER = 1
2040     N$ = LEFT$(ANS$,1) : IF N$ < "A" OR N$ > "G" THEN ER = 1
2050     O$ = RIGHT$(ANS$,1) : IF O$ < "Ø" OR O$ > "8" THEN ER = 1
2060      IF LEN(ANS$) > 2 THEN A$ = MID$(ANS$,2,1)
2070      IF A$ <> "+" AND A$ <> "-" THEN ER = 1
2080      IF ER = 1 AND N$ <> "Q" THEN 2ØØØ
2089 :
2090     RETURN
```

Let's examine the subroutine in more detail. First, we use several temporary variables to store our parsed code values. In this case N$ holds the note name, A$ holds the accidental character (the next character after the first one in ANS$), and O$ holds the octave number.

As mentioned above, the variable ER (for ERror) is a "flag" to indicate whether any input errors have been encountered. The procedure is relatively simple. We set ER to 0 upon entering the subroutine. At any point where invalid data are encountered, ER is set to 1. Line 2070 then checks the value of the ER flag at the end of the subroutine, and if its value is 1 and N$ is not equal to "Q" (for Quit), a branch is made to the top of the subroutine to allow reentry of data.

Line 2010 initializes variables to the null value (the quotation marks enclosing nothing, or null) in order to safeguard that no previous information exists (say, from a previous call of the subroutine) when the subroutine is entered. After line 2020 calls for input, line 2030 determines whether the length of the input code is valid (it can't be longer than four characters, including "++", double sharp, or "−−", double flat). If it is not valid, the ER flag is set to 1. Lines 2040 and 2050 determine the validity of letter name and octave code and set the ER flag if either is invalid. Line 2060 determines whether the input code is longer than two characters, and if it is puts the second character of the code (the accidental type) in the variable A$. Then A$ is checked for validity; it must be either "+" or "−" (double accidentals will be checked later in the program).

Exercises 2.1

1. Revise the subroutine above to check for double sharps (++) or double flats (−−) and whether A$ contains the correct accidentals before returning to the calling program.
2. Revise the subroutine so that if an error is encountered and the error flag ER is set, the user is notified by a "bell". ASCII code 7 is the bell sound. The statement PRINT CHR$(7) will "ring" the bell.

Creating New Strings from Old: Concatenation

Concatenation is the joining together of alphanumeric data to form a longer string. For example, the expression

```
NST$ = "M" + "U" + "S" + "I" + "C"
```

will assign the string "MUSIC" to NST$. The "+" in connection with character data means to add in the sense of joining, not numerical addition.

It is often necessary in string manipulation procedures to create new strings from old ones. For example, the program segment below will create a LTTR/ACC/OCT string "G−5" from separate elements.

```
10 N$ = "G" : A$ = "-" : O$ = 5
20 NST$ = N$ + A$ + O$
```

The following short program will read characters from a DATA statement one at a time and build a string containing them.

Example 2.3

```
10 FLG$ = "X" : NST$ = ""
20 READ CH$
30  IF CH$ = FLG$ THEN 70
40 NST$ = NST$ + CH$ + " "
50 PRINT NST$
60 GOTO 20
70 END
80 DATA A,D,F,G,E,D,C,B,A,X
```

Note carefully line 40, which can be read: "Replace the current contents of NST$ with the current contents of NST$ concatenated with CH$ and a blank." The listing below simulates the output of the program.

```
A
A D
A D F
A D F G
A D F G E
A D F G E D
A D F G E D C
A D F G E D C B
A D F G E D C B A
```

How long is NST$ at the end of the process? (Remember that blanks count as characters.)

Finding Patterns in a String: Imbrication

Imbrication is the process by which consecutive overlapping patterns of a certain number of notes are found. For example, in the string below, the imbricated three-note patterns are marked:

A B C D E A G D B C E F

Suppose we wanted to perform imbrication on a string of pitches. In the next chapter we'll develop a generalized program that will imbricate patterns of any size, but for now we'll design the procedure so that successive three-note patterns are found and printed. First we'll show the procedure in pseudo-code.

```
10 Define a flag to denote the trailer character
20 Read three characters (C1$, C2$, C3$)
30 Print the concatenated characters with a blank
      separating each one
40 Save the second character as the first, the third as
      the second
50 Read the next character as C3$
60  If C3$ <> flag, then goto 30
90 End
```

The "trailer" character mentioned in the first line refers to a common practice in marking the end of the data in DATA statements. If we didn't know how many characters the DATA contained, we would eventually encounter an OUT OF DATA error which might cause the program to cease operation. (Some call this situation a program **crash**.) To safeguard against this kind of error, we add a character at the end of the data string that is different in nature from the data the program needs. Each time we READ a character from DATA, we test whether the trailer character has been encountered and branch accordingly if it has been.

Note carefully line 40. So that line 30 prints each successive three-note pattern, we save the second and third characters and read the next and join it with them to form the next pattern. An illustration (Figure 2.3) may make this procedure clearer. The enclosed note names in the top line are the contents of the variables C1$, C2$, and C3$ after the first READ statement. The arrows in the second line show the contents of the three variables the second time READ is encountered. The BASIC code for the program appears in Example 2.4.

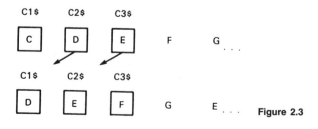

Figure 2.3

Example 2.4

```
1    REM ###############
2    REM # an imbrication program
3    REM ###############
4    :
10       FLG$ = "X" : BLNK$ = " "            :REM initialize
20       READ C1$, C2$, C3$                  :REM read three notes
30       PRINT C1$ + BLNK$ + C2$ + BLNK$ + C3$ :REM print pattern
35   :
40       C1$ = C2$ : C2$ = C3$               :REM save C2$, C3$
45   :
50       READ C3$                            :REM read next note
60        IF C3$ <> FLG$ THEN 30             :REM loop
80   :
90       END
100      DATA C,D,E,F,G,E,C,E,D,C,X
```

In addition to the importance of line 40, notice also line 10. In line 60 we could have simply used the literal "X" in place of the variable FLG$, and in line 30 we could have written the literal blank, " ", instead of the variable BLNK$. However, in "pattern matching" programs such as this one, when the patterns are sought frequently, as in a loop, it is more efficient to assign the string constant to a variable and use the variable in pattern matching statements. It is also easier to change such simple assignment statements if you decide to change string constants than it is to go through the program and change the constants in the various pattern matching statements.

Exercises 2.2

1. Use concatenation to retrograde a string of encoded note values in the LTTR/ACC/OCT format.
2. Use the MID$() function to find the fifth through the eighth characters in a string. You might do this in a loop, finding one character at a time, or you might find all characters at once.
3. Replace the fifth through the eighth characters in a string by four other characters. (Hint: Build a new string from the old one containing the new characters.)
4. Given a LTTR/ACC/OCT/LNTH code, print each character in turn moving from left to right through the string.
5. Given a LTTR/ACC/OCT encoded melody with some notes containing accidentals and others not, print only the notes with accidentals. (How can you do this without looking for specific accidentals?)

6. Given a LTTR/ACC/OCT encoded melody, find each octave code and print the string containing all the octave codes in the melody.

7. Given a string of LTTR codes, find all imbricated two-note patterns and print a message indicating which note of the pair, first or second, is higher in pitch. (In this exercise, assume that "A" is lower than "B" is lower than "C", etc.)

8. Print the ASCII codes of each LTTR in a string of LTTR/ACC encoded pitches.

NUMERICAL DATA REPRESENTATION AND MANIPULATION

Pitch Class and Letter Class

The term **pitch class** (abbreviated "pc") refers to a note and any and all octave and enharmonic duplications of the note, assuming equal-tempered tuning. Thus "C" stands for all C's, B sharps (B+ on the computer), D−− (D double flat), and so forth. There are twelve pitch classes representing the twelve notes of the chromatic scale. Pitch classes are often represented as the twelve numbers 0, 1, 2, 3, 4, 5, 6, 7, 8, 9, 10, and 11, in which the distance between any pair represents an interval in semitones (half steps). Any chromatic scale member may be thought of as the zero element, though it is common practice to think of C as zero. Pitch class letter names and associated numbers are shown below.

B+/C	C+/D−	D	D+/E−	E/F−	E+/F	F+/G−	G	G+/A−	A	A+/B−	B/C−
0	1	2	3	4	5	6	7	8	9	10	11

The term **letter class** (abbreviated "lc") refers to the seven letter names C, D, E, F, G, A, and B, irrespective of octave. By parallel with pitch classes, letter classes may be represented as the set of seven numbers 0, 1, 2, 3, 4, 5, and 6. The distance between any pair of letter classes represents a "generic" interval. For example, the distance 1 represents the distance between adjacent letters, or all qualities of "seconds," the distance 2 represents all qualities of thirds, and so forth. Letter class names and numbers appear below.

Letter class names:	C	D	E	F	G	A	B
Letter class numbers:	0	1	2	3	4	5	6

Both pitch classes and letter classes are very important to computer applications in music, and we will see uses of each of the classes in the following sections and chapters.

Transposition and Inversion
mod12 and mod7

The number of integers in each of the pitch class and letter class number systems is called the **modulus** of the system. Frequently, the term **mod12** is used to refer to the pitch class numbers, and **mod7** is used for the letter class numbers.

In keeping with the idea of a number system, any "operation" (for example, addition and subtraction), on numbers within the system must yield a number in the system. For example, transposition in these systems is addition mod12 or mod7. In the pitch class system, if C = 0, then transposition by perfect fifth upward is found by adding 7 (7 semitones, or a perfect fifth) to 0, thus giving 7, or G. Similarly, if C = 0, then transposition of G (pc 7 relative to C) upward by perfect fifth is 7 + 7, or 14. However, 14 is greater than 11, so we must reduce 14 to a mod12 number by subtracting 12 from it, which gives pc 2, or D.

Transposition of letter class numbers gives "generic" intervals, that is, seconds, thirds, fourths, and so forth, irrespective of quality. A fifth in letter class numbers is 4. Thus adding a fifth to any letter class, say 2 (D), will give the generic fifth above that letter, in this case 6 (or A above D). Adding a fifth to A will give E, or (6 + 4) − 7 = 3 (E).

Inversion of pitch and letter class numbers is equivalent to subtraction mod12 or mod7. To find the inversion of a pitch class number or an interval in semitones, subtract the number from 12. For example, the inversion of a perfect fifth (7) is a perfect fourth (5), or 12 − 7. The inversion of 0 is 0. That is 12 − 0 = 12, but since 12 is greater than 11, 12 must be subtracted from it, to give 0.

With letter classes, inversions are found similarly in the mod7 system, and again the resultant intervals or letter class numbers are generic types. For example, a sixth (5) inverts to a third (2), that is, 7 − 5 = 2. Again, 0 inverts to 0.

Finally, transposition can be applied to an inverted interval or note name. In the mod12 system, a C major triad can be inverted to produce the F minor triad and be transposed up a major third to produce the A minor triad:

C major triad:	0	4	7
Invert mod12:	0	8	5
Transpose by 4:	4	0	9

The following musical notation will help make transposed inversion easier to visualize:

0   4   7   0   8   5   4   0   9

Remember that inversion produces the contour mirror of the starting interval or chord, so that C E G is mirrored by C A− F, the latter of which is transposed to E C A in this example.

Inversion followed by transposition can also be applied to letter class numbers. Try the similar mod7 process with the letter classes C E G (0 2 4). First invert relative to 0, giving C A F (0 5 3); remember that inversion mod7 is generic, not interval specific. Then transpose up a third (1c 2), giving the letter class triad E C A (2 0 5).

A MODulus Function

While some BASICs (such as IBM PC BASICA) include a built-in mod function, these functions are not sufficient for all modulus operations that are needed in numerical pitch/letter class manipulations. For this reason, we must resort to defining both a mod7 and a mod12 function to accommodate our needs.

User-defined functions within the BASIC language make this possible. Here are the function definitions we need:

Example 2.5

```
DEF FN M7(X) = INT((X/7 - INT(X/7)) * 7 + 0.05)
DEF FN M12(X) = INT((X/12 - INT(X/12)) * 12 + 0.05)
```

The name of each function is M7 and M12, respectively. We'll follow the mod7 function through one application, getting the mod7 equivalent of the number 13:

```
FN M7(13) = INT((13/7 - INT(13/7)) * 7 + 0.05)
          = INT((1.86 - INT(1.86)) * 7 + 0.05)
          = INT((1.86 -        1)  * 7 + 0.05)
          = INT(0.86              * 7 + 0.05)
          = INT(6.02                   + 0.05)
          = INT(6.07)
          = 6
```

One thing to remember about user-defined functions is that the function definition (as shown above) must precede any use of the function. The function can be called as in the statement below:

> PRINT FN M7(LN), where the variable LN in the function argument is any whole number.

Note that the argument in the function definition given above used the variable name X, while we called the function with the variable LN. This is legal, for the variable named in the definition argument is a place holder, or a dummy, name which is filled by the value passed from the function call. Function arguments can be constants, variables, and subscripted variables (array variables), the latter of which are discussed in the following chapter on data structures. Note that the call must contain the FN in the call, for example, PRINT FN M7(12).

Converting Letter Names
to Letter Class Numbers

It is often necessary to convert letter class names to letter class numbers. A formula for performing the conversion is given in Example 2.6

Example 2.6

```
LTTR = FN M7(ASC(LTTR$) - 67)
```

In the formula, LTTR$ contains any legal letter class name. The ASCII codes for the alphabet begin with "A" = 65, "B" = 66, "C" = 67. Since C is the zero reference point for the letter classes, the argument of the function yields -2 for the letter "A" (that is, $65 - 67 = -2$). The value -2 is passed to the function definition, and the value returned from the function application and assigned to LTTR is 5, the letter class number for the letter "A." Similarly, the letter "B" will yield a -1, which converts to a value of 6. The table below shows the mod7 conversion of the letters to letter class numbers.

$$\text{"A"} = \text{mod7}(-2) = 5$$
$$\text{"B"} = \text{mod7}(-1) = 6$$
$$\text{"C"} = \text{mod7}(0) \quad = 0$$
$$\text{"D"} = \text{mod7}(1) \quad = 1$$
$$\text{"E"} = \text{mod7}(2) \quad = 2$$
$$\text{"F"} = \text{mod7}(3) \quad = 3$$
$$\text{"G"} = \text{mod7}(4) \quad = 4$$

The above formula does not account for accidentals. This is accomplished by the following formula, assuming "+" = sharp, and "−" = flat.

Example 2.7

```
ACC = 44 - ASC(ACC$)
```

The ASCII code for "+" is 43 and for "−" is 45. Thus a flat becomes $44 - 45$, or -1, and a sharp becomes $44 - 43$, or $+1$. We'll see how conversions from note names to numbers are carried out and stored in arrays in the next chapter in greater detail.

Exercises 2.3

1. Use the mod7 function to convert the C major scale note names to letter class numbers. Print the letter name of each note followed by its letter class number.
2. Given a LTTR/ACC encoded melody or phrase, parse the string for the note

names and the accidentals. Convert the letter class names to numbers mod7. For each number, convert it to a string data type by the STR$ function, and use the concatenation process described earlier in this chapter to create a string of all letter class numbers, separating each one by a blank from the next. At the end of the process, print the string of numbers.

3. Develop a mod12 drill game from the pseudo-code below. Be sure to use structured code. For example, lines 20 to 50 could be one subroutine, lines 60 to 110 could be another, while lines 120 to 140 could be designed to include a flag that could be set if the student answered "N(o)" to the question in line 120. The flag could then be tested in the main calling program to determine whether to continue or to print the concluding message and end.

```
10   Define the mod12 function
20   CLS    : REM CLear the Screen
30   Print the message "I'LL SHOW YOU A NUMBER, AND YOU GUESS"
                        "WHAT MOD12 (SIMPLE) INTERVAL IT IS."
40   Print a message to type any key to begin
50   Get the KEY$ entered and continue
60   Generate a random number between 12 and 99
```

(Note: $N = INT(RND(1) * (100 - 12)) + 12$ will provide the numbers you need)

```
70   Print "YOUR NUMBER IS  "; N
80   Print "WHAT'S YOUR GUESS?"
90   Input G(uess)
100   If G = FN M12(N) then print "CORRECT!": Goto 120
110    Else print "TRY AGAIN." : Goto 80
120  Print "WANT ANOTHER NUMBER (Y/N)?"
130  Input ANS(wer)$
140   If ANS$ = "Y" then goto 60
150    Else print goodbye message
160  END
```

4. Modify the mod12 program in Exercise 3 above so that one incorrect guess is allowed. If more than one incorrect answer is given, provide a HELP session for the student to review how mod12 numbers are determined. The HELP session should be on a separate screen display.

Brinkman's Binomial Representation

Alexander Brinkman of the Eastman School of Music has developed a code that combines both mod12 and mod7 numbers and that also can be manipulated to include octave designations. He calls this code a Binomial Representation, or BR code.*

A BR encoded note may be symbolized <pc,lc>, where pc is the pitch class number mod12 and lc is the letter class number mod7. The advantage of this code is that it enables the user to specify precisely the note desired, whereas a pitch class number alone gives no details about the particular letter name on which it is based. That is, 2 mod12 could be D, E−−, C++, or any other enharmonic equivalent of the pitch class.

Suppose we wanted to encode the note D precisely in BR code. The pc portion of the code is 2, the lc portion is 1, that is, <2,1>. The note A− is <8,5>, whereas G+ is <8,4>.

To transpose any BR code, we simply add the mod12 interval to the pc portion and the mod7 interval to the lc portion of the code. For example, to transpose A up a perfect fifth to E:

$$
\begin{array}{rl}
A & = & \langle 9,5 \rangle \\
\text{P5th} & = & \underline{\langle 7,4 \rangle} \\
\text{summed} & = & \langle 4,2 \rangle = \text{the note E}
\end{array}
$$

Remember that 16 mod12 is 4, while 9 mod7 is 2.

Subtraction of BR codes can give us intervals between BR codes. The following formula applies.

Example 2.8

```
< | pc1 − pc2 | mod12, | lc1 − lc2 | mod 7 >
```

This means to take the **absolute difference** of the pcs and find their mod12 value, and then take the absolute difference of the lcs and find their mod7 value. Absolute difference, symbolized by the vertical lines in the formula, means the difference between two numbers irrespective of the sign, for example, the absolute difference between 7 and 3 or between 3 and 7 is 4. The interval between two notes C+ and A is found as follows:

```
C+ = <1,0>, A = <9,5>
< |1 − 9| mod12, |0 − 5| mod7 > = <8,5>, the interval m6
```

However, note carefully that this procedure assumes that the note A (pc9,lc5) is the higher note. If A were taken to be the lower note, then the equivalent of an

---

*We are indebted to Professor Brinkman for permitting us to present this as yet unpublished code.

octave in both mod12 and mod7 would have to be added to the pc/lc representation of C+ in order to get the correct interval, that is, we have to know which note is higher and adjust accordingly. In this case, C+ would be modified to <13,7>. Subtracting <9,5> from it gives <4,2>, or a M3, the inversion of the m6 interval.

Intervals can be found much more easily when octave information is added to BR codes. The octave numbers are the same as in the LTTR/ACC/OCT code, in which middle C is 4. To add the octave to the pc component, multiply the octave number by 12 and add it to the pc number. Then multiply the octave number by 7 and add it to the letter class number. Here are some examples:

```
C+0  = <1 +  (0*12), 0 + (0*7)> = <1,0>
C4   = <0 +  (4*12), 0 + (4*7)> = <48,28>
E−3  = <3 +  (3*12), 2 + (3*7)> = <39,23>
```

To reduce such information to pc and lc equivalents, do the following: derive the mod12 equivalent of the pc element and the mod7 equivalent of the lc element. Given <39,23>, 39 mod12 = 3, and 23 mod7 = 2, giving <3,2>.

With the octave information added in, we can determine simple interval equivalents of any two BR encoded notes using the procedure given above: take the absolute difference of the two pitch classes mod12 and the absolute difference of the two letter classes mod7. For example, C3 = <36,21>, G4 = <55,32>

```
< |36 − 55| mod12, |21 − 32| mod7 >
= < 19 mod12, 11 mod7 >
= <7,4>
```

As a final refinement of the BR code, Brinkman adds what he calls a Continuous Binomial Representation (CBR) for the purpose of determining a set of single numbers encoding all pitches. To determine a CBR-encoded pitch, we first find a single numerical value for a BR code as shown in Example 2.9:

Example 2.9

```
encode:  BR = pc * 10 + lc
decode:  lc = BR mod10
         pc = INT(BR / 10)
```

For example, to encode the note A+ with the BR code <10,5>,

```
encode:  10 * 10 + 5 = 105
decode:  lc = 105 mod10 = 5
         pc = INT(105 / 10) = 10
```

which gives the original BR code <10,5>.

Then we add the octave number * 1000 to produce the CBR value:

Example 2.10

$$CBR = OCT * 1000 + BR$$

Given the note A+5, the BR value is 105 (see Example 2.9):

encode: 5 * 1000 + 105 = 5105
decode: BR = CBR mod 1000
            = 5105 mod 1000 = 105
       OCT = INT(CBR / 1000)
           = INT(5105 / 1000)
           = 5

Codes such as Brinkman's BR or CBR provide preciseness for determining pitch. Since the codes are themselves algorithmically determined, they can easily be programmed. In the next chapter when we take up the use of arrays, we shall see how such codes can be employed with efficiency.

Exercises 2.4

1. Read a pitch at a time from a DATA statement containing a LTTR/ACC code. Convert each note to its BR code and print both the original code and the BR equivalent on the same line.
2. Using the DATA from the previous exercise, compute the interval succession using the BR code. Convert each numeric interval to its string equivalent and put it in a string to be printed when all intervals have been determined. Pseudo-code for a generalized interval succession procedure is given below. Note that it is similar in principle to the procedure given earlier for the imbrication program (see p. 31, Ex. 2.4).

```
100 Get note 1 (P1)
110 Get note 2 (P2)
120  If P2 = trailer flag then 170
130 NTRVL = P2 - P1
140 Put converted NTRVL in string of intervals
150 P1 = P2              :REM replace P1 with current P2
160 Goto 110
170 ...(go on)...
```

3. Write a program to encode LTTR/ACC/OCT data in the CBR code. Develop the encoding procedure in the order shown in Example 2.10 above. Then decode each CBR number into its BR and OCT parts. Print each original LTTR/ACC/OCT code, its encoded CBR equivalent, and the decoded BR and OCT parts on one line.

DATA STRUCTURES
FOR MUSIC APPLICATIONS

In this chapter we discuss two types of **data structures,** arrays and linked lists. A data structure is a way of organizing data to facilitate its manipulation. Arrays provide a convenient way to store data so that each element within the array can be retrieved individually. We will discuss arrays of both one and two dimensions, the latter of which can also be called **tables**. Linked lists are data structures whose elements change in number and ordering within a program. We will discuss both singly and doubly linked versions of the linked list data structure. As in the previous chapter, exercises are provided to test your understanding of the ideas introduced.

SUBSCRIPTED VARIABLES: ARRAYS

Arrays in One Dimension

An **array** is most easily thought of as a variable with subscripts. Like other variables in BASIC, an array may be of numeric or alphanumeric data type. An example of both types is given in the table. NUM is the name of the numeric, and LTTR$ is the name of the alphanumeric array. Note that the latter array takes the "$" identifier as do all string variables. The top row of numbers refers to the subscript element, or cell, within the array.

SUBSCRIPT	0	1	2	3	4	5	6	
NUM	5	49	34	1	14	102	11	. . .
LTTR$	C	D−	D	E−	E	F	F+	. . .

In the table, we indicate by the dots that the arrays may be extended. The data we have placed in the arrays are arbitrary: any data that conform to the type of array variable defined (numeric or alphanumeric) may go in the cells. To refer to any subscripted position, the number of the subscript is placed in parentheses following the array name. For example, NUM(5) refers to the **contents** of the sixth subscripted position of the NUM array, which is the integer 102. LTTR$(3) refers to the encoded note "E−".

To use arrays the following rules must be noted:

1. The first subscript of an array is numbered 0, and the subscript numbers range upward to the limit you define in the DIMension statement (see rule 2). The upward limit will vary for each implementation of BASIC; you should consult your particular system manual for specifics. In practice, limitations tend to be related to available memory. Note that you need not begin your arrays with the number 0; some programmers prefer numbering subscripts starting with 1. But you may not exceed the upper limit number (the DIM number). The number of subscripts of an array will be the number in the parentheses of the DIM statement plus 1 (to accommodate the subscript zero).

2. You must first DIMension the array to reserve in memory the number of subscripts needed. This is done by placing the following statement **before** any reference to a particular array subscript is made in a program. Assume the array NUM will contain 51 numbers:

```
10 DIM NUM(50)
```

This will reserve 51 subscripted elements in the array NUM. Whether you use reserved locations is immaterial, but you may not use more than you reserve or you'll get an error message indicating that the subscript you referenced is out of range, and the program will terminate abnormally.

3. As an exception to the above rule, you may use as many as 11 subscripts (subscripts 0 to 10) without dimensioning the array in most BASIC implementations. All you need do is build the array and refer to its subscripted elements as needed.

4. Once dimensioned, never pass through the DIM statement a second time or a fatal program error will result. Thus be sure to place your DIM statements out of the flow of other statements.

To demonstrate how an array may be defined, we'll "load" an array called NTE$ (for NoTEs) with LTTR/ACC codes and print it.

Example 3.1

```
10    DIM NTE$(14)                    :REM reserve 15 cells
20    FOR  S = 0 TO 14               :REM load NTE$ array
30      READ NTE$(S)
40    NEXT S
50    FOR  S = 0 TO 14               :REM print NTE$ array
60      PRINT NTE$(S); SPC(1);
70    NEXT S
80    END
100   DATA F+,F+,G,A,A,G,F+,E,D,D,E,F+,F+,E,E
```

In the program, the array NTE$ is loaded a note at a time and printed the same way with a single space separating each; the SPC(1) function provides the space. The value of an array can be seen from this simple program: if an array were not available to hold the notes, once the DATA were READ they would be lost, unless of course fifteen different variable names were used, one to hold each different note!

A Program to Sort Data: The Exchange Sort

One of the advantages of an array is that it allows one to sort contents into some order. Numerical arrays can be sorted into ascending or descending order, while alphanumeric arrays can be sorted into similar ordering based on the ASCII ordering. The most common sorting done on the alphanumeric data type is to sort words into alphabetical order. The topic of sorting is a complicated one: sort procedures are numerous and depend on the nature and amount of data to be sorted. We'll demonstrate only one sort procedure in this book, the so-called "exchange" sort, but it will likely be adequate for most of your sorting tasks.

Suppose you wish to sort an array of numbers into ascending order. The exchange sort compares the first element with each of the following, then the second with the remaining elements, and so forth, until all pairs of elements have been compared. For each comparison that finds a pair out of order, the elements of the pair exchange places. The array NUM and the procedure employed are shown in Example 3.2.

Example 3.2

Subscript	1	2	3	4

NUM	10	7	9	2

RESULT AFTER COMPARISONS: *COMPARISONS:*

7	**10**	9	2	1.	If NUM(1) > NUM(2), then exchange contents
7	10	9	2	2.	If NUM(1) > NUM(3), then exchange contents
2	10	9	**7**	3.	If NUM(1) > NUM(4), then exchange contents
2	**9**	**10**	7	4.	If NUM(2) > NUM(3), then exchange contents
2	**7**	10	**9**	5.	If NUM(2) > NUM(4), then exchange contents
2	7	**9**	**10**	6.	If NUM(3) > NUM(4), then exchange contents

For any set of N elements, there will always be N * (N−1) / 2 comparisons in the exchange sort procedure.

The following program in Example 3.3 will perform the exchange sort on the array NUM defined above. The variable TTL is the ToTaL of the elements to be sorted, in this case, four.

Example 3.3

```
10  REM   ###############
11  REM   # exchange sort
12  REM   ###############
13  :
20          FOR  FRST = 1 TO TTL − 1        :REM from the FiRST
                                                 to next−to−last element
30              FOR  NXT = FRST + 1 TO TTL  :REM from the NeXT to the
                                                 last element
```

```
40              IF NUM(FRST) < = NUM(NXT) THEN 80
50               TEMP = NUM(FRST)              :REM save N(FRST) as TEMP
60               NUM(FRST) = NUM(NXT)          :REM replace NUM(FRST) with
                                                NUM(NXT)

70               NUM(NXT) = TEMP               :REM replace NUM(NXT) with
                                                TEMP
80            NEXT NXT
90          NEXT FRST
```

In the program, a nested loop is set up so that all pairs of items can be compared. Line 30 determines whether array items are out of (ascending) order. If the statement fails, then the exchange process in lines 40 to 60 swaps the two array elements being compared. Study the program carefully, especially the nested loop structure.

NOTE: For those who use IBM PCs, a command SWAP makes life simpler. Instead of lines 40 to 60, all you'll need is one line with the statement SWAP NUM (FRST), NUM(NXT).

Finding the Largest (or Smallest) Number

It is frequently necessary to find the largest (or smallest) item in a list. Assume that we have an array NTRVL that contains a collection of twenty intervals measured in semitones. The pseudo-code for a program to find the largest of these intervals is shown in Example 3.4.

Example 3.4

```
100 Set LaRGe to NTRVL(1)
110 For S = 2 to 20
120  If NTRVL(S) is larger than LRG
     then set LRG to NTRVL(S)
130 Next S
```

To find the SMallest interval, simply change LRG to SM and change line 120 to test for "smaller than."

Finding the Interval Succession
of a Collection of Pitches

A typical use of the computer in music analysis is to perform tasks that are too tedious and/or error-prone to do manually. One example is determining interval successions within strings of pitches, to use, for example, as the basis of comparisons among different melodic phrases. This is common in much musicological style analysis.

Below is the BASIC code for a subroutine that will find each interval in the array PTCH which contains fifteen subscripts ranging from 1 to 15. The subroutine also prints the interval succession. The procedure is straightforward. In lines 220 to 240 a loop subtracts each pitch number from the one to its right and prints the value followed by a space.

Example 3.5

```
200 REM ***************
201 REM * determine intervals
202 REM ***************
203 :
210      FOR  N = 1 TO RNG - 1              :REM RNG = 15
220        NTRVL = PTCH(N+1) - PTCH(N)
230        PRINT NTRVL; SPC(1);
240      NEXT N
250      PRINT
289 :
290      RETURN
```

Before leaving this subroutine, note carefully line 250, which "turns on" the line feed (that is, nullifies the semicolon in line 230) so that subsequent printing is not done on the same line as used in statement 230.

A Generalized Imbrication Program

In the previous chapter, we showed an imbrication procedure (see pp. 29–30) for determining successive patterns of three notes. However, the earlier program could not be generalized to find patterns of various sizes because arrays were not used to hold and reference the data. Now we provide a more complete program that will enable the user to enter the size of the imbrication pattern desired. We'll assume that a range of from two to six notes within a pattern are MINimum and MAXimum sizes, for these are common lengths of patterns in musical lines.

Here is the pseudo-code for the main program followed by the BASIC code.

Example 3.6

```
10  Gosub title/initialization
20  Gosub read data into array
```

```
30   Gosub size of pattern
40   Gosub imbricate and print patterns
50   Gosub more patterns?
60    If quit flag is set then goto 90
70      Else goto 30
90   End
```

The BASIC code for the program appears in Example 3.7.

Example 3.7

```
1     REM ################
2     REM # Imbrication program
3     REM ################
4   :
10          GOSUB 400                          :REM title, init.
20          GOSUB 500                          :REM read data
30          GOSUB 100                          :REM get SZE$
40          GOSUB 200                          :REM imbricate/print
50          GOSUB 300                          :REM more?
60            IF QFLG = 1 THEN 90
70          GOTO 30                            :REM loop back
89   :
90          END
91   :
100 REM ***************
101 REM * get SZE$
102 REM ***************
103 :
110         CLS                                :REM clear screen
120         INPUT "ENTER SIZE OF PATTERN (2 - 6)" ; SZE$
130          IF SZE$ < MIN$ OR SZE$ > MAX$ THEN 120
140         SZE = VAL(SZE$)
189 :
190         RETURN
191 :
200 REM ***************
201 REM * imbricate and print
202 REM ***************
203 :
205         CLS : PRINT "PATTERNS OF "; SZE; " NOTES" :REM header
210         FOR T = 1 TO CNT - (SZE - 1)
220           PTN$ = ""
230             FOR S = T TO T + (SZE - 1)              :REM one pattern
240               PTN$ = PTN$ + NTE(N) + BLNK$
250             NEXT S
260           PRINT PTN$
280         NEXT T
289 :
290         RETURN
291 :
300 REM ***************
301 REM * more patterns wanted?
302 REM ***************
303 :
310         QFLG = 0
320         PRINT:PRINT "TYPE 'M' FOR MORE, ANYTHING ELSE TO QUIT"
330         INPUT M$
340          IF M$ <> "M" THEN QFLG = 1
```

```
389 :
390        RETURN
391 :
400 REM ***************
401 REM * title and initialization
402 REM ***************
403 :
410        DIM NTE$(50) : MIN$ = "2" : MAX$ = "6" : BLNK$ = " "
420        CLS
430        PRINT TAB(10) "IMBRICATION PROGRAM"
440        PRINT: PRINT "PRESS ANY KEY TO CONTINUE"
450        GET K$ : IF K$ = "" THEN 450
489 :
490        RETURN
491 :
500 REM ***************
501 REM * read data into NTE$
502 REM ***************
503 :
510        FLG$ = "X"
520        CNT = 1
530        READ NTE$(CNT)
540          IF NTE$(CNT) = FLG$ THEN 590
550        CNT = CNT + 1 : GOTO 530
560 :
570        DATA F+4,F+4,G4,A4,A4,G4,F+4,E4,D4,D4,E4,F+4,F+4,E4,E4,X
589 :
590        RETURN
591 :
```

Subroutine 400 initializes main variables used in the program and displays a program title. DIM sets the number of memory locations reserved for the data. If the number of data is not known, the number of locations reserved will have to be at least as large as the number of notes in any melody that might be encoded. The variables MIN$ and MAX$ set the range of pattern sizes allowed. BLNK$ is assigned the literal blank as its contents. In most cases, if literal characters, that is, string constants, are to be used in pattern building or matching loops, it is more efficient to give them a name and to use the name whenever the constant is needed. The remainder of the subroutine prints the program title and waits for the user to press a key before going on. (Note that the second statement on line 450 is not necessary in Applesoft BASIC. In IBM-PC BASICA, line 450 should read K$ = INKEY$: IF K$ = "" THEN 450.)

Subroutine 500 reads the DATA into the array NTE$, using a trailer character to mark the end of the data to be read. FLG$ is assigned the trailer and checks are made as data are read to determine when the trailer is encountered. The variable CNT counts the number of characters read into NTE$ to be used as a loop variable in subroutine 200.

The subroutine beginning at line 100 defines the SiZE$ of the imbricated patterns. Line 120 defines a string variable SZE$ to hold the number entered to ensure that the program will not terminate if the user enters something other than a number. Then line 130 checks SZE$ for validity against the MIN$ and MAX$ permissible values. If the value is in error, a branch is made to line 120 to reenter code. If SZE$ is within range, then line 140 converts the string to a number and returns to the calling program.

The subroutine at 200 uses a nested loop, with the inner loop defining one pattern whose length is determined by the variable SZE, for every time through the outer loop. The loop range variables are rather complicated. Recall that CNT is the number of notes in NTE$. We want to define patterns of SZE characters, so the upper range has to be the number of notes minus (SZE − 1). To illustrate, if SZE is 4 and CNT is 25, then the upper range is 25 − (4 − 1), or 22. This means that a complete pattern of four notes can be found starting at subscript 22. The patterns to be found are defined in the inner loop, whose upper range is defined as the current value of T (the counter for the outer loop—T stands for Total notes) plus (SZE − 1). Thus if we were in the third iteration of the outer loop where T = 3 and SZE = 4, then the pattern would be found in the array NTE at positions 3 through 6. Study these range specifications carefully to be sure you understand how they are determined and control the looping.

The pattern itself is defined in line 240 by concatenation using the string building process defined in the previous chapter. The blank is added for spacing in the string. Line 260 prints the string pattern each time the inner loop is completed. Note that line 220 is very necessary, for if it were not there, the pattern would continue to grow each time the inner loop was performed.

Subroutine 300 determines whether the user wants to find and print more patterns. The variable QFLG (QuitFLaG) is set if the user does not enter the letter "M". Then QFLG is tested in the main program to control whether to loop back to line 30 or to end the program.

Study the imbrication program carefully to be sure that you understand how it operates. We suggest that you enter and run the program for practice.

Exercises 3.1

1. The imbrication program assumes that at least one pattern of the required length is present in NTE$. How would you program in a "fail-safe" to ensure that the program doesn't fail if it happens that SZE is greater than CNT?
2. Adapt this program so that imbricated patterns are found for each of several individual phrases. You will have to encode the phrases so that a trailer character marks the end of each one, or alternatively, so that each one begins with a number indicating the number of notes it contains. A loop would then have to be included that would perform the imbrication process for each phrase. If the whole program is to be redone for imbrication of different size patterns, then a RESTORE command would have to be inserted at the appropriate location in the program to reset the DATA pointer to the beginning of the data.

Indirect Referencing of Arrays

Suppose we had a LTTR/ACC/OCT encoded melody and we wanted to put the notes in each octave segment in separate strings. We would like to be able to build a new array OSEG$, each cell of which contains the notes found in each octave so that we can print the content of each cell to show the octave segment pitch activity. When we parse the code we can pick up the octave designation as the rightmost character in the string. We cannot, of course, refer to the subscript by writing OSEG\$(OCT\$), where OSEG\$ is the octave number, but we can convert OCT\$ to its numerical equivalent and use it as the array reference. This is the meaning of the word "indirect" in our subsection title above. Since the octave segment identifiers range from 0 through 8 (the lowest octave is incomplete and the highest contains only the note C8 on the 88-key piano), we need not even dimension the array. Example 3.8 shows an octave segment parsing subroutine. Assume that the string MEL\$ contains a melody of 25 notes in the appropriate encoding.

Example 3.8

```
300 REM ****************
301 REM * octave segment subroutine
302 REM ***************
303 :
305     BLNK$ = " "
310     FOR  N = 1 TO 25
320        OCT$ = RIGHT$(MEL$(N),1)
325        NTE$ = LEFT(MEL$(N),LEN(MEL$(N))-1)
330        OCT = VAL(OCT$)
340        OSEG$(OCT) = OSEG$(OCT) + NTE$ + BLNK$
350     NEXT N
389 :
390     RETURN
391 :
```

Each time through the loop, the subscript of array OSEG\$ (for OctaveSEGment) corresponding to the value of OCT is referenced, and pitches in that octave are added to that cell. The pitch contents added are defined in line 325 in which the LTTR and ACC portion of each NTE\$ are assigned to the appropriate subscript in OSEG\$. At the end of the process, those cells corresponding to octave segments with notes in them will have contents and the others will be null.

Counting Each Pitch in a Melody

It is sometimes of interest to count the number of each different item (LTTR, ACC, etc.) in a melody. Say we wanted to provide a tally of the number of different pitches in a melody. To simplify things for the moment, assume that the melody is in C major and that there are no accidentals.

We can determine the array subscripts in a way similar to that used in the octave segment program in Example 3.8. In Example 3.9 the expression FN M7 (ASC(LTTR$) − 67) will convert each letter name (LTTR$) into a letter class number 0 through 6 using procedures described in the previous chapter. Note that you will have to provide a function definition for FN M7 before attempting to call the function in line 130. Program Example 3.9 will find each LTTR$ in an array MEL$ of 25 elements and store the count in an array named NTE whose subscripts are the letter class numbers.

Example 3.9

```
110    FOR  N = 1 TO 25
120       LTTR$ = MEL$(N)             :REM find LTTR$
130       L = FN M7 ASC(LTTR$) − 67   :REM convert to number mod7 (C = 0)
140       NTE(L) = NTE(L) + 1         :REM increment array count
150    NEXT N
```

Counting Pitches with Accidentals

As a variant on the procedure in Example 3.9, following is a way to accommodate not only letter names but accidentals as well in the pitch count problem. Assume that each letter name can have associated with it five pitch inflections—double flat, flat, natural, sharp, double sharp—and that these values can be numbered as shown below:

0	1	2	3	4	5	6	7	8	9	10	11	12	13	14	...
C−−	C−	C	C+	C++	D−−	D−	D	D+	D++	E−−	E−	E	E+	E++	...

If we carried out this sequence through all seven letter names, we would observe that each natural note (C, D, E, etc.) differs from the next by 5. By applying the following formula,

$$\text{FN M7}(\text{ASC}(\text{LTTR\$}) - 67) * 5 + 2$$

we can convert any letter name to a number in the set 2, 7, 12, 17, 22, 27, 32. The subscript referenced would be one of these values plus the value of the accidental (if any) associated with the LTTR value. The accidental values are:

double flat:	−2
flat:	−1
natural:	0
sharp:	+1
double sharp:	+2

We leave it to you to modify the program segment in Example 3.9 to implement the procedure just described.

Exercises 3.2

1. Given a collection of letter class (LC) numbers 0 to 6, how would you use the function CHR$() to print the letter name of the note?
2. Suppose you want to convert a LTTR/ACC code to a Binomial Representation (BR) code defined earlier in Chapter 2 (pp. 36–39). For example, given C+ (C sharp), the BR code is <1,0>. The following formula will perform the conversion (CPC = Converted Pitch Class, LC = letter class number, PC = pitch class number):

   CPC = INT((LC * 1.8) + 0.5)

   For example, if LC = 5 (the note A), then the CPC value is 9. If we knew both the pitch class and the letter class numbers, we could determine the accidental by the following formula:

   ACC = PC − CPC

   ACC values will run from −2 to 2 for double flats to double sharps, respectively. For example, given PC = 10 and LC = 5, the CPC value from the earlier formula is 9. Supplying these values in the above formula gives ACC = 1, that is, one sharp.

   Using the formulas given, write a program that will allow the user to enter the LC and PC numerical values for any LTTR/ACC code and that will determine and print the letter name and its associated accidental (if any).

Using Parallel Arrays to Convert PC Letters to Numbers

Suppose we had a string of LTTR/ACC encoded notes that we wanted to convert to pitch class numbers. One simple way to do this is to define two parallel arrays, one containing pitch class numbers, the other LTTR/ACC code:

Example 3.10

PC	0	0	1	1	2	3	3	4	4	5	5	6	6	7	8	8	9	10	10	11	11
LTTR$	B+	C	C+	D−	D	D+	E−	E	F−	E+	F	F+	G−	G	G+	A−	A	A+	B−	B	C−

In all, there are 21 cells in each array. By searching through the LTTR$ array until the appropriate encoded item is found, the subscript associated with that item will reference the corresponding item in the PC array. Example 3.11 shows a short program for carrying out the LTTR/ACC to PC conversion. L$ is the name of the variable that holds the note to be converted.

Example 3.11

```
100 FOR  P = 1 TO 21
110   IF LTTR$(P) = L$ THEN PRINT PC(P) : GOTO 130
120 NEXT P
130. . .(more code) . . .
```

Creating a Set of Pitches:
Eliminating Duplicates

Much analysis of twentieth-century music deals with **sets** of notes, that is, collections of notes in which there are no duplicates, such as the set (C,E,G). Given a succession of pitches, the computer can determine sets. In the computer language SNOBOL (for String Oriented Symbolic Language), there are built-in procedures for parsing a string and eliminating any duplicates in the string. Unfortunately, BASIC does not provide this convenience, yet often it is helpful to be able to determine sets in a melody or phrase.

A short program that creates a set from the first four measures of Chopin's "A Major Prelude for Piano" is shown in Example 3.12. The encoding is in MUSTRAN (see Chapter 2). The pseudo-code appears below.

Read the notes of a melody into the array N$
Print the melody for reference
Begin loop: FOR I = 1 to number of notes in N$
    Put each unique note in a new string NST$
    Put "X" in its place in N$ to indicate duplicate
End loop: NEXT I
    If the last note of N$ is not "X" add it to NST$
Print the set NST$

```
10   REM ###############################
11   REM # Create a set from Chopin's #
12   REM # A Maj. Prelude, mm. 1-4     #
13   REM # using MUSTRAN code          #
14   REM ###############################
15   :
20       GOSUB 500                    :REM  init., load N$, print
30       GOSUB 100                    :REM  build set and print
89   :
90   END
91   :
100 REM ****************
101 REM * create and print the set
102 REM ****************
103 :
110      FOR  I = 1 TO 11
120       IF N$(I) = X$ THEN 170
130         NST$ = NST$ + N$(I) + CMA$
140         FOR  J = I + 1 TO 12
150          IF N$(J) = N$(I) THEN N$(J) = X$
160         NEXT J
170      NEXT I
```

```
180           IF N$(12) <> X$ THEN NST$ = NST$ + N$(12)
181 :
185           PRINT "SET FROM THE MELODY ABOVE:"
187           PRINT NST$
189 :
190           RETURN
191 :
500 REM ****************
501 REM * initialize, load N$, print melody (N$)
502 REM ****************
503 :
510           DIM N$(12)                  :REM N$ holds 12 notes
520           CMA$ = "," : X$ = "X"
525 :
530           FOR  I = 1 TO 12
540             READ N$(I)
550             PRINT N$(I) CMA$;
560           NEXT I
570           PRINT : PRINT
575 :
580           DATA 4E,8*C+.,16D+,4B,4B,2B
585           DATA 4*F+,8*D+.,16E+,4A+,4A+,2A+
589 :
590           RETURN
```

Output from a run of the program will look like this:

4E,8*C+.,16D+,4B,4B,2B,4*F+,8*D+.,16E+,4A+,4A+,2A+
SET FROM THE MELODY ABOVE:
4E,8*C+.,16D+,4B,2B,4*F+,8*D+.,16E+,4A+,2A+

Subroutine 500 is straightforward and needs no comment. The search for duplicates begins in subroutine 100. Note line 120: the search for an "X" must be placed in this outer loop even though the statement will clearly fail the first time through. For each time the test in line 120 fails, line 130 adds an item and a comma to the new string NST$. Lines 140 to 160 create an inner loop that searches through the remainder of the string N$ for subsequent occurrences of the character contained in N$(I). For each duplicate found, an "X" is put in its place. Since this effectively alters the original melody string, the original has to be printed when the string N$ is first created. Line 180 is necessary because the last character of N$ may contain an item not yet encountered in the search, as is the case in this melody.

Exercises 3.3

The set creation program is not generalized, for before the melody can be searched we have to know just how many notes it contains. Moreover, we can deal with but one melody in this program. Alter the set creation program in the following ways:

1. Change the DIMension of N$ to a variable. Then let the user enter the number to be used for this variable. The number will be the number of notes in a melody in any run of the program.

2. Provide for user entry of the notes to be stored in N$. Entry should be phrase by phrase, with a trailer character marking the end of each phrase and a separate trailer character marking the end of the melody.

TWO-DIMENSIONAL ARRAYS

Arrays in two dimensions, also called tables (by analogy with the typical table format of rows and columns), can be thought of as a collection of single arrays. For example, the following illustration is a two-dimensional array of LTTR encoded data, each row of which is a major scale a fifth removed from the next.

		COLUMNS 1	2	3	4	5	6	7	8
ROWS	1	C	D	E	F	G	A	B	C
	2	G	A	B	C	D	E	F+	G
	3	D	E	F+	G	A	B	C+	D
	4	A	B	C+	D	E	F+	G+	A
	5 . . .								

Assuming we were to include all fifteen major scales in an array SCL$, and that we wanted to count row and column positions with the usual counting numbers 1, 2, 3, . . . , we would dimension this array by the statement DIM SCL$(15,8), which would reserve 16 * 9, or 154 memory locations to hold the data. (Why not 15 * 8, or 120?) Again, whether we use all the reserved space is immaterial, but we must reserve as much as we might need.

We can think of this array as a matrix of 15 rows by 8 columns. To reference any cell in the matrix, we index the (row,col) position. For example, SCL$(2,5) finds the fifth column in the second row, the note D. It really makes no difference how we think about the array, that is whether rows by columns or columns by rows, so long as we load the array accordingly.

To load the array of scales, we could use a nested loop structure as demonstrated in Example 3.13.

Example 3.13

```
10   DIM SCL$(15,8)
20   FOR  R = 1 TO 15          :REM R = Row
30      FOR  C = 1 TO 8        :REM C = Column
```

Exercises 5.1

1. Write a subroutine that will draw a single or multi-line border around the graphics portion of the monitor screen.
2. Plot your name on the screen within the borders.
3. Add bar lines and repeat signs to each staff set in the staff drawing subroutine. (HINT: Use offsets so that your graphics can be added to all the staves drawn.)

DRAWING SHAPES: COMPLEX TASKS

If our musical graphics needs were always as simple as drawing lines, computer graphics would be no problem. Unfortunately, many (if not most) musical graphics requirements are much more complex than line drawings.

Take, for example, drawing a whole note. Using the line command would require eight different (X,Y) coordinates just to plot a simple "stick" figure of the shape. Certainly it can be done, but it is time consuming and is a relatively crude representation of the note. The shape in Figure 5.3 is what is drawn by the program following:

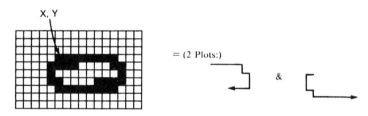

Figure 5.3

```
1400 REM ***************
1401 REM * Plot a note
1402 REM ***************
1403 :
1410      line (X1,Y1) to (X2,Y2) to (X3,Y3) to (X4,Y4)
             to (X5,Y5) to (X6,Y6)
1420      line (X7,Y7) to (X8,Y8) to (X9,Y9) to (X10,Y10)
             to (X11,Y11) to (X12,Y12)
1489 :
1490      RETURN
```

Not only is this code cumbersome, but all the values would first have to be set in the calling program. More important still is the fact that BASIC executes such multi-statement code very slowly. We could eliminate much of the calling program by using offsets in the subroutine. For example, line 1410 could be rewritten as follows:

```
1410  line (X,Y) to (X+7,Y) to (X+7,Y+1) to (X+8,Y+1) to
      (X+8,Y+3) to (X+5,Y+3)
```

and line 1420 could be rewritten correspondingly. The calling program would have only to set an initial X and Y value, but the speed of execution is still unacceptably slow. And if this is the case for a relatively simple shape such as a whole note, consider the problem of drawing a complex shape, such as a treble clef!

Defining a Shape

There is a way around the problem of execution speed and coding difficulty, namely by using predefined shapes that can be drawn on the screen, usually with one or two simple BASIC statements. The following paragraphs present a general discussion of shape creation and manipulation. As with the previous discussion of graphics, machine specifics follow at the end of this section. Because shape creation and manipulation on the Apple is especially complex, we have provided code for a shape-maker program and additional information on using Apple shapes in Appendix B.

In order to use a shape, we must first define it. To do this, we define a string of command characters that represent motions of plotting (or nonplotting) on the screen, and we assign them to a string variable. Following is a list of some of the more commonly used command characters. Our pseudo-code equivalent command for drawing a shape is **draw.**

    U = up   D = down
    L = left R = right

    B (preceding a command) means to move without plotting
    X ends a string

Let's go through an actual example by defining the note shape shown earlier and reproduced in Figure 5.4.
We begin by defining a starting point. This is important because this point will correspond to the (X,Y) values supplied to our draw command. For this example

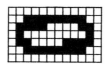

Figure 5.4

we may start with the center point of the shape, work out to one edge, and then trace through the entire shape until all the pixels are plotted. In Figure 5.5, the arrows in the plotting diagram indicate moves.

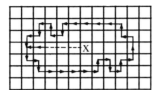

Figure 5.5

To incorporate this procedure into an actual shape definition, we assign to a string variable, say, NTE$, the command characters shown earlier that correspond to moves in our diagram. The following line of code defines our note shape.

```
10    NTE$ = "BL BL BL BL D R D R R R R U R D R"
20    NTE$ = NTE$ + "U R U U L U L L L L L D L U L D L D X"
```

In the case of a long string such as in this example, we can define substrings and concatenate them. This can also be helpful for debugging your code because you can build the shape by adding a section at a time and then drawing the shape. As soon as an error appears in the display, you know that the error is in the segment most recently added to the string.

In some BASIC implementations, multiple moves can be redefined as a single command followed by an integer denoting the number of repetitions needed for that command. For example, the above code might be rewritten as shown below:

```
10 NTE$ = "BL4 D R D R5 U R D R U R U2 L U L5 D L U L D L D X"
```

Note that while we have left a space between each command character for clarity of reading, the spaces are not necessary and in fact should be removed in actual code to increase speed of execution.

Drawing a Shape

Once we have defined our variable, it is a simple matter to draw the shape: we can simply write **draw var$ at (X,Y),** where **var$** (**var** in Applesoft) is the variable containing the information for the shape we want to draw, and (X,Y) is the starting point for our shape.

Often it is desirable to be able to draw several shapes within the same drawing routine, for example, notes of different durations within a global note drawing routine. One way to do this is to include one draw command for each value:

```
3500 REM *******************
3501 REM * draw notes
3502 REM *******************
3503 :
3550        ON (duration value) GOTO 3560,3570,3580
3559 :
3560        draw WNTE$ at (X,Y) : GOTO 3590        :REM Whole NoTE
3570        draw HNTE$ at (X,Y) : GOTO 3590        :REM Half NoTE
3580        draw QNTE$ at (X,Y) : GOTO 3590        :REM Quarter NoTE
3589 :
3590        RETURN
```

However, it is conceptually easier to define a one-dimensional array—DIM SHAPE$(3)—that would contain all the definitions and then index it as needed.

```
3500 REM *******************
3501 REM * draw notes
3502 REM *******************
3503 :
3550        draw SHAPE$(index) at (X,Y)
3589 :
3590        RETURN
```

Before we can actually implement such a procedure, there are some required parameters that must first be defined. First, we must define a **scale** to govern the size of our shape. The default value 1 will scale our shape to a 1:1 ratio, that is, just as we have defined it. Other values (up to 255) will enlarge each dimension of the shape by a ratio equal to the number defined in our pseudo-code **scale** command. For example, if we entered the statement **scale = 4**, all shapes will be drawn with both the horizontal and the vertical dimensions enlarged by a factor of 4.

Next we need to define a **rotation**. Depending on the BASIC implementation, shapes can be rotated on their axis. In some versions, the scale has a direct effect on the number of permissible angles that a shape can be rotated. For example, in Applesoft BASIC, **scale=1** recognizes four rotations: 0, 16, 32, and 48 (on a scale of 0 to 63). If **rotation=0**, the shape will be rotated 0 degrees, that is, it will appear in its original position, while **rotation=16** will rotate the shape

90 degrees clockwise, **rotation**=**32** will rotate the shape 180 degrees clockwise, and **rotation**=**48** will rotate the shape 270 degrees clockwise. For **scale**=**2**, eight rotations are recognized: 0, 8, 16, 24, 32, 40, 48, and 56. The diagram below helps illustrate the relationship between rotation settings and degrees of rotation in Applesoft BASIC.

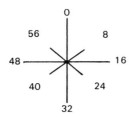

Figure 5.6

An important point to consider is that shapes are not rotated on their central axis, but rather are rotated about the point at which you started creating the shape. Thus if you wanted to create a quarter note so that it could rotate 180 degrees (say, to put the stem down instead of up), you would have to be sure to create the shape starting in the center of the note head. Figure 5.7 demonstrates the effect of rotation 180 degrees starting in two different places in the shape.

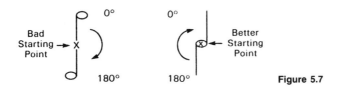

Figure 5.7

Once scale and rotation values are defined, these values remain in effect until redefined. With the following generalized subroutine, we can initialize our graphics to allow for the use of shapes.

```
1900 REM ***************
1901 REM * Graphics Initialization
1902 REM ***************
1903 :
1910       color = B/W : rotation = 0 : scale = 1
1920       (load or define shapes here)
1989 :
1990       RETURN
```

This subroutine should be called near the beginning of any program that requires graphics and shapes. Once it is run, then you may enter graphics at any point in the program by the command **hi-res** = ON and exit graphics by the command **hi-res** = OFF.

After initializing graphics, the draw command can be used to place shapes on the screen. Two parameters are required:

1. We need to supply an integer that corresponds with the order of the shapes in the array. For example, if the treble clef is the third shape, to draw it we would write draw SHAPE$ (3).
2. We need to supply a screen coordinate at which the shape is to be drawn. Remember, however, that the coordinate will correspond to the point in the shape at which we began creating it.

As an example, the following code will cause shape number 3 to be drawn at the (X,Y) location 50,100:

```
50 draw SHAPE$(3) at (50,100)
```

Erasing a Shape

Erasing a shape can be done by using an **undraw** command, which draws a shape in its complementary color. In effect, **undraw** erases the shape from the screen. A simple loop will demonstrate how to make a shape blink on the screen.

```
10  REM ***************
11  REM * Blinking shape demonstration
12  REM ***************
13  :
20      GOSUB 1900                      :REM initialize graphics
30      FOR I = 1 TO NUM
40        draw SHAPE$(1) at (X,Y)       :REM draw shape
50          FOR J = 1 TO 500 : NEXT J
60        undraw SHAPE$(1) at (X,Y)     :REM erase shape
70          FOR J = 1 TO 500 : NEXT J
80      NEXT I
```

In this example, we initialize graphics, draw a shape, wait a short time (with a timing loop), erase the shape with the undraw command, wait again, and then repeat the entire process any NUMber of times.

With more complex shapes, we begin to run into some problems with the undraw command. If at any time during the creation of a shape we cause drawing to double back over any part of the shape, then the pixels involved in the "retracing" may not erase with **undraw** and we will be left with residual dots on the screen.

The solution to the problem with **undraw** turns out to be rather simple. Instead of using the **undraw** command, we simply change the color setting to black and **draw** the shape again. Here is the modification necessary for the previous program:

```
10 REM ****************
11 REM * Blinking shape demonstration
12 REM ***************
13 :
20      GOSUB 1900
30      FOR  I = 1 TO NUM
40        color = WHT : draw SHAPE$(1) at (X,Y)
50         FOR J = 1 TO 500 : NEXT J
60        color = BLK : draw SHAPE$(1) at (X,Y)
70         FOR J = 1 TO 500 : NEXT J
80      NEXT I
```

Animation

We can actually do crude animation simply by incrementing the X and/or Y coordinates each time we pass through the loop. A simple modification to the previous program will suffice to demonstrate this possibility:

```
10 REM ****************
11 REM ** Simple shape mover
12 REM ***************
13 :
20      GOSUB 1900
30      FOR  I = 1 TO NUM
40        color = WHT : draw SHAPE$(1) at (X+I,Y+INT(I/2))
50         FOR J = 1 TO 500 : NEXT J
60        color = BLK : draw SHAPE$(1) at (X+I,Y+INT(I/2))
70      NEXT I
```

Here we have used offsets to move the shape and have reduced the length of the timing loop so that time from drawing to erasure is kept to a minimum. Study the program. In what direction will the shape move?

Note the use of the INT function within the draw command. The intent is to make the shape move down half the distance that it moves to the right. Unfortunately, we cannot move by half dots. Therefore, the INT command is

The final step is to do the actual coding of the shape using the codes discussed earlier. Once the treble (or any other) clef is created and stored in the shape array, we can incorporate it into the staff drawing subroutine we discussed earlier. However, before writing any actual code, we must decide on a way to allow the programmer to choose a clef for any staff. In this way we don't lose the flexibility we wrote into the original routine.

In order both to preserve flexibility and to be able to have access to the particular clef as needed, we can build a one-dimensional array, called **CLF,** and store the shape numbers corresponding to the various clefs as successive array elements. We will assume the following ordering and numbering of the clefs for our purposes:

1. G-clef = shape#1
2. C-clef = shape#2
3. F-clef = shape#3

If we plot two staves and wish to place the G-clef on the top staff and the F-clef on the bottom, we simply assign the value 1 to CLF(1) and the value 3 to CLF(2), for example, CLF(1) = 1 : CLF(2) = 3. We can now alter our staff drawing subroutine to include the following line:

```
1335 draw CLF(J) at X+fctr1,Y+fctr2
```

Here is the complete routine:

```
1300 REM ****************
1301 REM * Draw staff
1302 REM ****************
1303 :
1305      FOR  J = 1 TO NUM
1310        FOR  I = 0 TO 24 STEP 6
1320          line (X,Y+I) to (X+200,Y+I)
1330        NEXT I
1335        draw SHAPE$(CLF(J)) at (X+fctr1,Y+fctr2)
1340        Y = Y+36
1350      NEXT J
1389 :
1390      RETURN
```

In the above program, note that in line 1335 we need to add some factor (fctr) to the X and Y coordinates required for the staff line sets. Here we can use a constant for the value of the factor, since once the clefs are defined, their starting location will always remain the same distance relative to the staff on which they are drawn.

The calling code for this subroutine must add the assignments for the various clefs. If we use one staff only, we need only one assignment. Two staves will require two assignments, etc. Here is the updated calling statement:

```
20 NUM=2 : X=40 : Y=39 : CLF(1)=1 : CLF(2)=3 : GOSUB 1300
```

NOTES ON THE IBM-PC

In BASICA, shapes are defined as string variables. The following list of commands is a partial summary of those available:

"U" = Up	"D" = Down
"L" = Left	"R" = Right
"E" = Up to right (diagonal)	"F" = Down to right
"H" = Up to left	"G" = Down to left
"B" = (Preceding a command) = move without plotting	

Note that any command may be repeated a number of times indicated by a number following it, such as "U5".

The definition for a simple box shape would be as follows.

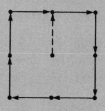

```
BOX$ = "BU R D2 L2 U2 R"
```

Once the shape is defined, it can be drawn with the following commands:

PSET (X,Y) : DRAW string variable   draws a shape defined as the string variable at the location starting at X,Y; location is set by the PSET (X,Y) command. If the first move is without plotting, substitute the command PRESET (X,Y).

TA n   if placed in a string, this command changes the rotation, or Turning Angle, where n may be any integer −360 to 360 (degrees).

The following statements will cause the box above to be rotated 45 degrees:

```
10 ANGLE$ = "TA 45"
20 PSET (X,Y) : DRAW ANGLE$ + BOX$
```

Note that by concatenating these commands in line 20 we preserve flexibility in that a given turning angle is not tied to any one shape.

NOTES ON THE C-64

In Simon's BASIC, shapes are defined as string variables. The following commands may be placed in a string:

Move without plotting	Move with plotting
0 = right	5 = right
1 = up	6 = up
2 = down	7 = down
3 = left	8 = left

All shape definitions must end with "9". As an example, a simple box shape might be:

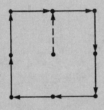

```
BOX$ = "1577886659"
```

Notice that the first move is without plotting and the use of the obligatory "9" at the end of the string.

Once a shape is defined, it can be drawn with the following statements:

DRAW string variable, X,Y, plot type   string variable is the predefined string variable, which will be drawn at X,Y, where plot type may be any integer in the range 0 to 2; 0=erase, 1=draw, 3=XOR

ROT rotation, scale   sets rotation and scale of any shape DRAWn after executing this statement, where rotation may be any integer 0 to 7 (0=0 degrees, 7=315 degrees), and scale may be any integer 0 to 255 (1=normal)

NOTES ON THE APPLE II FAMILY

On the Apple we can define numerous shapes and store them together in a binary file called a **shape table**. This assemblage of shapes is stored on disk and can be loaded and called into use from within a BASIC program.

Every shape table has several components:

1. a number from 1 to 255 indicating the number of shapes in the table;
2. a series of offsets pointing to the beginning of each shape in the table; and
3. the actual coded definition of each shape.

If we had a shape table beginning at location 32768 in memory, the following information would appear: one byte containing the number of shapes in the table followed by an unused byte, and a series of offsets of two bytes each pointing to the beginning of each shape defined in the table. The offsets denote the distance from the first byte in the table (e.g. at 32768) to the location of the first byte of each respective shape. For example, if our first shape started at location 32812, the distance from 32768 to 32812 would be 44 bytes. This value would be stored in locations 32770 to 32771, that is, the location of the first offset. Following is an example of what our shape table might look like:

32768	32769	32770 . . . 32770+(2*(n−1))	etc.
no. of shapes	(unused)	offset 1 . . . offset n	shape 1 . . . shape n

As you can see, the process gets very involved. Moreover, the actual definition of shapes gets even more complicated.

One of the solutions to creating graphics on the Apple is to acquire one of the numerous commercially available programs designed to help you in the task. For the convenience of our readers, we have written an easy-to-use program to aid in building shape tables. The listing is given in Appendix B, along with information on its operation and how to load and initialize the tables. We suggest you enter the code, SAVE it, and then experiment with it to see how it works.

Once the shapes are created, the drawing commands in Applesoft BASIC are the following:

DRAW shape# AT X,Y   draws one shape from a predefined shape table AT a given X,Y, where shape# may be any number from 0 to 255 so long as it is an existing shape in the table

XDRAW shape# AT X,Y   like DRAW, but drawing is in the inverse color, which in effect erases the shape

ROT=n   rotation, where n is a scale of 0 (0 degrees) to 63 (355 degrees)

SCALE=n   defines the relative size of a drawn shape, where n is any integer from 0 to 255; 1 = normal size

For those who are interested in more detail, we recommend the following two sources for information:

Applesoft BASIC Programming Reference Manual (which comes with the Apple computer at time of purchase).

Apple Graphics and Arcade Design, by Jeffrey Stanton. Los Angeles: The Book Company, 1982. (11223 South Hindry Ave., Los Angeles, CA 90045).

Exercises 5.2

1. Define a series of clef shapes and implement the new staff/clef drawing routines.
2. Make the program in Exercise 1. above versatile so that a user can INPUT the number of staff line sets and the type of clef to be drawn, and then have the program draw examples.

Manipulating Shapes: Moving Notes

Once one knows how to create and draw shapes, the next step is to move them wherever they are needed on the screen, which is relatively uncomplicated.

One of the most common manipulations in music graphics is plotting notes on a staff. If notes were always placed at the same location, this task would be as simple as drawing staff lines, but since notes may appear anywhere on, above, or below the staff, the information needed to orient their placement is dynamic and changes according to values supplied by the program and interactively by the user.

To accommodate this dynamic information, we must have two things: (1) some predetermined code for entering note data, that is, a music code; and (2) a procedure (an algorithm) for converting this code into information usable by the computer. We must also know what information will be required to implement the graphics and sound, as well as what information is necessary for evaluating the correctness of information being supplied by the user. This latter information is particularly important if we are designing a computer-assisted instruction (CAI) lesson.

Since CAI is one of the most common uses of the microcomputer in music, we'll design an instructional program that drills a student on spelling triads. Our first task will be to define a judging procedure for evaluating student input. Recall that we did this in Chapter 2 (see pp. 27–28) using the LTTR/ACC/OCT encoding scheme in which a student response might contain a LeTTeR name for a note, one or two ACCidentals, and an OCTave code. We also discussed there how to parse the code to enable isolating any of the input symbols and presented a parsing subroutine. Then in Chapter 3 (pp. 55–58), we discussed how this information could be converted to numbers and stored in a two-dimensional array in which each row contained the information for one note of a triad. We repeat the relevant code here for convenience, but we refer you to the earlier chapters for related discussion.

Example 5.1

```
2000 REM ***************
2001 REM * Input ANS$
2002 REM ***************
2003 :
```

```
2010        ER=0 : N$="" : O$="" : A$="" : AN$=""
2020        INPUT AN$ : IF AN$= "" THEN 2020
2030         IF LEN(AN$) > 4 THEN ER = 1
2040        N$ = LEFT$(AN$,1) : IF N$ < "A" OR N$ > "G" THEN ER=1
2050        O$ = RIGHT$(AN$,1) : IF O$ < "0" OR O$ > "8" THEN ER=1
2060         IF LEN(AN$) > 2 THEN A$=MID$(AN$,2,1)
2070         IF A$ <> "+" AND A$ <> "-" THEN ER=1
2080         IF ER=1 AND N$ <> "Q" THEN 2000
2089 :
2090        RETURN
2091 :
2100 REM ****************
2101 REM * Compute letter name
2102 REM ****************
2103 :
2110        NTE(n,LTTR) = FN M7(ASC(N$) - 67)
2189 :
2190        RETURN
2191 :
2200 REM ****************
2201 REM * Compute accidental
2202 REM ****************
2203 :
2210         IF A$ = "" THEN NTE(n,ACC) = 0 : GOTO 2290
2220        NTE(n,ACC) = 44 - ASC(A$)
2230         IF LEN(AN$) > 3 THEN NTE(n,ACC) = NTE(n,ACC) * 2
2289 :
2290        RETURN
2291 :
2300 REM ****************
2301 REM * Octave value
2302 REM ****************
2303 :
2310        NTE(,OCT) = VAL(O$)
2389 :
2390        RETURN
2391 :
```

To refresh your memory, these subroutines will return the following ranges of values:

```
LTTR = 0,1,...,6 ("C" = 0, "B" = 6)
ACC  = -2,-1,...,2 ("-" = -1, "+" = 1)
OCT  = 0,1,...,8 (where C4 is middle C)
```

The subroutines can be called with the following code:

```
500    REM ##############
501    REM # Enter and compute note values
502    REM ##############
503    :
510         GOSUB 2000             :REM get input
520         GOSUB 2100             :REM compute LTTR
530         GOSUB 2200             :REM compute ACC
540         GOSUB 2300             :REM compute OCT
```

Plotting the Notes

The final step in the plotting process is to convert note values into a usable plotting coordinate so that we can draw the note at a desired screen position. Several factors have to be taken into consideration.

First, we know that our LTTR numbers are consecutive (that is, 0, 1, 2,...,6), while consecutive notes on the screen (e.g., C, D, E) must be three pixels apart. That is, if the Y value for the note C4 is n, then the Y value for D4 is n-3 (remember that Y values decrease from bottom to top on the screen). If we multiply LTTR by 3, then each value will be three numbers apart and will correspond to our desired screen spacing.

Second, we need to determine the placement based on OCT. Again, there are seven notes in an octave (not including the octave duplicate, of course) and each note must be three pixels apart. We thus multiply each octave by 3 pixels × 7 notes (or 21). For example, if our note is C4, we compute the following value:

```
position = 3 * (7 * NTE(n,OCT) + NTE(n,LTTR))
```

That is, first the OCT is multiplied by 7 and then it is added to LTTR. This combined value is then multiplied by 3. In the case of the note C4, the value is equal to 84.

Third, we must remember that screen plotting position values decrease numerically as they ascend, while note values increase as they ascend. To accommodate these differences, we subtract the computed position value from some larger factor (FCTR). That is, the larger our note position number, the smaller the remaining value after the subtraction. For example, if FCTR = 200, then

```
FCTR - 100 = 100 , while FCTR - 150 = 50.
```

If we assume that middle C (C4) will be located at vertical position 70 (as determined from our earlier staff drawing subroutine), then the necessary FCTR value must be 154. The equation follows:

```
note            = C4
position        = 3*(7*NTE(n,OCT)+NTE(n,LTTR) )
                = 3*(7*     4     +     0     )
                = 3*(      28     +     0     )
                = 84
if FCTR         = 154
then FCTR - 84  = 70 (middle C)
```

If we also assume that each successive note should be 25 pixels to the right of the previous (thus displaying the triad linearly), then the following code will draw a note at the proper vertical position and increment the horizontal position by 25:

```
2500 REM ***************
2501 REM * Draw note
2502 REM ***************
2503 :
2510     X = X + 25: Y = 154 - 3*(7*NTE(n,OCT)+NTE(n,LTTR))
2520     draw note at (X,Y)
2530     IF NTE(n,ACC) <> 0 THEN draw accidental at (X-FCTR,Y)
2589 :
2590     RETURN
```

Then add the following line to the earlier calling program:

```
550         GOSUB 2500      : REM draw note
```

Exercises 5.3

1. In the subroutine above, we included a line (2530) that will check for an accidental if one is needed. As an exercise, write the subroutine that will draw the accidental where needed relative to the drawn note, and then change line 2530 to a GOSUB call to that subroutine.
2. Combine the previous subroutines (lines 2000 to 2390, 2500 to 2590, and 500 to 540) together with a user interface routine (a subroutine that will prompt a user to enter some value) that will allow the user either to enter two notes for an interval or three notes for a triad.
3. Rewrite the circle of fifths triad algorithm in Chapter 4 (pp. 92–94) and combine it with the previous exercise so that the answer entered by the user will be evaluated.

An Alternative Method of Input: Cursor Driven Input

We have seen how one might go about converting keyset (alphanumeric) input into computer usable information. While this method works well and is acceptable, it can become an annoyance to the user because each command must be entered by typing. For those who are not adequate typists, a typewriter keyset is not an efficient means of data entry, particularly for music data. One effective solution is called **cursor driven input,** which we abbreviate as **CDI** for our discussion.

In a typical CDI scheme, the user is required to use only two to four keys to control up, down, left, and right motions of a small pointer, called a **cursor,** on the screen. Any four keys can be "redefined" to suit our needs, but whichever keys are chosen, they should lie comfortably under the hand and be representative of the actions the keys control.

A common scheme uses four keys in a diamond pattern to represent the four compass points:

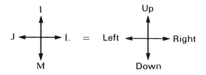

On some keysets we can use the left (←) and right (→) arrow keys for left and right movement, respectively, and the up and down arrow keys for up and down movement.

Typically, a selection of all possible responses is displayed somewhere on the screen. To access any response, the user simply uses the appropriate key to move the cursor until it points to, or overlays, the desired choice. Then the user enters the response by pressing some other key, commonly the RETURN key or the space bar.

Once the user enters the response, the program must use the X,Y coordinates of the cursor to determine the user's choice. For example, if we wanted four possible choices to be represented by the numbers 1 to 4, we could place the choices on the screen at X locations 20, 50, 80, and 110. The user would move the cursor to one of these screen locations to make a selection and enter it. The X value of the cursor can be translated to the numbers 1 to 4 by the following simple equation:

```
CHOICE = (X + 10) / 30
```

Besides being used as simple pointing mechanisms, CDIs can also represent physical actions. For example, the cursor may be an actual note that is moved up and down on a staff in order to simulate actual music writing.

Overall, CDIs can greatly simplify the use of a program by eliminating the need to concentrate on typing. For children, especially, this simplification enhances the use of computers.

A Simple CDI Example

Let's look at a relatively simple example of CDI, in this case for entering one of the five solfege syllables DO, RE, MI, SOL, and LA associated with a basic CAI lesson utilizing Kodaly teaching methods. The syllables will be required in order to build short melodic fragments using a pentatonic scale set.

Instead of having the student type in each syllable name, a better strategy is to set up a simple two-key CDI routine in which the five syllables are placed horizontally on the screen and a small arrow (the cursor) can be moved left and right above the syllables in the selection process. After positioning the arrow, the user would simply press RETURN.

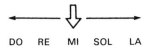

DO   RE   MI   SOL   LA

With this general description of the process, we can now define our requirements more specifically:

1. The arrow needs to be a graphics shape because there is often no down-arrow character available in a computer character set.
2. The actual solfege syllables can best be represented as text characters "printed" to the graphics screen (see specifics on each machine for how to accomplish this).
3. Two keys will be required to move the arrow. In this case, the left- and right-arrow keys will work well.
4. Provisions must be made for dealing with unwanted key strokes, that is, all keys except the two arrow keys and the RETURN key.
5. A procedure is needed for capturing the correct key strokes and moving the arrow.
6. A procedure is needed for evaluating the X coordinate of the arrow and converting it to computer-usable information.

We will likely want to set up the screen so that the text lies horizontally near the bottom (out of the way of other graphics) and the arrow will move horizontally above it. Let's assume that each character on the screen is positioned eight pixels apart horizontally. The following subroutine will set up the screen as desired.

```
1100 REM ***********************
1101 REM * draw input screen
1102 REM ***********************
1103 :
1110     LFT   = 24    :REM leftmost arrow position
1112     RHT   = 152   :REM 16 characters × 8-pixels
1114     YPNTR = 155   :REM 20 characters down
1116     XPNTR = 88    :REM centers on 8th character from left
1120     CLS
1130     (SCR LOC 21):  PRINT TAB(3) "DO  RE  MI  SOL  LA"
1140     draw arrow shape at (XPNTR,YPNTR)
1189 :
1190     RETURN
```

Lines 1110 to 1116 set up the required variable and constant values. XPNTR,YPNTR are the starting X,Y coordinates of the arrow. Because the arrow will move horizontally only, YPNTR will not change, but XPNTR will be incremented and decremented as needed to reposition the shape. LFT (LeFT) and RHT (RigHT) represent the furthest points to the left and right that will be allowed for arrow movement. Line 1120 simply clears the text screen while line 1130 sets the vertical position to 21 (so that the next text will appear at line 21) and does the actual printing of the answer choices.

Assuming that we have initialized our graphics and properly defined our shapes, we should see an all blank screen with a row of solfege syllables and an arrow pointing down directly above the center of the middle choice. This will be our "default" arrow position, that is, the place where the arrow will appear at the beginning of each new question. (NOTE: While on the C-64 and IBM-PC every character is eight pixels wide, on the Apple II, characters are only seven pixels wide. The same routine can be used on the Apple by simply converting the values as follows: LFT=21, RHT=133, YPNTR=155, and XPNTR=74.)

Next we need a subprogram that accepts input from the keyset and takes one of four actions based on the value of the key:

1. LEFT ARROW: move arrow left one choice and check LFT
2. RIGHT ARROW: move arrow right one choice and check RHT
3. <RETURN>: record (enter) the choice
4. (any other key): ignore and continue subprogram

To "capture" a single keystroke, we need to invoke the GET or the INKEY$ command (see page 263 for an example of their syntax). Here we'll simply write **get KEY$,** as in line 1220 below. If we elect to use keys that represent alphanumeric characters, then checking is very easy, for example:

```
1220 get KEY$
1230 IF KEY$ = "J" THEN take the appropriate action
```

Unfortunately, none of the three keys (for LFT, RHT, and <RETURN>) can be checked simply in this manner. Instead, we need to determine their ASCII code and check for it by using the CHR$(ASCII code) command. For example, the ASCII code for "J" is 74. Line 1230 could therefore be rewritten:

```
1230 IF KEY$ = CHR$(74) THEN take the appropriate action.
```

With this information, we are nearly ready to complete a CDI subroutine. However, one other element needs to be incorporated, namely the code for drawing and erasing the arrow shape. Thinking back through the design of the algorithm, we have three steps:

1. Call the screen setup subroutine
2. Call the CDI input subroutine
   a. draw the arrow at some location (X,Y)
   b. get the input (KEY$)
   c. take the appropriate action(s)
   d. erase the old arrow
   e. repeat if necessary
3. Evaluate the choice of response

Step 1 is already complete. The following code will take care of most of step 2:

```
1200 REM ***************
1201 REM * Get input (KEY$)
1202 REM ***************
1203 :
1210     draw arrow shape at (XPNTR,YPNTR)
1220     get KEY$
1225     FL = 0
1230      IF KEY$=CHR$(ascii for ←) THEN GOSUB 1300 :FL=1
1240      IF KEY$=CHR$(ascii for →) THEN GOSUB 1400 :FL=1
1250      IF KEY$=CHR$(ascii for <CR>) THEN GOTO 1290
1260       IF FL=1 THEN undraw arrow shape at (XOLD,YOLD)
1270     GOTO 1210
1289 :
1290     RETURN
```

In this subroutine the initial arrow shape is drawn at XPNTR, YPNTR. These values represent either the initial values defined in the screen setup subroutine or the new values updated after pressing the left- or right-arrow key. Before updating these values, however, we need to store them somewhere in order to have them available when we are ready to erase the old arrow. This is accomplished within the two arrow mover subroutines. Upon entering either of those subroutines, the current values of XPNTR and YPNTR are stored in the variables XOLD and YOLD before being updated. After exiting either of those subroutines, the old arrow shape is erased using the previous values of XPNTR and YPNTR (now stored as XOLD and YOLD), after which the program flow returns to the top of the main input subroutine where the arrow is redrawn with the updated X,Y information.

Note that the new arrow is drawn at the start of the subroutine (see line 1210 above) and not at the end so that if we exit from the subroutine we will not redraw an unwanted arrow on the screen. If an unwanted key is pressed, all the conditional checks will fail and the flag (FL) will remain set at 0, which will cause the program to bypass line 1260 and return to line 1220 (via line 1270) where it will await the next keystroke.

Here is the LEFT ARROW subroutine:

```
1300 REM ***************
1301 REM * Arrow left
1302 REM ***************
1303 :
1310     XOLD = XPNTR : YOLD = YPNTR
1320     XPNTR = XPNTR - 32 :REM move arrow left 4 chars.
1330      IF XPNTR < LFT THEN XPNTR = RHT
1389 :
1390     RETURN
```

The procedure above is relatively simple. Line 1310 assigns the current values of XPNTR and YPNTR to the variables XOLD and YOLD, respectively. XPNTR is then updated in line 1320 by moving it 32 pixels to the left (a distance of four characters). Line 1330 implements what is commonly referred to as a "wrap-around" feature. Back in the initial screen setup subroutine, we declared two constants which corresponded to the leftmost (LFT) and rightmost (RHT) positions for our arrow. Line 1330 checks whether we have gone too far to the left by comparing the value of the updated XPNTR with the constant value stored in LFT. If we have gone too far, we compensate by moving the cursor all the way around to the rightmost position, that is, as if we had "wrapped around" the display.

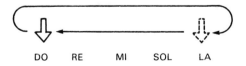

DO   RE   MI   SOL   LA

The code for the right arrow is nearly identical, except for the direction of motion and the wrap-around.

```
1400 REM ****************
1401 REM * Arrow right
1402 REM ***************
1403 :
1410      XOLD = XPNTR: YOLD = YPNTR
1420      XPNTR = XPNTR + 32: REM move arrow right 4 characters
1430       IF XPNTR > RHT THEN XPNTR = LFT
1489 :
1490      RETURN
```

With the completion of these two subroutines, we are basically done. Operationally, the input subroutine starting at line 1200 will continue to loop until the <RETURN> key is pressed, at which time this subroutine is left and the choice of response will have to be evaluated.

NOTES ON THE IBM-PC

In BASICA, all the normal text commands work on the graphics screen. Be careful, however, as some text commands (such as CLS and the scrolling commands) will also affect graphics drawn on the screen.

NOTES ON THE C-64

In Simon's BASIC, text can be printed on the graphics screen with one of two special commands:

CHAR X,Y, poke code, plot type, height   plots a single character on the hi-res screen. The actual character plotted is determined by the value of the poke code which corresponds to the screen poke codes found in the *Commodore Reference Manual.* The plot type may be any integer from 0 to 2 (0=erase, 1=draw, 2=XOR draw). The height may be any integer from 1 to 8 (1=normal height).

TEXT X,Y "<CTRL-A> character string", plot type, height, spacing   plots a string of characters starting at X,Y. Plot type may be 0, 1, or 2, height may be any number 1 to 8, and spacing may be any integer 0 through 255 (the normal spacing is 8).

Note: <CTRL-B> instead of <CTRL-A> will produce lower case characters. The two may be interspersed throughout the string so that selected characters or words may appear in either upper or lower case.

NOTES ON THE APPLE II FAMILY

The first two requirements of the sample CDI program present an immediate problem on the Apple, namely using both graphics and text in close proximity to each other. On the Apple, there is no simple way to put text on the hi-res graphics screen, and there is no way to put graphics on the text screen. However, the solution to this problem turns out to be straightforward.

If you recall from earlier comments, the bottom one-sixth of the Apple hi-res graphics screen provides a small (four-line) text window. If we place our solfege syllables on the top line of this window area and place our graphics arrow at the bottom of the graphics screen, then the two will be adjacent:

CDI Diagram

The following line of code will place the solfege syllables (the text) on line 21, which is the first line of the text window.

```
1130        VTAB 21 : PRINT " DO RE MI SOL LA"
```

As we mentioned earlier, printing text on the graphics screen requires a "character generator" program. Such a program is beyond the scope of this book, but there are numerous commercially available character generator programs available at a reasonable cost (around $25 to $50).

Exercises 5.4

1. Assume that the X coordinates for our five response choices are as follows:

DO	=	24
RE	=	56
MI	=	88
SOL	=	120
LA	=	152

   Assume also that these five values are to be converted into numbers representing the musical scale degrees 1, 2, 3, 5, and 6. Develop a short algorithm that will carry out this conversion.

   (Hint: It can be done by one line of code in which each number is divided by some factor and the remainder is truncated with the INT function.)

2. Try to devise an easy method to allow you to set up a CDI procedure in which all the choices are not evenly spaced. For example, you may want to space the response choices to more closely represent actual keyboard spacing:

```
DO  RE  MI    SOL  LA
```

(Hint: Try using a one-dimensional array.)

3. Convert the note drawing program from the last section so that it incorporates the above CDI. Design it so that the notes G4, A4, B4, D5, and E5 can be drawn by using the arrow and the solfege syllables.

A MORE COMPLEX CDI PROGRAM: A MUSIC EDITOR

Given a basic understanding of how CDIs work, let's now examine a much more complex problem: a music editor that will allow us to write and edit melodies. In this section we discuss the basic operation of the editor program and include a number of its necessary subroutines. Further details, including the program code for the three different microcomputers and a discussion of machine language requirements, appear in the final chapter of the book.

We begin by defining criteria for the editor. We need to be able to:

1. Move a cursor up, down, left, and right on a grand staff. This will require a wrap-around feature for moving the cursor arrow up and down so that when it reaches the upper limit, it will wrap around to the bottom of the staff and vice-versa.
2. Add, that is, insert, a note at any point within a melody
3. Delete a note at any point
4. Add accidentals to any note
5. Change duration values of any note
6. Scroll the music left or right to accommodate writing a melody longer than one "screen"

Because our needs involve inserting and deleting notes, the ideal data structure to use for this project is the linked list structure defined and illustrated in Chapter 3 (see pp. 37–40). For each note (or node in the linked list) in our melody, we will need the following information:

LTTR	= Letter name (0,1,...,6)
ACC	= Accidental (−2, −1, ..., 2)
OCT	= Octave (2, 3,...,6)
LNTH	= Note duration (3, 6, 12, 24, 48)
LL	= Left link (points to previous node)
RL	= Right link (points to next node)

The linked list will be defined in BASIC as a two-dimensional array: DIM NTE(60,7). Note that we must define a maximum number of array subscripts in a DIMension statement. In this case we allow as many as 60 notes (we will not use subscript 0).

As in our example in Chapter 3, we will use an X pointer variable (XX) and a Y pointer variable (YY). Because our melody may be longer than can be displayed on a screen (0 to 279 on the Apple, and 0 to 319 on the C-64 and IBM-PC), we must protect against the value of XX exceeding allowable limits. We do this by providing two constants, LFT and RHT that will hold the allowable LeFTmost and RigHTmost plotting coordinates.

We will also need a second X pointer variable (XPNTR) that will be used to store the actual X coordinate of every note of the melody regardless of how high the value may become. For example, Figure 5.11 shows a simulated melody in terms of its durations. The dotted box represents the screen. Numbers at the top of the example denote XPNTR values of each note. Numbers below the box denote screen values marking locations on the screen.

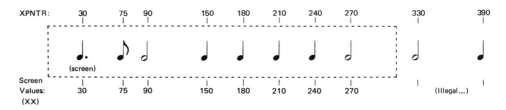

Figure 5.11

We can store the XPNTR value of each note by adding one more record to our linked list node structure, thus completing the structure as shown:

LTTR
ACC
OCT
LNTH
LL
RL
XPNTR

There is still one more problem we must address. As the melody scrolls to the right, the X coordinate values stored in each node (NTE.XPNTR) will still be out of range and must be recalculated to compensate for the distance scrolled, thus bringing the value within allowable screen coordinates. We can accomplish this by using a variable XOF (for X OFfset) to keep track of the total number of pixels scrolled from the starting point. By subtracting this value from NTE.XPNTR, we will arrive at a legal X coordinate value: XX = NTE(CRNT, XPNTR) − XOF, where CRNT is the current note. For example, in Figure 5.11 we showed the screen in the unscrolled position in which XOF will be 0 and the XPNTR value for each of the first seven notes will remain unchanged, that is, XPNTR − 0 = XPNTR. Now, if we want to plot the eighth note, we have to scroll the screen to the right approximately 40 pixels. XOF will thus have the value 40. This is illustrated in Figure 5.12.

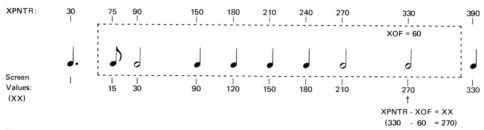

Figure 5.12

The XPNTR value of the eighth note is 350, an X coordinate too great to be plotted on the screen. But by using the formula shown above, XX = NTE(8,350) − 40, we arrive at a value of 310, which is a legitimate X coordinate and the proper one to plot.

In reality, we don't want to scroll the entire screen. We want to be able to keep clef signs on the screen at all times, and we want the staff lines to remain on the screen also. Thus we will scroll only a small portion, or window, of the screen as shown in Figure 5.13.

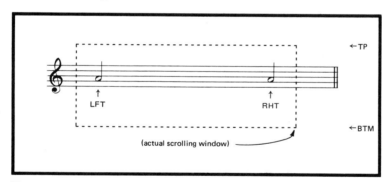

Figure 5.13

We use the previously defined plot-limiting variables LFT and RHT to designate the first allowable plotting locations within the scrolling window. We will also use two other variables, TP and BTM, to hold appropriate values for ToP and BoTtoM, the up and down wrap-around values. By use of these variables, we ensure that we never attempt to plot outside the scrolling area. It will be necessary further to define a minimum distance to move the screen (MVE). We set this at 24 pixels; every move will then be some multiple of MVE, such as 24, 48, 72.

The following subroutine will move the cursor one move unit (MVE) to the right. If we are already at the far right of the screen, a scroll will occur and any newly exposed note will be drawn. Explanation of the code follows the listing.

```
1300 REM   ================
1301 REM   = move right
1302 REM   ================
1303 :
1310        IF CRNT = MAX THEN 1390
1320        LUMN=0 :GOSUB 2000 :LUMN=1                    :REM erase cursor
1325        IF NTE(CRNT,XPNTR)=XX THEN GOSUB 3500         :REM redraw note
1330        XX = XX+MVE
1340        IF XX > (RHT+XOF) THEN GOSUB 2200             :REM scroll left
1350        GOSUB 2000                                    :REM draw cursor
1360        IF XX>=NTE(NTE(CRNT,RL),XPNTR) AND NTE(CRNT,RL)<>0
                  THEN CRNT=NTE(CRNT,RL)
1370        IF XX = NTE(CRNT,XPNTR) THEN GOSUB 3500 :REM draw note
1389 :
1390        RETURN
1391 :
```

Line 1310 is simply a safeguard to insure that we cannot continue adding notes once we have reached the maximum size (MAX) of our melody data base. Line 1320 erases the cursor (CRSR) before the scroll, and line 1350 redraws it after the move. If the cursor was on top of a previously plotted note when it was erased, then the note underneath the cursor will likely be partially erased as well. Line 1325 takes care of redrawing the note. Line 1330 updates XX, and line 1340 calls the scrolling routine if the updated value exceeds the value of RHT + XOF.

Line 1360 updates the linked list pointer CRNT. If the new cursor moves up to or beyond the next note of the melody, CRNT must be reset to point to the next note. Figure 5.14 illustrates this resetting.

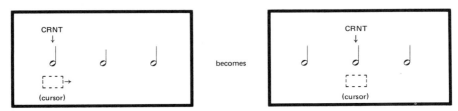

Figure 5.14

Finally, if the cursor is at the far edge of the screen and scrolls it farther to the right, any notes to the right whose (XPNTR − XOF) values have now come into range must be plotted on the screen. Line 1370 carries out this task. Figure 5-15 illustrates this procedure.

The following subroutine moves the cursor left one move if the test in line 1210 fails; line 1210 tests whether XX is at the left edge of the screen, which prevents scrolling left.

```
1200 REM   ================
1201 REM   = move left
1202 REM   ================
1203 :
1210        IF (XX=LFT) AND (XOF=0) THEN 1290
1220        LUMN=0 :GOSUB 2000 :LUMN=1                    :REM erase cursor
1225        IF NTE(CRNT,XPNTR)=XX THEN GOSUB 3500         :REM redraw note
1230        XX = XX-MVE
1240        IF XX < (LFT+XOF) THEN GOSUB 2100             :REM scroll right
1250        GOSUB 2000                                    :REM draw cursor
1260        IF (NTE(CRNT,XPNTR)>XX) THEN CRNT = NTE(CRNT,LL)
```

```
1270            IF XX = NTE(CRNT,XPNTR) THEN GOSUB 3500 :REM draw note
1289 :
1290            RETURN
1291 :
```

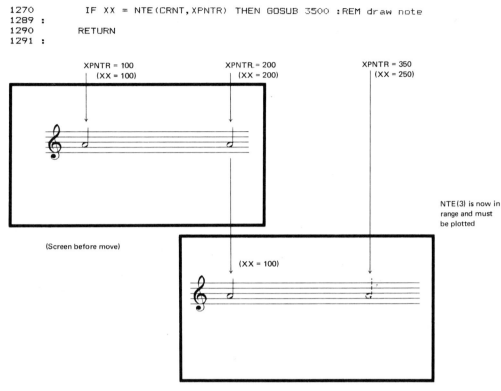

Figure 5.15

(Screen after move)

The following subroutines are called by the two previously discussed subroutines. Each of the subroutines should be self-explanatory.

```
2000 REM      ------------------
2001 REM      - draw/erase cursor
2002 REM      ------------------
2003 :
2010            color=LUMN :draw CRSR$ at (XX-XOF,YY)
2089 :
2090            RETURN
2091 :
2100 REM      ------------------
2101 REM      - scroll right
2102 REM      ------------------
2103 :
2120            FOR I=0 TO 2 : call ML scrolling routine : NEXT
2130            XOF = XOF-MVE
2189 :
2190            RETURN
2191 :
2200 REM      ------------------
2201 REM      - scroll left
2202 REM      ------------------
2203 :
2220            FOR I=0 TO 2 : call ML scrolling routine : NEXT
2230            XOF = XOF+MVE
2289 :
2290            RETURN
2291 :
```

The following subroutine moves the cursor up and down by one pitch distance (3 pixels). Similar to the previous routines, lines 1410 and 1440 (and 1510 and 1540) erase and redraw, respectively, the cursor. Lines 1430 and 1530 update YY, and lines 1435 and 1535 implement the wrap-around feature.

```
1400 REM   ================
1401 REM   = move up
1402 REM   ================
1403 :
1410       LUMN=0 :GOSUB 2000 :LUMN=1                :REM erase cursor
1420        IF NTE(CRNT,XPNTR)=XX THEN GOSUB 3500    :REM redraw note
1430       YY = YY-3
1435        IF YY<TP THEN YY=BTM
1440       GOSUB 2000                                :REM draw cursor
1489 :
1490       RETURN
1491 :
1500 REM   ================
1501 REM   = move down
1502 REM   ================
1503 :
1510       LUMN=0 :GOSUB 2000 :LUMN=1                :REM erase cursor
1520        IF NTE(CRNT,XPNTR)=XX THEN GOSUB 3500    :REM redraw note
1530       YY = YY+3
1535        IF YY>BTM THEN YY=TP
1540       GOSUB 2000                                :REM draw cursor
1589 :
1590       RETURN
1591 :
```

Lines 1000 to 1070 below implement the linked list insert algorithm discussed in Chapter 3. The subroutine called from line 1080 simply inserts all the proper values into the various records of the insert node.

```
1000 REM   ================
1001 REM   = insert (after)
1002 REM   ================
1003 :
1010       TEMP = NTE(NXT,RL)
1020       NTE(NXT,RL)  = NTE(CRNT,RL)
1030       NTE(CRNT,RL) = NXT
1040       NTE(NXT,LL)  = CRNT
1050       NTE(NTE(NXT,RL),LL) = NXT
1060       CRNT = NXT
1070       NXT  = TEMP
1080       GOSUB 1600                                :REM record/display note
1089 :
1090       RETURN
1091 :
1600 REM   ================
1601 REM   = record note
1602 REM   ================
1603 :
1610        IF CRNT = 0 THEN 1690
1620       NTE(CRNT,LTTR)  = FN MD7((154-YY)/3)
1625       NTE(CRNT,OCT)   = INT((154-YY)/21)
1630       NTE(CRNT,ACC)   = 0
1635       NTE(CRNT,LNTH)  = DR
1640       NTE(CRNT,XPNTR) = XX
1650       GOSUB 3500                                :REM draw note
1689 :
1690       RETURN
1691 :
```

Once a note has been inserted into the melody, we may add accidentals. Lines 1700 to 1891 provide for adding a sharp or flat. Since the note drawing routine (developed earlier but added here for convenience) takes care of drawing an accidental when it draws a note, we can save on code by setting the accidental to its proper value and then simply recalling the note-drawing routine to redraw the note, this time with the accidental.

```
1700 REM  ================
1701 REM  = add a sharp
1702 REM  ================
1703 :
1710        IF CRNT = O THEN 1790
1720        NTE(CRNT,ACC) = 1
1730        GOSUB 3500                           :REM draw accidental
1789 :
1790        RETURN
1791 :
1800 REM  ================
1801 REM  = add a flat
1802 REM  ================
1803 :
1810        IF CRNT = O THEN 1890
1820        NTE(CRNT,ACC) = -1
1830        GOSUB 3500
1889 :
1890        RETURN
1891 :
3500 REM  ================
3501 REM  = draw note
3502 REM  ================
3503 :
3520        XDRW = NTE(CRNT,XPNTR)-XOF
3530        YDRW = 154 - 3*( 7*NTE(CRNT,OCT)+NTE(CRNT,LTTR) )
3540        color=LUMN :draw NTE$(INT(NTE(CRNT,LNTH)/24)+1) at (XDRW,YDRW)
3550        IF YDRW = 70 THEN GOSUB 3700            :REM ledger lines
3560        IF NTE(CRNT,ACC) <> O THEN GOSUB 3600   :REM accidentals
3589 :
3590        RETURN
3591 :
3600 REM  ----------------
3601 REM  - draw accidentals
3602 REM  ----------------
3603 :
3610        ON NTE(CRNT,ACC)+2 GOSUB 3660, 3670, 3680
3639 :
3640        RETURN
3641 :
3660        draw F$ at (XDRW-12,YDRW) :RETURN
3670        RETURN
3680        draw S$ at (XDRW-12,YDRW) :RETURN
3691 :
3700 REM  ----------------
3701 REM  - ledger lines
3702 REM  ----------------
3703 :
3710        line (XDRW-7,YDRW) to (XDRW+7,YDRW)
2789 :
3790        RETURN
3791 :
```

Similarly, we can change a duration value (DR) in the same way. Lines 1900 to 1991 accomplish this task. Lines 1910 and 1920 test first whether a

melody is empty (contains no notes) and/or whether the note pointed to by
CRNT is off the screen, which means that it has not been drawn. If either of
these conditions is true, then the routine is bypassed. Line 1930 erases the old
note, while lines 1940 to 1950 reassign values to NTE(CRNT,LNTH) and redraw the note.

```
1900 REM    ================
1901 REM    = change note value
1902 REM    ================
1903 :
1910        IF CRNT = 0 THEN 1990
1920        IF NTE(CRNT,XPNTR)-XOF < LFT THEN 1990
1930        LUMN=0 :GOSUB 3500 :LUMN=1
1940        NTE(CRNT,LNTH)=DR
1950        GOSUB 3500
1989 :
1990        RETURN
1991 :
```

A last needed subroutine is one to delete a note. Once again, we use the
algorithm developed in Chapter 3, adding modifications where needed. Line
1110 forces the routine to be bypassed if the linked list is empty. Lines 1115 to
1120 erase the note to be deleted and redraw the cursor (which is likely also
partially erased in the process). Once all the lines have been reconnected, line
1170 clears out all the previously assigned values from the deleted node before it
is returned to the list of available nodes to be reused later if needed. This last
step is instructive, for if the values for nodes to be reused are not cleared, then
errors will result at some later point.

```
1100 REM    ================
1101 REM    = delete (after)
1102 REM    ================
1103 :
1110        IF CRNT = 0 THEN 1190
1115        LUMN=0 :GOSUB 3500 :LUMN=1      :REM erase note
1120        GOSUB 2000                      :REM draw cursor
1124 :
1125        NTE(NTE(CRNT,LL),RL) = NTE(CRNT,RL)
1130        NTE(NTE(CRNT,RL),LL) = NTE(CRNT,LL)
1140        NTE(CRNT,RL) = NXT
1150        NXT = CRNT
1160        CRNT = NTE(CRNT,LL)
1170        NTE(NXT,LTTR)=0:NTE(NXT,ACC)=0:NTE(NXT,OCT)=0:NTE(NXT,LNTH)=0
1189 :
1190        RETURN
1191 :
```

Once we have created all necessary subroutines, we need a calling loop to
access them. First, however, we need to define our input parameters. We will use
the keyboard for the following functions:

"→" = move right
"←" = move left
"↑" = move up (use "A" on the Apple)

"↓"	=	move down (use "Z" on the Apple)
"I"	=	Insert
"D"	=	Delete
"W"	=	Whole note
"H"	=	Half note
"Q"	=	Quarter note
"+"	=	Sharp
"−"	=	Flat
"X"	=	\<EXIT\>

By building a simple "GET" loop based on the algorithm we used in the discussion of the CAI drill program in Chapter 4 (see p. 85) we can control the operation of the routines.

```
500 REM ****************
501 REM * editor (calls)
502 REM ****************
503 :
550      GET NPT$ :IF NPT$="" THEN 550
555 :
570      IF NPT$ = CHR$(157) THEN GOSUB 1200 :GOTO 550          :REM left
590      IF NPT$ = CHR$(29)  THEN GOSUB 1300 :GOTO 550          :REM right
610      IF NPT$ = CHR$(145) THEN GOSUB 1400 :GOTO 550          :REM up
630      IF NPT$ = CHR$(17)  THEN GOSUB 1500 :GOTO 550          :REM down
650      IF NPT$ = "I" THEN GOSUB 1000 :GOTO 550            :REM insert
670      IF NPT$ = "D" THEN GOSUB 1100 :GOTO 550            :REM delete
690      IF NPT$ = "W" THEN DR=48 :GOSUB 1900 :GOTO 550
700          :REM whole note
710      IF NPT$ = "H" THEN DR=24 :GOSUB 1900 :GOTO 550
720          :REM half note
730      IF NPT$ = "Q" THEN DR=12 :GOSUB 1900 :GOTO 550
740          :REM quarter note
750      IF NPT$ = "+" THEN GOSUB 1700 :GOTO 550            :REM sharp
770      IF NPT$ = "-" THEN GOSUB 1800 :GOTO 550            :REM flat
900      IF NPT$ <>"X" THEN 550
989 :
990      RETURN
991 :
```

Finally, we need routines to set up the graphics screen (lines 3000 to 3391), to initialize all the variables values (lines 9000 to 9091), to define all the shapes (lines 9100 to 9491), to set up the linked list (lines 9500 to 9591), and to load the machine language screen scroller routine (lines 9600 to 9692). These are shown to conclude this chapter. (NOTE: A machine language scrolling routine is not necessary on the IBM-PC as the two graphics commands "GET" and "PUT" can be utilized to serve the same function.)

```
3000 REM ===============
3001 REM = setup screen
3002 REM ===============
3003 :
3005      cls
3010      hires=ON : rotation=0 :scale=1
3020      NUM=2 :X=8 :Y=40 :XX=LFT :YY=70
3030      LUMN=1 :GOSUB 3200                          :REM draw staff
```

```
3035        LUMN=1 :GOSUB 3300                          :REM draw melody
3040        LUMN=1 :GOSUB 2000                          :REM draw cursor
3099 :
3100        (scn loc 21) :PRINT"JOY STICK (OR CURSOR KEYS): U,D,L,R"
3110        (scr loc 22) :PRINT"JOY BUTTON (OR <CR>): RECORDS A NOTE"
3120        (scr loc 23) :PRINT"D: DELETES NOTE    +: SHARP   -:FLAT"
3130        (scr loc 24) :PRINT"W: WHOLE  H: HALF  Q: QUARTER  X: EXIT"
3189 :
3190        RETURN
3191 :
3200 REM     ----------------
3201 REM     - draw staff(s)
3202 REM     ----------------
3203 :
3205        FOR  J=1 TO NUM
3210          FOR  I=0 TO 24 STEP 6
3220            line (X,Y+I) to (X+295,Y+I)
3230          NEXT I
3240            IF J=1 THEN draw GC$ at (X+FX,Y+FY)
3250            IF J=2 THEN draw FC$ at (X+FX,Y+FY)
3260          Y=Y+36
3270        NEXT J
3289 :
3290        RETURN
3291 :
3300 REM     ----------------
3301 REM     - draw melody
3302 REM     ----------------
3303 :
3310        CRNT = NTE(0,RL)
3319 :
3320         IF NTE(CRNT,XPNT)>RHT OR CRNT=0 THEN 3380
3330        GOSUB 3500                                   :REM draw note
3340        CRNT = NTE(CRNT,RL)
3350        GOTO 3320
3379 :
3380        CRNT = 0
3385         IF NTE(NTE(CRNT,RL),XPNTR) <= XX THEN CRNT = NTE(CRNT,RL)
3389 :
3390        RETURN
3391 :


9000 REM****************
9001 REM* init variables
9002 REM****************
9003 :
9005    DR=48 :FX=10 :FY=24 :TP=37 :BTM=103 :LUMN=1
9010    LTTR=0 :ACC=1 :OCT=2 :LNTH=3 :LL=4 :RL=5 :XPNTR=6
9015    MAX=60 :LFT=71 :RHT=279 :MVE=24
9034 :
9035    GOSUB 9100                                  :REM define shapes
9040    GOSUB 9500                                  :REM setup nte()
9045    GOSUB 9600                                  :REM load scroller
9049 :
9050 REM--- DEF FN ---
9055    DEF FN MD7(Z) = INT((Z/7-INT(Z/7))*7+.05)
9089 :
9090    RETURN
9091 :
9100 REM   ===============
9101 REM   = define shapes
9102 REM   ===============
9103 :
9105 REM   --- CLEFS ---
9110        REM (insert 'machine specific' code here for defining shapes)
9199 :
```

```
9200 REM    --- NOTES ---
9210         REM (insert 'machine specific' code here for defining shapes)
9299 :
9300 REM    --- ACCIDENTALS ---
9310         REM (insert 'machine specific' code here for defining shapes)
9399 :
9400 REM    --- CURSOR ---
9410         REM (insert 'machine specific' code here for defining shapes)
9489 :
9490         RETURN
9491 :
9500 REM    ================
9501 REM    = setup nte()
9502 REM    ================
9503 :
9510         DIM NTE(MAX,6)
9519 :
9520         FOR  I=1 TO MAX
9530           NTE(I-1,RL) = I
9540         NEXT I
9545         NTE(MAX,RL)=0 :NTE(0,RL)=0
9550         CRNT=0 :NXT=1 :XOF=0
9589 :
9590         RETURN
9591 :
9600 REM    ================
9601 REM    = load scroller(ml)
9602 REM    ================
9603 :
9610         REM (load 'machine specific' machine language scroller)
9689 :
9690         RETURN
9691 :
9692 REM****************
```

While a discussion of the machine language scrolling routines is beyond the scope of this book, complete program listings have been included in Appendix D for the C-64 and Apple machines.

Exercises 5.5

1. Modify the accidental routines to allow for double sharps, double flats, and for a natural.
2. Write a description of how you might implement a PLAY function within the program outlined above. (See Chapter 7 for the complete program and a description.)

6

COMPUTER-GENERATED SOUND

In this chapter we investigate how to incorporate sound into music programs. For instructional lessons dealing with notation of music, with note reading, or with the relationships between music's sounding elements, we believe sound is a necessity. Even for noninstructional music programs, it is often desirable to have sound, if only for entertainment value.

We first briefly explore the physics of sound production as applied to music and to the electronic circuits used in computer-generated sound. Then for each of our three microcomputers, we discuss how sound is produced, how sound may be programmed and incorporated into different programming contexts, and we illustrate sound production with examples of music-related programs, all developed with attention to the principles set forth in Chapter 1. Finally, we conclude the chapter with a program for each of the IBM, C-64, and Apple microcomputers that plays melodies entered by the user and that makes use of the linked list data structure introduced in Chapter 3 and demonstrated in Chapter 5.

FUNDAMENTALS OF MUSICAL SOUND

Sound is heard with the ears. Study the path of sound waves through the ear and into the brain shown in Figure 6.1. The physical motion of the eardrum is transferred through the bones of the middle ear and creates disturbances in the

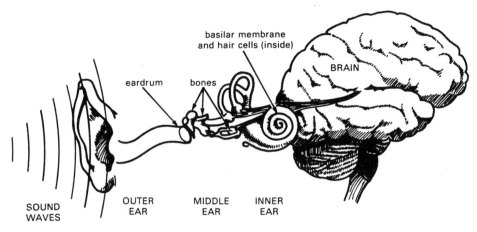

Figure 6.1 The Path of Sound from Ear to Brain

fluid of the inner ear. These disturbances cause the hair cells of the basilar membrane to be stimulated, and through mechanisms that we do not yet fully understand, this stimulation is passed along to the brain and interpreted as sound.

This perceptual process—hearing—is the final step in sound's existence. But what causes the eardrum to move? The process begins with some **sound source** that is set into vibration. This vibration can be regular and long-lasting, as that of a vibrating and undamped string, or it can be irregular and short-lived, as that of a falling rock crashing onto a ledge below. In both cases the sound source vibrates; indeed, vibration is the necessary antecedent to the perception of any sound.

After vibration creates sound, the sound must be transmitted somehow. To visualize this transmission, imagine a row of dominoes standing on edge. At the end of the row is a cup of water. Push the first domino with your finger, and it knocks over the second, which in turn knocks over the third, and so forth. As the last domino falls, it tips over the cup. Your finger is the sound source; the cup is the ear of the hearer. The energy of your finger is transferred to the first domino, and from there through the entire row. Finally, the energy of the last domino is transferred to the cup and sets it into (a possibly messy) motion.

The dominoes are the **medium** through which the energy is transferred indirectly from your finger to the cup. The medium for most sounds we hear is air, although we can hear sounds also underwater, in which case water is the medium. Like the dominoes, air molecules are bumped, or excited, and in turn excite others. Thus a **sound wave** travels through the air. Eventually, some of the air molecules will excite our eardrums, causing them to vibrate, and this completes the cycle, as shown in Figure 6.2.

Like the dominoes, the air molecules themselves do not move very much (did the first domino do little but fall over?); they are merely the transferrers of

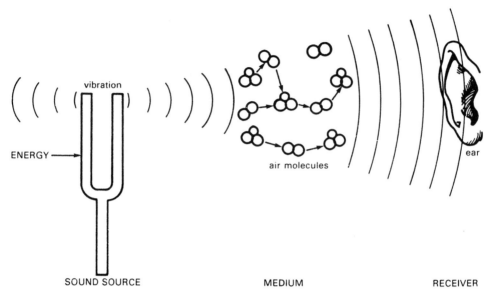

Figure 6.2   The Path of Sound from the Source to the Ear

energy. Moreover, sound energy disperses over an increasingly large area as it travels, thus dissipating its energy, like water rushing out of a broken dam. That is why distant sounds are not as loud as nearby ones.

What distinguishes musical sound (specifically pitched sound) from the sound of one rock striking another? Primarily it is the regularity of the vibrations. Regular vibrations repeat their patterns of motion periodically, and this **periodicity** is the key to pitch. The number of times in one second that the pattern of vibrations repeats itself is the **frequency** of the sound. We perceive frequency as pitch. Frequency used to be specified in cycles per second (cps), but now this same unit of measure is called Hertz (abbreviated Hz), after the nineteenth-century German physicist Heinrich R. Hertz. Thus to say that a musical instrument produces a frequency of 440 Hz (the A that orchestras tune to) is to say that the instrument is repeating its pattern of vibration 440 times each second. It doesn't matter whether the source of vibration is a piano string, an oboe reed, or a brass player's lips; in each case the rate is the same for the same pitch.

If you strike the A key (A 440 Hz) on the piano softly, the sound is soft, and if you strike it forcefully the sound is loud. In both cases the vibration rate (the frequency) is the same, but in the second case the greater amount of energy transferred from your finger through the piano action to the string causes the string to vibrate with more force. The force causes the air molecules to excite each other more violently, and as a consequence the listener's eardrums are forced to move in and out farther. This physical characteristic of vibrating bodies is called **amplitude**, and the magnitude of amplitude in the sound waves is referred to by the term **intensity**. The perception of intensity by the listener is called **loudness**.

A piano, an oboe, and a trombone may all produce the same frequency and the same intensity, and yet we know that they do not sound the same. Two factors account for much of the perceived differences among instruments. These factors are called **harmonics** and **envelope**.

While the whole piano string (or the reed, or the lips) may vibrate at 440 Hz, there are other vibrations taking place. The sound source also vibrates in parts and produces irregular vibrations due to its construction and condition. The vibrations having frequencies that are multiples of the basic, or **fundamental**, frequency, such as 880 Hz, 1320 Hz, and so forth, are called **harmonic partials**, or **overtones**. The other, "odd" vibrations present in the sound, for example 937.2 Hz, are called **inharmonic partials**. The relative intensity of these various partials varies a great deal according to the instrument producing them. Physically, this is reflected in the **waveform** of the sound, that is, the shape of one vibration cycle. Perceptually, this is one of the two principal ingredients of **timbre** or tone color.

The second ingredient of timbre is called the **envelope**, which refers to the change over time in the amplitude and waveform of a sound. The beginning and ending of a sound are particularly crucial for identification of the sound source. Experiments have demonstrated that even experienced listeners misidentify recorded instrumental sounds if the beginning (called the **attack**) and/or the ending portion of the sound (called the **release**) are removed. Reversing the attack and release portions is also confusing, as you may have noted if you have ever heard a tape recording played backwards. Some instruments have a short attack time (for example, the xylophone), while some have a relatively long attack time (such as the flute). Other instruments have a short release time (for example, the trumpet) or a long release time (such as the harp). Attack and release are mostly factors of amplitude, but the waveform changes over time as well, thus influencing the envelope and, therefore, the perceived timbre of a tone.

ELECTRONIC SOUND GENERATION

So far we have spoken of the energy of a person's fingers or lungs causing an instrumental sound source—which could be the voice as well as any other instrument—to vibrate. However, computers create their sound differently. Physical energy is replaced by electrical energy, and the speaker translates those patterns of electricity into physical motions. The speaker thus becomes the musical instrument of electronic and computer-generated sound. The speaker, by the way, is properly called a **transducer,** for it transforms one form of energy into another.

Because the computer uses electrical signals in the sound creating pro-

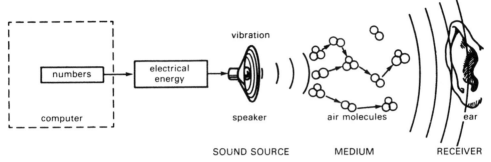

Figure 6.3 Computer Sound Generation

cess, it is similar to the needle and cartridge assembly of a record player. There is one important difference, however, in the nature of the record player's sound source. The physical motion of the needle in the grooves of the record transmits electrical energy through the cartridge. The needle-cartridge assembly is thus another instance of a transducer. The range of possible electrical energy values is continuous, similar to the positions of the needle in the grooves of the record, and there is a direct relationship between the two. Because of the analogy between the range of electrical values and the needle positions, a record player is an example of an **analog** device.

The computer, on the other hand, is a **digital** device in that it uses numbers to communicate its electrical signal values to its sound generating sources. These numbers are discrete. That is, a number can have one value or the next possible value, but it can have no values between the two. As a related aside, digital audio disks are produced by using numbers to control production of conventional analog records. And video disks, as well as the new compact audio disks, both record and play back digitally. To demonstrate the difference between analog and digital sound sources, compare Figures 6.2 and 6.3.

Let us now examine the capabilities of each computer for musical sound generation, develop routines to take advantage of those capabilities, and incorporate those routines in program examples.

Before going on, we note that in this chapter, as in others previously, specific pitches are designated by attaching an octave number to a letter name, such as C4, where 4 is the octave starting with middle C, 5 is next octave higher, and so forth, as determined by the Acoustical Society of America (ASA).

COMPUTER-GENERATED SOUND ON THE IBM-PC

Of the three computers, the IBM-PC is the one on which it is easiest to produce musical sound. One reason for this is its very restricted capabilities: only one voice may be generated at a time; there is no control for loudness or timbre;

and only the pitch and duration of the sound may be varied. Another reason is that IBM-PC BASICA contains commands that produce tones. The programmer simply includes these commands in any BASIC program in order to produce anything from beeps to bagatelles.

SOUND

Try typing the following statements and listen to their effects. (Typing BASIC statements without line numbers will cause them to be executed immediately, and then the computer will print "Ok" on the screen to let you know that it is ready for your next statement.)

```
SOUND  440,18
```

This is A4 and it lasts about one second. Doubling the frequency of the pitch raises it one octave. Doubling the second number similarly doubles the duration of the sound, in this case to about two seconds. For example:

```
SOUND  880,36
```

The following command produces the lowest pitch possible on the PC.

```
SOUND  37,54
```

It is just slightly higher than the pitch D1. The number 54 will set the duration to about three seconds. The next "sound" lasts for almost four seconds (note how long it took to print "OK") and is the highest possible on the PC.

```
SOUND  32767,72
```

However, it is higher than humans can normally discern (although your dog may hear it!). In fact, you can test your pitch hearing acuity by adjusting the frequency downward until the sound becomes audible. This is your "upper threshold" frequency, and it decreases with age.

The syntax (rules for legal expressions) of the SOUND statement is

```
SOUND  f,d
```

where "f" and "d" are arguments. In actual statements, they are replaced by either numbers representing the frequency and duration of the tone or variables standing for these quantities. Frequency is stated in Hertz and must be some integer between 37 and 32767. The duration is specified in "ticks" and may be any value from 0 to 65535. There are 18.2 ticks per second, so that our tone of 72 ticks sounded 72/18.2, or approximately 3.96 seconds.

It is possible to use the SOUND statement in a program to produce music. Enter and RUN the following short program. Note carefully that it follows the principles of programming style that we have used throughout the book. As an exercise, figure out what the resulting sounds are in terms of pitch and duration before RUNning the program.

Example 6.1

```
20   REM #######################
21   REM #--------------------#
22   REM * Fire up the Troops! #
23   REM *--------------------#
24   REM #######################
25   :
100          GOSUB 1000             :REM first phrase
110          GOSUB 9000             :REM pause
120          GOSUB 2000             :REM second phrase
130          GOSUB 9000             :REM pause
140          GOSUB 3000             :REM third phrase
150   :
200          END
201   :
1000 REM ================
1001 REM = First phrase
1002 REM ================
1003 :
1010         SOUND 196,8
1020         SOUND 262,8
1030         SOUND 330,8
1040         SOUND 392,18
1050         SOUND 330,6
1060         SOUND 392,24
1089 :
1090         RETURN
1091 :
2000 REM ================
2001 REM = Second phrase
2002 REM ================
2003 :
2010         SOUND 208,8
2020         SOUND 277,8
2030         SOUND 349,8
2040         SOUND 415,18
2050         SOUND 349,6
2060         SOUND 415,24
2089 :
2090         RETURN
2091 :
3000 REM ================
3001 REM = Third phrase
3002 REM ================
3003 :
3010         SOUND 220,8
3020         SOUND 294,8
3030         SOUND 370,8
3040         SOUND 440,18
3050         SOUND 370,6
3060         SOUND 440,48
3089 :
```

```
3090        RETURN
3091 :
9000 REM ==================
9001 REM = Short pause
9002 REM ==================
9003 :
9010        FOR I = 1 TO 1000 : NEXT I :REM Timing loop
9089 :
9090        RETURN
9091 :
```

PLAY

Calculating and entering the numbers for every SOUND statement needed to play an entire piece would be tedious, time-consuming, and error-prone. Fortunately, PC BASICA provides a very powerful sound statement called PLAY. Using PLAY allows one to think more naturally about music, that is, in note names, than does the SOUND command.

The syntax of the PLAY command is

```
PLAY string
```

where "string" stands for a character string, which is a list of letters, numbers, and other symbols enclosed in quotation marks. Of course, string variables may also be used. Try this example:

```
PLAY "F# F# G A A G F# E"
```

No doubt it was much easier to figure out the resulting melody in this case than in the earlier SOUND examples! Blanks between notes are not necessary, but they help in reading the code.

The example just shown also points up another powerful aspect of the PLAY statement. Unless you explicitly define certain musical elements in your string, PLAY will make decisions for you. For example, our string contained no information about tempo, duration, or octave position. PLAY strings may contain such information (and more), but if it is lacking, default values are used. These details will be covered in the following discussion.

Pitch

Before discussing other string elements, here is a summary of pitch characters.

The letters "C", "D", . . . , "B" denote pitch letter names;
"#" or "+" denote sharp, but "E#" or "E+" and "B#" or "B+" are not allowed; and
"−" denotes flat, but "C−" and "F−" are not allowed.

If you wish, you may also specify pitch with "N" followed by the number of half-steps above the pitch B1. The lowest pitch allowable is "N1", two octaves below middle C. The symbol "N0" indicates a rest. The pitch D#4 is "N28". The highest pitch allowed is "N84", the B nearly five octaves above middle C.

To specify octaves, use octave numbers preceded by the letter "O" as in the following example:

```
PLAY "O3B B O4C D D C O3B A"
```

It is necessary to add the octave number only when octaves change and to begin a string. As an exception, you may omit octave numbers and all pitches will be played in the default octave, namely octave 4 in IBM-PC BASICA, which corresponds to ASA octave 5. In PC BASICA, octave numbers range from 0 (ASA 1) to 6 (ASA 7).

The same result obtained with octave numbers in the example above may be given as below:

```
PLAY "B B> C D D C <B A"
```

The character ">" raises the octave by 1, while "<" lowers the octave by 1.

Duration

By now you may be a bit tired of the "Ode to Joy" melodic fragment we have been using for examples thus far. You may wish to "jazz it up" a bit (you wouldn't be the first). For example,

```
PLAY "L8F# F# L8.G L16A A L8G L8.F# L8E"
```

Since this version is more complex, we show it in music notation also.

Beethoven, "Ode to Joy" Theme

The default duration is the quarter note. It and other durations may be specified in the form "Ln", where n = 1 for whole note, = 2 for half note, = 4 for quarter note, and so forth. Note especially that once a duration is established, it continues until it is changed explicitly, as in the case for octave designations. Dots may follow the duration number to increase the length of the note by one half the specified duration. The longest duration is L1 (whole note), while the shortest is L64 (sixty-fourth note). As with octaves, there is an alternate, simpler way to specify durations: the number may follow the pitch name without the "L". Our "Ode" fragment then becomes

```
PLAY "F#8 F#8 G8. A16 A16 G8 F#8. E8"
```

Rests may be included in PLAY strings in the form "Pn", where "n" may take any of the values allowed for duration. Tempo control is also provided for. The form of the tempo string is "Tm", where "m" is the Maezel Metronome (M.M.) number for a quarter note in the tempo. The default tempo is M.M. 120, but any value from 32 to 255 is possible.

Having introduced a number of the PC BASICA music code symbols, try deciphering the following PLAY statement:

```
PLAY "T16Ø 04L8G F# L16F F# F E L8E- D C# D E E- L16D D#
      D C# L8C 03B B- B 04D 03L16A A L8G# A 04 D 03L16A
      A L8G# A"
```

Now translate the following melody into PC BASIC PLAY code.

J.S. Bach, Fugue in C minor WTC I No. 2

Other Capabilities

The last example points out one of the drawbacks of music generated by a small microcomputer: it often sounds unmusical. This is primarily because all the sounds are played exactly alike. However, PC BASICA has a unique feature which helps to overcome this drawback. It is possible to simulate different articulations by controlling the proportion of a note's duration during which sound is actually being produced. Try the following PLAY strings and note how much improved these versions are.

```
PLAY "T16Ø 04MSL8G F# MNL16F F# F E MLL8E- MND MLC# MND
      MSE E- MNL16D D# D C# MLL8C 03 MNB MLB- MNB 04MSD
      03L16A A MLL8G# MNA 04MSD 03L16A A MLL8G# MNA"
```

```
PLAY "T6Ø 04MSC16 <B16 >C8 <MLG8 MNA-8 >MSC16 <B16 >C8
      MLD8 <MNG8 >MSC16 <B16 >C8 MLD8 <MSF16 G16 MNA-4
      MSG16 F16 MLE-4"
```

"MS" stands for "music staccato"; the sound portion of a staccato note is 3/4 of its notated duration. "MN" stands for "music normal" and is the default articulation; it is 7/8 of the notated duration in length. "ML" stands for "music legato"; the sounding portion of a legato note is its specified duration.

The examples given above also illustrated how difficult such strings, especially long ones, are to read. For this reason we have included spacing (blanks) in the code. Such strings can easily exceed the limit of 255 characters allowable per statement of code. Long strings are generally synonymous with poorly organized programs. The solution here is the same as in structured programs, namely, modularize. Small groups of notes should be gathered together in one string as we did with the melody playing program examples in the first chapter. Consider the following program.

Example 6.2

```
20   REM ================
21   REM = Circus time
22   REM ================
23   :
100  REM --define parameters--
105  :
110       T$ = "160"              :REM Tempo
120       O$ = "O4"               :REM Octave
130       S$ = "MS"               :REM Staccato
140       N$ = "MN"               :REM Normal
150       L$ = "ML"               :REM Legato
155  :
157   REM --define phrases--
158  :
160       P1$ = "XO$; XS$; G8 F#8 XN$; F16 F#16 F16 E16 XL$; E-8
                 XN$; D8 XL$; G#8 XN$; D8"
170       P2$ = "XS$; E8 E-8 XN$; D16 D#16 D16 C#16 XL$; C8 <
                 XN$; B8 XL$; B-8 XN$; B8"
180       P3$ = "XS$; D8 < A16 A16 XL$; G#8 XN$; A8"
185  :
197  REM --define melody--
198  :
200       M$ = "XT$; XP1$; XP2$; XP3$; XP3$;"
205  :
247  REM --play melody--
248  :
250       PLAY M$
255  :
999       END
```

The sort of organization demonstrated by this program makes it easy to read and understand. Both the use of variables and the definition of substrings within other strings help. The expression "Xsubstring;", where "substring" denotes a PLAY string variable, instructs the computer to execute the given string sequentially as shown in line 200. Modularity has another advantage as well, in that it is relatively easy to change the tempo and the octave in this version.

A few other string elements and sound commands exist in PC BASICA. These deal with playing music continuously while a program is executing. Interested readers may find details in the PC BASICA manual. Table 6.1 summarizes the PLAY command and its string elements that we have presented in the preceding discussion.

Table 6.1   The PLAY Command

Syntax: PLAY string, where "string" is a string constant or variable consisting of combinations of the following:

Pitch

Note names	C, D, . . . , B;
Accidentals	#, +, −, (no E#, E+, F−, B#, B+, or C−)
Half-steps above B1	Nn (0 ≤ n ≤ 84); N0 = rest
Octaves	On (0 ≤ n ≤ 6) O3 = ASA 4
>	raises octave of succeeding pitches
<	lowers octave of succeeding pitches

Duration

Note values	Ln (1 ≤ n ≤ 64) (1 = whole, 2 = half, etc.) Number may appear without "L" if after pitch letter name
Rest	Pn (1 ≤ n ≤ 64) (1 = whole, 2 = half, etc.)
Dot	
Tempo	Tn (32 ≤ n ≤ 255) M.M. for quarter note

Other

Articulation	MS = staccato (3/4 specified duration) MN = normal (7/8 specified duration) ML = legato (full specified duration)
Xsubstring	means to execute (PLAY) a substring

Exercises 6.1

1. Translate a melody of your choice into a PLAY statement.
2. Write a program to translate simple PLAY statements into numbers that can be stored in an array and used as input for execution by a SOUND statement. The word *simple* means that the entire melody will be in a single string, spaces may be used freely, octaves will be specified by "On", or by "<" or ">", and notes will be in the form LAD, where L is the letter name, A is the accidental (none, "+", "−", or "#"), and D is the duration (1, 2, 4, 8, or 16, with no dotted values). If this task is too complicated, then restrict the possibilities further.

Hint 1: Use LEFT$, RIGHT$, and/or MID$ to parse the elements of the melody and interpret them as you go.

Hint 2: In order to derive a frequency from a pitch name, you will need the following formula which calculates equal-tempered frequencies:

frequency = base.frequency *12th root of 2 raised to the power equal to the number of half steps above the base.frequency.
Use C1 = 32.703192 as the base.frequency.
Use ROOT = 1.0594631 as the 12th root of 2.

SOUND ON THE COMMODORE 64

The C-64 Sound Interface Device (SID) chip provides far more powerful sound production capabilities than either the IBM-PC or the Apple. Its three sound oscillators allow the simultaneous generation of three voices. The programmer may control these voices not only in terms of pitch and duration but also in terms of their collective loudness and their individual timbres. The timbre control is especially sophisticated for a general-purpose microcomputer. The envelope generators are each capable of creating over 65,000 different loudness envelopes, and a filter will permit removing or passing certain ranges of frequencies for further timbre control. To control the sounds possible on the C-64, twenty-nine memory locations are used.

Unfortunately, lack of programming commands in Commodore BASIC complicates effective use of the SID chip. Normally, the commands POKE (to place something in a memory location) and PEEK (to examine a value in a memory location) must be used to control sound generation on the C-64. Further, the bits within a single memory location must be used for multiple functions, such as to control volume, the filter, and a switch to bypass voice 3. This requires the use of logical operators (OR and AND) to set the correct bits, since POKE cannot work with anything smaller than an entire memory byte (eight bits).

If you didn't fully understand the previous paragraph, you will be relieved to know that the software product Simon's BASIC does simplify the use of the C-64 SID chip through the BASIC language. For the most part, our explanation of C-64 sound programming will use Simon's BASIC statements. If you want to learn more about the SID chip or make use of capabilities that Simon's BASIC does not support, see the list of references at the end of this chapter.

Preliminary Statements

Three statements are used before any music is played in order to set up various aspects of that music. These are VOL, ENVELOPE, and WAVE.

VOL

The VOL command sets the volume of succeeding music. Sixteen loudness levels are possible, ranging from 0 (volume off) to 15 (maximum volume). The syntax of the command is

    VOL n

where **n** is the loudness level number.

ENVELOPE

The ENVELOPE command is used to create a sound envelope for a particular voice. The SID chip envelope generator creates an ADSR-type envelope. The **Attack** time is the time it takes the sound to reach its peak loudness as set by the VOL statement. The **Decay** time is the time it takes the sound to decay from peak loudness to the sustain loudness level. The **Sustain** level is the loudness of the sustain portion of the sound in relation to the peak loudness. And the **Release** time is the time it takes the sound to decay from the sustain level to the end of the note. See Figure 6.4.

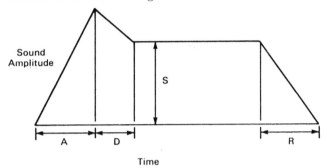

Sound Amplitude

S

A   D   R

Time

Figure 6.4 The ADSR Envelope

The syntax of the ENVELOPE command is

```
ENVELOPE vn,a,d,s,r
```

where **vn** is the voice number for which the envelope is being defined (1, 2, or 3), **a** is that attack time (0 = none to 15 = maximum), **d** is the decay time (0 = none to 15 = maximum), **s** is the sustain level (0 = none to 15 = maximum), and **r** is the release time (0 = none to 15 = maximum).

WAVE

The WAVE command is used to define the waveform for a particular voice. The available waveforms are triangle, sawtooth, and rectangle. The triangle wave contains only the odd partials of a tone, the sawtooth contains all partials, and the rectangle wave depends on its pulse width, that is, the relationship between the time the electrical energy is high and the time it is low. Figure 6.5 shows three different rectangle waves. The middle one is a special type called the square wave, and it contains only odd partials, but with different amplitude relationships among those partials as compared with the triangle wave. The practical effect of these different waveforms is different timbres.

The syntax of the WAVE command is

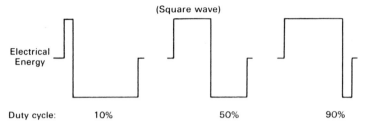

Duty cycle:　　10%　　　　　50%　　　　90%

Figure 6.5 Rectangle Waves

```
WAVE vn,number
```

where **vn** is the voice number (1, 2, or 3) and **number** is an eight-digit binary number of the form

```
pnmlOkjO
```

where

　　l = 1 denotes triangle wave (0 otherwise),
　m = 1 denotes sawtooth wave (0 otherwise),
　n = 1 denotes rectangle wave (0 otherwise), and
　p = 1 denotes white noise (mixed random frequencies) (0 otherwise).

Only one of the values l, m, n, and p may be set to 1; the other three must be zero. The digits in positions j and k are used in advanced sound generation and will not be explained here.

Here are some examples of the WAVE statement:

```
10   WAVE 1,00100000    :REM voice 1, sawtooth wave
20   WAVE 3,00010000    :REM voice 3, triangle wave
30   WAVE 2,01000000    :REM voice 2, rectangle (pulse) wave
40   WAVE 3,10000000    :REM voice 3, white noise
```

Experiment with the voice and timbre settings to familiarize yourself with the possibilities.

One final comment on waveforms: Simon's BASIC has no provision for controlling the pulse width (also called the duty cycle) of a rectangle wave. This may be accomplished by using POKE, however. As an example of how code to control pulse width looks, we give a short subroutine below. For more information on this and other C-64 sound capabilities, we suggest you consult a book dealing with C-64 sound. (See the bibliography at the end of this chapter for two such books.)

```
1000   REM ****************
1001   REM * Pulse width control
1002   REM ***************
1003   :
1010   REM —The variable PW must contain a
1011   REM —pulse width number from 0 (0% duty cycle)
1012   REM —to 4095 (100% duty cycle) before this
1013   REM —subroutine is called.
1014   :
1015   REM —The variable VN must contain the voice
1016   REM —number for which the pulse width is
1017   REM —being defined.
1018   :
1020        W2 = INT(PW/256)          :REM split number between
1030        W1 = PW — (W2*256)        :REM two memory locations
1035   :
1040        POKE 54267+7*VN,W1
1050        POKE 54268+7*VN,W2
1089   :
1090        RETURN
1091   :
```

Defining and Playing Music

MUSIC

The MUSIC command is used to define a character string similar to the one used in the IBM-PC PLAY command. The elements of this string are not as sophisticated as those used in the IBM string, but it is nevertheless possible to define simple musical examples easily.

PLAY

After a string has been defined, the PLAY command is used to instruct the computer to play the defined music. Its syntax is very simple:

```
PLAY n
```

where

n = 0 means to turn the sound oscillators off,

n = 1 means to play the MUSIC string (see below) and suspend program execution until done playing, or

n = 2 means to play the MUSIC string while continuing program execution. (Note: this cannot be done if the program uses hi-res or multi-color graphics.)

Try the following example. [Note: in the strings, (CLR) stands for the shifted CLR/HOME key, and (Fn) stands for function key number n.]

Example 6.3

```
20   REM ################
21   REM # A HEROIC example
22   REM ****************
23   :
100  REM --prepare to play
105  :
110       VOL 6
115  :
120       ENVELOPE 1,5,1,12,6
130       WAVE 1,00010000              :REM triangle
135  :
140       ENVELOPE  2,3,3,9,2
150       WAVE 2,00100000              :REM sawtooth
155  :
160       ENVELOPE 3,3,3,12,4
170       WAVE 3,01000000             :REM rectangle
175  :
200  REM--define music string
205  :
210       TM = 15                      :REM Tempo
215  :
220       M1$ = "(CLR)1 D4(F7) Z(F7) Z(F2) A4(F7) Z(F7) Z(F2)
              A3(F7) Z(F7) Z(F2) (CLR)G"
225       M2$ = "D4(F7) Z(F7) Z(F2) D4(F7) Z(F7) d4(F7) Z(F7)
              D4(F2) Z(F7) e4(F7) (CLR)G"
230       M3$ = "f4(F7) d4(F7) D4(F7) a3(F7) A3(F2) Z(F2) (CLR)G"
240       M4$ = "(CLR)1 D4(F2) (CLR)2 D5(F7) Z(F7) (CLR)1 A4(F2)
              (CLR)2 A5(F7) Z(F7) (CLR)G"
245       M5$ = "(CLR)1 A3(F2) (CLR)2 A4(F7) Z(F7) (CLR)1 D4(F2)
              (CLR)2 D5(F7) Z(F7) (CLR)G"
250       M6$ = "(CLR)1 D4(F7) (CLR)2 D5(F7) (CLR)1 d4(F7) (CLR)2
              d5(F7) (CLR)1 D4(F7) (CLR)G"
255       M7$ = "(CLR)2 D5(F7) Z(F7) (CLR)3 e4(F7) f4(F7) d4(F7)
              D4(F7) a3(F7) A3(F2) (CLR)G"
260  :
270       M$ = M1$ + M2$ + M3$ + M4$ + M5$ + M6$+ M7$
275  :
280       MUSIC TM M$
285  :
300  REM --play the music
305  :
310       PLAY 1
315  :
999       END
```

When you type the (CLR) and (Fn) characters, you will notice that the computer displays unrelated graphics characters. Both this and the string element composition make Simon's BASIC harder to read than IBM-PC PLAY strings. This can be overcome by typing the following command before entering the code:

```
PRINT CHR$(14)
```

The syntax for the MUSIC statement itself (line 280) is very simple. The first argument is the tempo value, which can range from 1 (fastest) to 255 (slowest); it has no relation to M.M. markings. The second argument is the music character string. These strings contain three kinds of elements. The first is a voice number specification in the form **(CLR)v,** where v = 1, 2, or 3. There must be a voice specification at the beginning of a music string, and others may be used within the string to change voices. Line 240 is instructive in this regard.

The second kind of element needed in a music string is a marker indicating when a music string has been completed. This occurs at the end of a string, in the form **(CLR)G.** Note that each of the seven music strings contains this marker at its end.

The final element type is a note specification. It has three subparts which must appear in order in the specification of each note. The first subpart is a letter name: c, d, e, . . . , b for natural pitches, C, D, E, . . . , B for sharps (no flats are possible), and Z for a rest. The second subpart is an octave number from 0 to 8, where 4 means the same as ASA octave 4 (middle C). The third subpart is a duration character. Duration is specified by the function keys according to the following scheme: (Fn = Function key n)

(F1) equals ♪

(F3) equals ♪

(F5) equals ♪

(F7) equals ♪

(F2) equals ♩

(F4) equals 𝅗𝅥

(F6) equals 𝅝

(F8) equals ▤

Dotted notes are not possible, which is a major drawback. An exception to the ordering of the elements in the pitch code is that the octave subpart is not needed in a rest. As in the case of IBM-PC strings, blanks added to the code improve readability.

Multiple Voices

A major drawback of Simon's BASIC is that it makes no provision for producing multi-voice sound. Thus one of the chief advantages of the C-64 over the other two microcomputers, namely its built-in three voice capability, is lost. The following program will produce multi-voice output. With slight modification, it could be converted into a subroutine for some other program. The ENVELOPE and WAVE commands may be added to it to provide a variety of two- or three-note harmonies. It assumes as input an array P, which contains letter class numbers (0,1,2, . . . , 6), accidental values (-1, 0, or 1), and the octave specification of each pitch.

Example 6.4

```
20   REM ###############
21   REM #-------------#
22   REM # C-64 chords  #
23   REM #-------------#
24   REM ###############
25   :
100  REM ***************
101  REM * Main routine
102  REM ***************
103  :
110      GOSUB 200             :REM initialize
120      FOR I = 1 TO 3
130        GOSUB 300           :REM calculate and store
140      NEXT I
150      GOSUB 400             :REM play
155  :
190      END
191  :
200  REM ================
201  REM = initialize
202  REM ================
203  :
210      VOL = 0               :REM turn off sound
220      LC = 1 : A = 2 : O = 3 :REM array subscripts
230      CO = 16.351625        :REM CO frequency
240      RT = 1.059463092      :REM 12th root of 2
289  :
290      RETURN
291  :
300  REM ================
301  REM = calculate and store
302  REM ================
303  :
310      PC = INT(1.8 * P(I,LC) + .5)  :REM pitch class
320      HS = PC + P(I,A) + 12 * P(I,O):REM half steps
330      F = CO * RT ^ HS      :REM frequency
340      FN = F / .059605      :REM freq. # for C-64
350      F2 = INT(F / 256)     :REM split into two parts
355      F1 = INT(F - (F2 * 256))
360      POKE 54265 + 7 * I, F1 :REM and store both parts
365      POKE 54266 + 7 * I, F2
389  :
390      RETURN
```

```
391 :
400 REM ================
401 REM = play
402 REM ================
403 :
410         FOR J = 1 TO 3
415             POKE 54269 + 7 * I,  (PEEK(54269+7*I) OR 1)
                                        :REM trigger oscillators
420         NEXT J
425 :
430         VOL 12                      :REM turn on sound
440         FOR T = 1 TO 1500 : NEXT T  :REM timing loop
445 :
450         FOR J = 1 TO 3
455             POKE 54269+7*I,  (PEEK(54269+7*I) AND 254)
                                        :REM trigger oscillators
460         NEXT J
489 :
490         RETURN
491 :
```

Line 330 is the key to this program. It calculates an equal-tempered frequency using a base of C0. Lines 415 and 455 set and reset bit 0 of each voice's control register without affecting the setting of other bits. (Bit 0 is a trigger for the oscillator; setting it starts the ADS portion of the envelope and resetting it starts the R portion.) For further details, see one of the suggested books on C-64 sound.

Exercises 6.2

1. If you haven't entered and executed the program listed on p. 164, try now to figure out the result before executing it.
2. Translate the following string into musical notation.

```
M8$ = "(CLR)1  f4(F7)  a4(F7)  f4(F7)  c5(F7)  f4(F7)  f5(F7)  e5(F5)
        d5(F5)  c5(F5)  d5(F5)  c5(F5)  A4(F5)  a4(F5)  A4(F5)  a4(F5)
        g4(F5)  f4(F7)  (CLR)G"
```

3. Translate the following melody into music string notation:

Brahms, Symphony No. 4 Theme

4. Write the statements needed to define voice 1 as a rectangle wave with ADSR values of 4, 4, 5, and 15.
5. Write the statements needed to define voice 3 as a triangle wave with ADSR values of 6,1,8, and 12.

SOUND ON THE APPLE

There are no built-in sound or music commands in Applesoft BASIC, as there are in IBM-PC BASICA and Simons' BASIC for the Commodore 64. There is a small speaker, however, which the user can control. We will see how this speaker can be used to create a one-voice rectangle wave sound very similar to that of the PC. The speaker is connected directly to one of the Apple's memory locations (location 49200). Every time that memory location is examined (by using PEEK) or written to (by using POKE), the speaker's cone changes position. Try RUNning this very short program:

```
20 REM **************
21 REM * Make the speaker click
22 REM **************
23 :
100     POKE 49200,0
```

If you are in a quiet place, you may hear the slighest click as the speaker cone changes position. (Note: it doesn't matter what value is POKEd into location 49200; the POKE itself causes the speaker to move.)

But how can this help us make music? To answer that question we first graph the click:

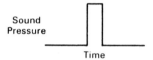

Now let's click the speaker repeatedly at regular time intervals. Our graph now looks like this:

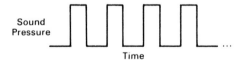

This looks like a rectangle wave! In fact, if we can control the time interval between clicks, we can control the frequency of the resulting tone. (Why?) How can we write a BASIC program that clicks the speaker repeatedly and at regular time intervals? Try this:

```
20 REM ***************
21 REM * Create a pulse wave
22 REM ***************
23 :
100     POKE 49200,0 : GOTO 100
```

(This is a very tight infinite loop indeed!) Now try this one:

```
20 REM ****************
21 REM * A lower-pitched pulse wave
22 REM ****************
23 :
100      POKE 49200,0 : JUNK = JUNK : GOTO 100
```

Can you explain the difference between the sounds produced by these two programs?*

The first tone-producing program above creates the shortest time interval between clicks possible in BASIC, and therefore the highest frequency. However, much higher frequencies are needed for music making (the first tone was only about C#3).

For that reason, our speaker-clicking program must be written in machine language, which runs much faster than BASIC. Since we assume no knowledge of machine language, two versions of a sound-production subroutine (assembly language and machine language) will be given. Assembly language and machine language are closer to what the computer "understands," and thus are called "low-level" languages, in contrast to the "high-level" languages that people understand, such as BASIC. BASIC code must be translated into machine language before it can be run. Assembly language must also be so translated, but the translation is a simpler process. If you know machine language or assembly language for the Apple's microprocessor (the MCS 6502), see if you can figure out how this subroutine works. The basic principle is the same as our BASIC programs—repeated clicks at precisely controlled time intervals.

The first version is assembly language; you may have to alter it slightly to conform to the syntactical rules of your own assembler. Save this routine as "MUSE" at location 300 hex (768 decimal).

```
PITCH1      EPZ 0           ;memory location 0
PITCH2      EPZ 1           ;memory location 1
LENGTH1     EPZ 2           ;memory location 2
LENGTH2     EPZ 3           ;memory location 3
TRASH       EPZ 4           ;memory location 4
SPEAKER     EQU $C030†      ;location 49200
```

---

*Answer: the meaningless (as far as we are concerned) step "JUNK = JUNK" simply lengthens the time interval between clicks and thereby lowers the frequency of the resulting tone.

†Using address $C020 instead will make the sound signal come out of the cassette port on the back of the Apple.

```
START:      LDX #01          ;initialize
            LDY #01
DELAY:      DEX              ;count time between
            BNE DELAY        ; clicks (control pitch)
            DEY
            BNE DELAY
            LDA SPEAKER      ;make speaker click
            LDX PITCH1       ;reload pitch counters
            LDY PITCH2
            DEC LENGTH1      ;this routine controls
            BEQ COUNT2       ; duration too
            STA TRASH        ;waste a little time
            SEC              ; (simplifies
            BCS DELAY        ;   calculations)
COUNT2:     DEC LENGTH2      ;more duration control
            BNE DELAY
            RTS              ;return
```

The machine language version can be entered directly from the Apple's machine language monitor. You may not even have known that your Apple has a machine language monitor, but if you type "CALL −151" you will see its "*" prompt. Then enter the routine exactly as shown below, pressing <RETURN> at the end of each line. When you are done, leave the monitor by pressing <CTRL-C> and immediately save the subroutine on disk by typing "BSAVE MUSE,A$300,L$20".

```
300: A2 01
302: A0 01
304: CA
305: D0 FD
307: 88
308: D0 FA
30A: AD 30 C0*
30D: A6 00
30F: A4 01
311: C6 02
313: F0 06
```

*Or "AD 20 C0" for cassette port. See previous note.

```
315:  8D 04 00
318:  38
319:  B0 E9
31B:  C6 03
31D:  D0 E5
31F:  60
```

Now you know why programmers prefer assembly language over machine language.

To use this subroutine within a BASIC program, three things must be done:

1. The subroutine must be loaded into memory from the disk on which it is stored (or use the BASIC loader program discussed below).
2. Pitch numbers must be loaded into memory locations 0 and 1 and duration numbers must be loaded into locations 2 and 3.
3. The subroutine must be executed (CALLed).

The next program illustrates these three steps.

```
20     REM ***************
21     REM * Make some music!
22     REM ***************
23     :
100           PRINT CHR$(4)"BLOAD MUSE"       :REM Step 1
105    :
110           P1 = 227 : P2 = 1        :REM Pitch numbers
112           R = 1760                 :REM Duration number
115           GOSUB 1000
120    :
130           PRINT "I CAN SING!"
140    :
150           END
1000   REM  ==============
1001   REM  = Play a pitch
1002   REM  ==============
1003   :
1010           POKE 0,P1 : POKE 1,P2       :REM Step 2
1015           R = R+256
1020           R2 = INT(R/256)
```

```
1025          R2 = R − (R2 * 256)
1030          POKE 2,R1 : POKE 3,R2
1035     :
1040          CALL 768                    :REM Step 3
1045     :
1060          RETURN
```

Line 100 loads the sound production subroutine into the computer's memory. Line 110 sets the pitch number values and line 112 sets the duration number value. After the playing subroutine is called in line 115, the program indulges in a little gloating (line 130). The playing subroutine begins in line 1000. The values of P1 and P2 may be placed directly into memory locations 0 and 1, but the rhythm value R must be split into two pieces (in lines 1020 and 1025) before being POKEd into locations 2 and 3. Line 1040 executes (CALLs) the machine language subroutine. Experiment with the effects of changing the numbers in lines 110 and 112. (Note: 0 should not be POKEd into any of the locations used in the playing routine; if it is, the subroutine won't work. For that reason, neither of the numbers in line 110 may be 0, and the number in line 112 must be at least 257 and may not be divisible by 256.)

The intonation quality of the machine language sound subroutine is excellent; moreover, both pitch and rhythm can be computed exactly. However, the formulas to do so are very complicated. For that reason, the values given in Table 6.2 should be stored and recalled when needed. (They may be stored either in an array—see below—or in a machine language file which is PEEKed at later.) The column labeled Pitch 1 contains the values that are to be POKEd into location 0 while the column labeled Pitch 2 contains the values that are to be POKEd into location 1. The values in the column labeled Rhythm must be adjusted by the formula

$$R = RR * B * 60 / MM$$

where

R is the rhythm value to be sent to the subroutine,
RR is the value from the Table,
B is the number of beats in the note, and
MM is the metronome marking of the tempo.

Another, perhaps easier, way to load and use a machine language program is to convert our machine language code into BASIC DATA statements. In this way, we can simply READ the codes and POKE them into appropriate memory locations. Before this can be done, however, all the hexadecimal codes (base 16 numbers) of the machine language program must be converted to

Table 6.2 Values Needed for the Apple Sound Generation Subroutine.

PITCH	PITCH VALUE PART 1	PITCH VALUE PART 2	RHYTHM VALUE (1 SEC DURATION)
A1 (55 Hz)	56	8	110
A#1/B♭1	209	7	117
B1	110	7	123
C2	17	7	129
C#2/D♭2	186	6	139
D2	103	6	147
D#2/E♭2	25	6	156
E2	208	5	165
F2	138	5	175
F#2/G♭2	73	5	185
G2	11	5	196
G#2/A♭2	209	4	208
A2	154	4	220
A#2/B♭2	101	4	233
B2	52	4	247
C3	6	4	262
C#3/D♭3	219	3	277
D3	177	3	294
D#3/E♭3	138	3	311
E3	101	3	330
F3	66	3	349
F#3/G♭3	33	3	370
G3	2	3	392
G#3/A♭3	230	2	415
A3	202	2	440
A#3/B♭3	176	2	466
B3	152	2	494
C4	128	2	523
C#4/D♭4	106	2	554
D4	86	2	587
D#4/E♭4	66	2	622
E4	48	2	659
F4	30	2	698
F#4/G♭4	14	2	740
G4	255	1	784
G#4/A♭4	240	1	831
A4	227	1	880
A#4/B♭4	214	1	932
B4	201	1	988
C5	190	1	1047
C#5/D♭5	179	1	1109
D5	168	1	1175
D#5/E♭5	159	1	1245
E5	149	1	1319
F5	141	1	1397
F#5/G♭5	132	1	1480
G5	125	1	1568
G#5/A♭5	117	1	1661
A5	110	1	1760
A#5/B♭5	104	1	1865
B5	98	1	1976
C6	92	1	2093

decimal numbers. For example, the first command LDX must be changed from its hexadecimal value, $A2, to its decimal equivalent, 162. To convert from hexadecimal to decimal, multiply the left digit by 16 and add the right to it. (Note: in hexadecimal, A = 10, B = 11, C = 12, D = 13, E = 14, and F = 15.) For example, $A2 = (A*16) + 2 = 162.

The following code can be used to load the previous machine language program from BASIC.

```
9100 REM ***************
9101 REM * BASIC loader
9102 REM ***************
9103 :
9110      FOR  LOC = 768 TO 799
9120         READ ML
9130         POKE LOC,ML
9140      NEXT LOC
9149 :
9150      DATA 162,1,160,1,202,208,253,136,208,250,173,48,192
9160      DATA 166,0,164,1,198,2,240,6,141,4,0,56,176,233,198
9170      DATA 3,208,229,96
9189 :
9190      RETURN
```

Exercises 6.3

1. What pitch is played by the program on pages 171–172? How long does it last?
2. Write POKE statements needed to prepare to play an eighth note F#5 at M.M. quarter note = 84. (Remember to add the offset to the rhythm value and then split it in half.)
3. Write the POKE statements needed to prepare to play a half note A3 at M.M. quarter note = 132.

A COMPLETE EXAMPLE

To draw together the sound generation concepts and capabilities into a larger context, we conclude this chapter with a complete program written with attention to good program design and programming principles. The program is a melody player that allows the user to enter the notes of any melody and then hear the melody played. The input is in the form LTTR/ACC/OCT for the pitch specification, and duration is entered in the form 1 = whole note, 2 = half note, 4 = quarter note, and so forth. (Dotted notes are not implemented.) The program is written to be compatible with the graphics input music editor program discussed in Chapter 5 and appearing in complete form in Chapter 7.

The following is pseudo-code for the main program.

```
GOSUB initialize
GOSUB print instructions
Begin loop: for each note
    GOSUB accept input
    GOSUB translate into a form compatible with the graphics input editor
    GOSUB store input
    GOSUB translate into a form to be played and store
End loop
GOSUB play the melody
```

Pseudo-code should now also be written for each of the subroutines called in the main program. We leave this for you as an exercise. Then compare your version of the subroutines with ours.

Before giving the program itself, a few comments on its structure are in order. Line numbers have been chosen so that this program could be integrated with the music editor discussed in Chapters 5 and 7. The same linked list data structure is used; the subroutine at line 1000 for insertion in the linked list is identical. In some cases, the same subroutine occurs two or three times to accommodate the different needs of each microcomputer. For example, one subroutine initializes volume, envelope, and waveform for the C-64. Another one loads the Apple sound routine, DIMensions a translated note array, and places the information of Table 6.2 into another array. Both the sound translation subroutine and the playing subroutine are different for each microcomputer. **You should implement only the code specific to your machine**. However, comparison of these subroutines is very instructive, for as you now know, sound generation is not equally difficult on each of the machines.

The program code follows.

Example 6.5

```
20 REM #########################
21 REM #=======================#
22 REM #=                     =#
23 REM #=    MELODY PLAYER     =#
24 REM #=                     =#
25 REM #=======================#
26 REM #########################
27 :
110      GOSUB 6000                  :REM initialize
130      GOSUB 6500                  :REM instructions
150      GOSUB 7000                  :REM input
199 :
200      INPUT "(P)lay, (S)ave, or (Q)uit";NX$
220       IF NX$ =  "S" THEN GOSUB 7400 :GOTO 490
240       IF NX$ =  "Q" THEN 490
260       IF NX$ <> "P" THEN 200
300          GOSUB 8000               :REM play (Apple only)
320          GOSUB 8200               :REM play (ibm-pc only)
```

```
340           GOSUB 8300              :REM play (c-64 only)
360           GOTO 200
489 :
490     END
491 :
1000 REM =======================
1001 REM = insert (after)
1002 REM =======================
1003 :
1010      TEMP = NTE(NXT,RL)
1020      NTE(NXT,RL)  = NTE(CRNT,RL)
1030      NTE(CRNT,RL) = NXT
1040      NTE(NXT,LL)  = CRNT
1050      NTE(NTE(NXT,RL),LL) = NXT
1060      CRNT = NXT
1070      NXT  = TEMP
1089 :
1090      RETURN
1091 :
6000 REM =======================
6001 REM = initialize
6002 REM =======================
6003 :
6010      N=0 :YS=1 :RPT=YS :NUMBER=0
6020      DEF FN M7(Z) = INT((Z/7-INT(Z/7))*7+.05)
6029 :
6030      GOSUB 6100              :REM c-64 only
6040      GOSUB 6200              :REM apple only
6050      GOSUB 6300              :REM init. linked-list
6089 :
6090      RETURN
6091 :
6100 REM   ----------------------
6101 REM   - init c-64
6102 REM   ----------------------
6103 :
6110      VOL 10
6120      ENVELOPE 1,6,2,11,9
6130      WAVE 1,00100000
6189 :
6190      RETURN
6191 :
6200 REM   ----------------------
6201 REM   - init apple
6202 REM   ----------------------
6203 :
6210      PRINT CHR$(4) "BLOAD MUSE"
6219 :
6220      DIM TRANS(50,3), SND(51,3)
6230      PLOW=1 :PHIGH=2 :DURTN=3
6239 :
6240      FOR  I=0 TO 51
6245        FOR  J=PLOW TO DURTN
6250          READ SND(I,J)
6255        NEXT J
6260      NEXT I
6269 :
6270      REM: enter data from table 6.2 as DATA statements
6289 :
6290      RETURN
6291 :
6300 REM   ----------------------
6301 REM   - init linked-list
6302 REM   ----------------------
6303 :
6310      DIM NTE(60,7)
6320      LTTR=0 :ACC=1 :OCT=2 :LNTH=3 :LL=4 :RL=5 :XPNTR=6
```

```
6330          CRNT=0 :NXT=1
6339 :
6340          FOR  I=1 TO 59
6345            NTE(I,RL) = I+1
6350          NEXT I
6360          NTE(60,RL) = 0
6365          NTE(0,LL)  = 0
6370          NTE(0,RL)  = 0
6389 :
6390          RETURN
6391 :
6392 REM ======================
6393 :
6500 REM ======================
6501 REM = instructions
6502 REM ======================
6503 :
6510          CLS
6520          PRINT"(INSTRUCTIONS)"
6579 :
6580          PRINT"<PRESS SPACE BAR>"
6585           GET Q$ :IF Q$="" THEN 6585
6589 :
6590          RETURN
6591 :
7000 REM ======================
7001 REM = input and save
7002 REM ======================
7003 :
7005          CLS :RPT=YS
7010          INPUT "Do you want an existing melody";MDE$
7020           IF LEFT$(MDE$,1)<>"Y" THEN 7050
7030           GOSUB 7100 :GOTO 7090
7049 :
7050          GOSUB 7200
7055           IF RPT=N THEN 7090
7060          GOSUB 7300
7070          GOSUB 7500            :REM apple only
7075          GOSUB 7600            :REM ibm-pc only
7080          GOSUB 7700            :REM c-64 only
7085          GOTO  7050
7089 :
7090          RETURN
7091 :
7100 REM      ----------------------
7101 REM      - input existing melody
7102 REM      ----------------------
7103 :
7110          CLS
7115          INPUT "File name";FLNM$
7119 :
7120          (machine specific code for opening a file)
7125          CRNT=0 :FLG=1
7129 :
7130            INPUT NTE(CRNT,LTTR)
7132            INPUT NTE(CRNT,ACC)
7134            INPUT NTE(CRNT,OCT)
7136            INPUT NTE(CRNT,LNTH)
7138            INPUT NTE(CRNT,LL)
7140            INPUT NTE(CRNT,RL)
7142            INPUT NTE(CRNT,XPNTR)
7150             IF CRNT<>0 THEN GOSUB (translate: 7500-7799)
7160             IF NTE(CRNT,RL) = 0 THEN 7180
7165              CRNT = NTE(CRNT,RL)
7170          GOTO 7130
7179 :
7180          (machine specific code for closing a file)
```

```
7185        FLG=0
7189 :
7190        RETURN
7191 :
7200 REM    ----------------------
7201 REM    - input IP$ and IR
7202 REM    ----------------------
7203 :
7210        L$="" :A$="" :O$="" :IP$="" :IR=0 :ER=0
7220        INPUT "ENTER PITCH: ";IP$
7230         IF LEN(IP$) > 3 THEN ER=1
7240        L$ = LEFT$(IP$,1)
7241         IF L$<"A" OR L$>"G" THEN ER=1
7250        O$ = RIGHT$(IP$,1)
7251         IF O$<"2" OR O$>"5" THEN ER=1
7260        IF LEN(IP$)=3 THEN A$=MID$(IP$,2,1)
7261         IF A$<>"+" AND A$<>"-" AND A$<>"" THEN ER=1
7269 :
7270         IF ER=1 AND IP$<>"Q" THEN 7210
7272         IF IP$="Q" THEN RPT=N :GOTO 7290
7274 :
7280        INPUT "ENTER RHYTHM: ";IR
7285         IF IR<>16 AND IR<>8 AND IR<>4 AND IR<>2 AND IR<>1 THEN 7280
7289 :
7290        RETURN
7291 :
7300 REM    ----------------------
7301 REM    - store in linked-list
7302 REM    ----------------------
7303 :
7310        NTE(NXT,LTTR) = FN M7(ASC(L$)-67)
7320        NTE(NXT,OCT)  = VAL(O$)
7330        NTE(NXT,LNTH) = 48/IR
7340         IF A$<>"" THEN NTE(NXT,ACC) = 44-ASC(A$)
7350 :
7360        GOSUB 1000           :REM insert note
7389 :
7390        RETURN
7391 :
7400 REM    ----------------------
7401 REM    - save a file
7402 REM    ----------------------
7403 :
7410        CLS
7415        INPUT "File name";FLNM$
7419 :
7420        (machine specific code for closing a file)
7425        CRNT=0
7429 :
7430         PRINT NTE(CRNT,LTTR)
7432         PRINT NTE(CRNT,ACC)
7434         PRINT NTE(CRNT,OCT)
7436         PRINT NTE(CRNT,LNTH)
7438         PRINT NTE(CRNT,LL)
7440         PRINT NTE(CRNT,RL)
7442         PRINT NTE(CRNT,XPNTR)
7450          IF NTE(CRNT,RL) = 0 THEN 7480
7460           CRNT = NTE(CRNT,RL)
7465        GOTO 7430
7479 :
7480        (machine specific code for closing a file)
7489 :
7490        RETURN
7491 :
7500 REM    ----------------------
7501 REM    - translate (Apple)
7502 REM    ----------------------
```

```
7503 :
7510          NUMBER = NUMBER+1
7515 :
7520          LF = INT(NTE(CRNT,LTTR)*1.8+.5)
7530          HS = LF + NTE(CRNT,ACC)+NTE(CRNT,OCT)*12
7540          TRANS(NUMBER,PLOW)  = SND(HS,PLOW)
7545          TRANS(NUMBER,PHIGH) = SND(HS,PHIGH)
7549 :
7550          B = NTE(CRNT,LNTH)/12
7560          R = B * SND(HS,DURTN)
7570          TRANS(NUMBER,DURTN) = R+256
7589 :
7590          RETURN
7591 :
7600 REM     -----------------------
7601 REM     - translate (IBM-PC)
7602 REM     -----------------------
7603 :
7605          IF FLG=1 THEN GOSUB 7800 :REM retranslate
7609 :
7610          O$ = STR$(VAL(O$)-1)
7620          O$ = "0" + O$
7630           IF IR = 16 THEN LG$="16" :GOTO 7650
7640             LG$ = CHR$(IR+48)
7650          M$ = M$+O$+L$+A$+LG$
7689 :
7690          RETURN
7691 :
7700 REM     -----------------------
7701 REM     - translate (C-64)
7702 REM     -----------------------
7703 :
7705          IF FLG=1 THEN GOSUB 7800 :REM retranslate
7709 :
7710          LF = ASC(L$)-(128*INT(ASC(L$)/128))
7715           IF A$=""  THEN 7765
7720           IF A$="+" THEN LF=LF+128 :GOTO 7765
7730             LF = LF+127
7740           IF LF=192 THEN LF=199
7750           IF LF=194 OR LF=197 THEN LF=LF-128
7760 :
7765          L$  = CHR$(LF)
7770          RF  = 139 - LOG(IR)/LOG(2)
7775          LG$ = CHR$(RF)
7779 :
7780          M$  = M$+L$+O$+LG$
7789 :
7790          RETURN
7791 :
7800 REM     :::::::::::::::::::::::::::
7801 REM     : re-translate input
7802 REM     :::::::::::::::::::::::::::
7803 :
7810            IF NTE(CRNT,LTTR) < 5 THEN L$=CHR$(NTE(CRNT,LTTR)+67)
7815            IF NTE(CRNT,LTTR) >=5 THEN L$=CHR$(NTE(CRNT,LTTR)+60)
7820            IF NTE(CRNT,ACC) = 0 THEN A$="":GOTO 7830
7825              A$ = CHR$(44-NTE(CRNT,ACC))
7830           O$ = STR$(NTE(CRNT,OCT))
7840           IR = 48/NTE(CRNT,LNTH)
7889 :
7890          RETURN
7891 :
8000 REM =======================
8001 REM = play Apple melody
8002 REM =======================
8003 :
8010      FOR  I=1 TO NUMBER
```

```
8020          P1  = TRANS(I,PLOW)
8030          P2  = TRANS(I,PHIGH)
8040          R   = TRANS(I,DURTN)
8050          GOSUB 8100              :REM play note
8060        NEXT I
8089 :
8090        RETURN
8091 :
8100 REM    ------------------------
8101 REM    - Apple sound
8102 REM    ------------------------
8103 :
8110          POKE 0,P1 :POKE 1,P2
8120          R2 = INT(R/256)
8130          R1 = R-(R2*256)
8140          POKE 2,R1 :POKE 3,R2
8150 :
8160          CALL 768
8189 :
8190        RETURN
8191 :
8200 REM ========================
8201 REM = play IBM-PC melody
8202 REM ========================
8203 :
8210        PLAY M$
8289 :
8290        RETURN
8291 :
8300 REM ========================
8301 REM = play C-64 melody
8302 REM ========================
8303 :
8305        TEMPO = 15
8310        M$ = CHR$(147)+"1" + M$ + CHR$(147)+CHR$(199)
8320        MUSIC TEMPO,M$
8330        PLAY 1
8389 :
8390        RETURN
8391 :
8392 REM #######################
```

Exercises 6.4

1. In the IBM-PC version, what adjustment does line 7610 make in the octave number?
2. Write a short description of what lines 7710 to 7750 do and why they are necessary in the C-64 version. (You'll need C-64 ASCII and CHR$ codes.)
3. What value will be stored in SOUND(23,PHIGH) by line 6250 in the Apple version?
4. Verify that the formula given in line 7520 in the Apple version does map from letter class numbers (0–6) to pitch class numbers (0–11).
5. Integrate the melody player with the graphics input music editor from Chapter 5. Allow alphanumeric input only, graphics input only, or a choice of either.

BIBLIOGRAPHY

Basic Acoustics

Appleton, J. and Perera, R. (Eds.). *The Development and Practice of Electronic Music.* Englewood Cliffs, NJ: Prentice-Hall, 1974.

Backus, J. W. *The Acoustical Foundations of Music.* New York: W. W. Norton, 1969.

Roderer, J. G. *Introduction to the Physics and Psychophysics of Music* (2nd ed.). New York: Springer-Verlag, 1975.

C-64 Sound

COMPUTE!'s First Book of 64 Sound & Graphics. COMPUTE! Publications, Inc.: Greensboro, NC, 1983.

Vogel, James, and Scrimshaw, Nevin B. *The C-64 Music Book.* Boston: Birkfräuer, n.d.

7

TOP-DOWN DESIGN: EXAMPLES

The purpose of this chapter will be to pull together many of the various routines developed throughout the preceding chapters, show how they might be used within the context of several full-scale programs, and review the necessary steps in designing complete programs. Let's begin by taking a closer look at the interval drill program discussed in Chapter 4.

AN INTERVAL DRILL CAI PROGRAM

The lesson was designed through a three-stage process. In the first stage (the lesson as a whole), we defined the basic criteria for the lesson. In the second stage (diagramming program flow), we took the criteria proposed in stage one and segmented them into various blocks, or modules. Within this diagram we also attempted to show program flow with single- and double-ended arrows, always striving to keep the flow as simple and unidirectional as possible. Finally, after examining each block in more detail and deciding what specific programming tasks were required for each, we created a more detailed "tree" diagram showing all the actual program modules. Once this was all completed, actual program code was written and tested one module at a time. This is often referred to as the "divide-and-conquer" approach. While many of the simple component parts were discussed, several specific routines needed to complete the lesson block were omitted and need to be discussed here.

Most importantly, the lesson block needs a special subroutine, called the **Main Lesson Loop**, to control the flow within the block. It must not only control the flow of activity, but it must also coordinate all of the preliminary tasks, such as setting up the graphics screen. The code for this routine is shown below.

```
500   REM * * * * * * * * * * * * * * *
501   REM * main lesson loop
502   REM * * * * * * * * * * * * * *
503   :
510        QFLG = 0
520        FOR  MAIN = 1 TO PRBL
540          GOSUB 1200              :REM generate screen display
560          GOSUB 1600              :REM generate interval
580            ON NX−1 GOSUB 1500, 3000  :REM visual/aural stimulus
600          GOSUB 2000              :REM answer routine
620            IF QFLG = 1 THEN 910  :REM quit?
900        NEXT MAIN
910        CLS
989   :
990        RETURN
991   :
```

This subroutine is the only one related to the lesson block that is called from the main calling program. All the others are called locally from within. From the main lesson loop we will call the staff-drawing subroutine developed in Chapter 5 (lines 1300 to 1399), a subroutine to generate an interval (a discussion of which follows), a routine to display the interval (using the note drawing routine from Chapter 5), or, if chosen, a sound routine to play the interval (from Chapter 6).

The remaining subroutines to be discussed are (1) a routine to allow users to define their own lesson and (2) a routine to generate the interval. Line number references are to the complete interval drill program that appears at the end of this chapter.

The function of the Define Lesson subroutine is to allow the user to choose from among the five interval qualities (perfect, major, minor, diminished, and augmented) to be drilled. Upon entering the subprogram (lines 5200 to 5299), the five subscripts of the array TYPE(n) are cleared to zero. The subscripts correspond to the five interval qualities, and if the value of the subscript is 1, the interval referenced by the subscript is a valid choice. As in the Main Index module, this one makes use of the same global input subprogram, which can be called more than once to allow the user to choose up to five interval types (qualities). If the input value is between 1 and 5, an asterisk ("*") is displayed by that choice, the value of the appropriate subscript in the array TYPE becomes 1, the flag variable FL will be set to 1, and the program segment will cycle back to get more input. Only when the user enters the number 9 can exit be made from the subprogram. Note that if no choices were made (FL = 0), then a loop will set all the interval types to 1 before leaving the subprogram. If this were not done, the interval generating module will hang in an endless loop because it cannot find a "1" in any of the array subscripts. (Note: if preferred, any combination of intervals could be selected in this case.)

Probably the most important subroutine is that which generates the intervals. It is also the most complex routine, as it calls four more subroutines in turn. The routine begins by calling the Get Quality routine which generates a random number between 1 and 5 and checks the array TYPE to determine whether it is a valid selection. As mentioned in the preceding discussion, these five numbers correspond to the interval qualities generated. A series of five short routines begin to build an answer string by assigning a quality type to the variable A2$, to which we will later add the interval size.

The next two local subroutines to be called each generate one of the two notes required for the interval. The basic procedure followed is based on the circle-of-fifths algorithm introduced in Chapter 4 (pp. 92). We will use a look-up table array, LT(n), to store our circle-of-fifths values. Each value will be stored as a two-number code containing a letter name value (C=0 through B=6) and an accidental value (0=flat, 1=natural, 2=sharp). For example, "02" represents C-sharp, while "50" represents A-flat. The first subroutine (get NTE #1) simply picks one note randomly from the array and assigns values for NTE(1,LTTR), NTE(1,ACC), and NTE(1,OCT).

Since we have already generated the interval quality, we can develop some simple equations to help us choose the second note of our interval. Recall from our discussion in Chapter 4 that we allow the algorithm to generate only perfect and major interval types, and that we derive the minor, diminished, and augmented interval qualities from these two through simple alteration. The first part of this task is accomplished by lines 1910 to 1930 of the "get NTE #2" subroutine. The main function of the remaining routine (minor/dim/aug) is to adjust accidental values for these three interval types. For example, if our quality choice is augmented, then we add "1" to NTE(2,ACC) (such as, P + 1 = augmented, MA + 1 = augmented).

We end this routine by adding the interval size to the answer string A2$. Our answer routine needs then only to compare this string with the user's response, AN$.

Example 7.1

```
1600 REM   =========================
1601 REM   = generate interval
1602 REM   =========================
```

```
1603 :
1610              A2$="": FL=0
1620              GOSUB 1700                        :REM get note quality (NTVL)
1630              GOSUB 1850                        :REM get note #1
1640              GOSUB 1900                        :REM get note #2
1650              SZE = ABS( NTE(1,LTTR)-NTE(2,LTTR) )+1
1660               IF FL=1 THEN FL=0: SZE = 9-SZE    :REM invert
1670               IF NTVL>2 THEN GOSUB 1800         :REM mi/dim/Aug
1675               IF ( NTVL=4 AND SZE=1 ) OR ABS( NTE(2,ACC) )>2 THEN 1610
1676                                         :REM flag dim1 & extra acc.
1680               IF SZE=1 THEN SZE = 1+( 7*INT(RND(1)*2) )
1681                                         :REM unison or octave
1685              A2$ = A2$ + RIGHT$(STR$(SZE),1)
1689 :
1690              RETURN
1691 :
1700 REM         ------------------------
1701 REM         - get quality (NTVL)
1702 REM         ------------------------
1703 :
1710              NTVL = INT(RND(1)*5)+1: IF TYPE(NTVL)=0 THEN 1710
1720              ON NTVL GOSUB 1750, 1760, 1770, 1780, 1790
1740              RETURN
1741 :
1750                A2$ = "P"    :RETURN
1760                A2$ = "MA"   :RETURN
1770                A2$ = "MI"   :RETURN
1780                A2$ = "D"    :RETURN
1790                A2$ = "A"    :RETURN
1791 :
1800 REM         ------------------------
1801 REM         - mi / dim / Aug
1802 REM         ------------------------
1803 :
1810              IF NTVL=5 THEN NTE(2,ACC) = NTE(2,ACC)+1 :GOTO 1840
1820              IF NTVL=3 THEN NTE(2,ACC) = NTE(2,ACC)-1 :GOTO 1840
1830              NTE(2,ACC) = NTE(2,ACC)-1
1835              IF SZE=2 OR SZE=3 OR SZE=6 OR SZE=7 THEN NTE(2,ACC)=NTE(2,ACC)-
1839 :
1840              RETURN
1841 :
1850 REM         ------------------------
1851 REM         - get NTE #1
1852 REM         ------------------------
1853 :
1855              PNTR = INT(RND(1)*15)+1
1860              NTE(1,LTTR) = VAL( LEFT$(LT$(PNTR),1) )
1865              NTE(1,ACC)  = VAL( RIGHT$(LT$(PNTR),1) )-1
1870              NTE(1,OCT)  = INT(RND(1)*2)+3
1889 :
1890              RETURN
1891 :
1900 REM         ------------------------
1901 REM         - get NTE #2
1902 REM         ------------------------
1903 :
1910              IF NTVL=1 THEN P2NTR = INT(RND(1)*3)-1
1920              IF NTVL=2 OR NTVL=3 THEN P2NTR = INT(RND(1)*4)+2
1930              IF NTVL>3 THEN P2NTR = INT(RND(1)*7)-1
1939 :
1940             NTE(2,LTTR) = VAL( LEFT$(LT$(PNTR+P2NTR),1) )
1955             NTE(2,ACC)  = VAL( RIGHT$(LT$(PNTR+P2NTR),1) )-1
1960             NTE(2,OCT)  = NTE(1,OCT)
1970              IF NTE(2,LTTR) < NTE(1,LTTR) THEN NTE(2,OCT)=NTE(2,OCT)+1: FL=1
1989 :
1990              RETURN
1991 :
```

At the end of this chapter you will find complete listings of this and other programs. In the case of the Interval Drill program, three complete versions have been included, one for each of the three machines. For interest, compare the ways in which some of the command structures vary from one implementation to another.

A MUSIC EDITOR PROGRAM

In this section we will develop a music editor for the purpose of writing, editing, and storing a melody. Once the melody is saved we can play it back, read it into an analysis program, or do anything else we choose. The program will be graphics oriented. In other words, the melody being written will be displayed on the screen in standard musical notation. It will also incorporate a CDI (cursor driven input) routine so that no complex music code has to be entered from the computer keyset.

First Stage: The Program as a Whole

First we must develop a concept of the program as a whole in terms of its overall deisgn and operation. Again, we begin by drawing up a list of desired criteria. We need:

1. A title page stating the intent of the lesson
2. A main index from which all components radiate and to which they should return
3. A graphic display of our melody in standard musical notation
4. The ability to insert and delete notes at any point in the melody
5. The ability to write a melody longer than what can be displayed on the screen at one time (this implies the ability to scroll the melody left and right so that different portions of the melody can be displayed as needed)
6. The ability to use a CDI that will accommodate motion up, down, left, and right with top and bottom wrap-around.
7. The ability to save and retrieve a melody at any point during the editing process.

At this point it should be apparent that the criteria we are asking for here are virtually the same as those required for the complex CDI editor developed at the end of Chapter 5. This is the time when a highly disciplined style of modular programming pays off. The ability of a module to be easily transported from one program to another can save an immense amount of programming time and effort. In other words, code developed for one program should be easily adaptable to any other program with similar requirements. The process of developing transportable routines can be an excellent method for helping us develop a more consistent and well organized style of programming. In practice

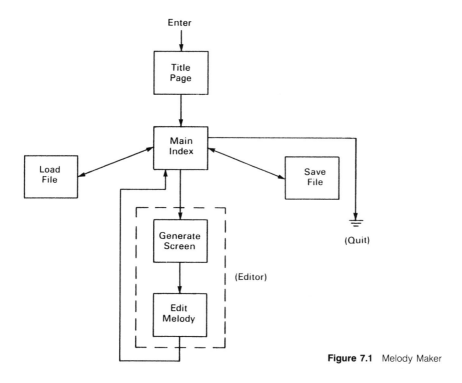

Figure 7.1 Melody Maker

we can lift out the entire series of routines from Chapter 5 and plug them into this program as our editor module, simply adding whatever routines are needed to complete the program.

Second Stage: Diagramming Program Flow

Following the list of criteria, we next need to diagram the flow of the program in order to reinforce in our minds that the flow is simple, organized, and without dead-end traps. Figure 7.1 shows the proposed flow. As previously discussed, the flow of the program should generally move sequentially in one direction, preferably down.

After entering the program we move into the Main Index module. From this point we can get to and return from any of the other three main modules. This is the time to make any desired changes. For example, if we should wish to be able to go from the Edit module directly to both the Save and Load routines, we should add the arrows now and evaluate the practicality of it before more concrete plans are put into place. As a general note, if the structure and flow of this diagram is not immediately clear to someone examining it, it is probably too complex and should be simplified (obviously the degree to which this can be done will relate specifically to the nature of the program).

Third Stage: Developing
Specific Program Strategies

The third stage in the development process requires that we begin to develop a specific strategy for dealing with each of the discrete units within our program. At this stage it is important to think in terms of solving specific problems. Frequently, one module may require several different programming tasks to complete it, in which case it is usually better to subdivide the module into several local subroutines. It is again important to stress the importance of not diving into complex tasks too hastily. The key to successful design can be found in the principle of divide-and-conquer! Let's begin by examining the previous modules and attempt to divide each into discrete tasks.

Title Page. The design of the title page is usually a relatively simple screen display and should present no programming problems. At some point near the beginning of the program we need to initialize all the variable values, DIMension arrays, and so forth. A good time to accomplish this task is to call an initialization subprogram while the user is reading the title page.

Main Index. The main menu is a simple module designed to let the user choose the desired path into and out of the program. This module will, like the previous one, not require any local subprograms.

Load a File/Save a File. These routines are relatively simple and will require no local subprogram calls. Since we are using a linked-list structure, we can utilize the read and write routines developed as exercises in Chapter 4.

Editor. As mentioned earlier in this discussion, the code for this entire module can be taken in its entirety from the complex CDI example and simply plugged into this program. Because of the complex nature of this module (actually, this module consists of two subcomponents, the first being the screen generator routine and the second the actual melody editor module), we use these transported routines as a guide and fashion all the remaining code to match them. (For a discussion of these routines refer to Chapter 5.)

Now, as in the previous example, it is a good practice to produce a new diagam (a tree diagram) of the program in order to make one last check of program flow and completeness. Figure 7.2 shows a completed tree diagram for this program.

The code for a completed version of this program appears at the end of this chapter. As in the previous example, three versions are included, one for each of the three machines.

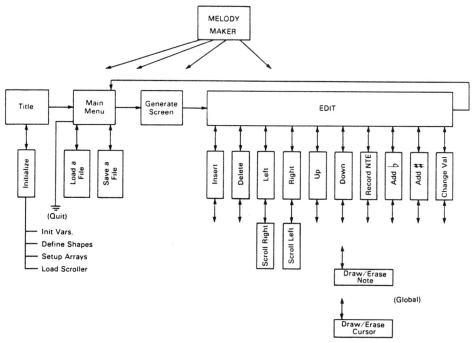

Figure 7.2

A FINAL DESIGN EXAMPLE

As a final example we will design a program that will carry out various analytical procedures on a melodic line. Unlike the graphics orientation of the previous two examples, this program will concentrate primarily on various ways of manipulating a linked-list structure, as well as demonstrating the use of "nested" menus.

First Stage: The Program as a Whole

As in the previous examples, we will begin the design of this program by developing a list of criteria:

1. A title page stating the intent of the lesson
2. A menu-driven design in which all features are readily available from either a main menu or sub-menus
3. The ability to enter a melody in a simple alphanumeric code containing a letter name, accidental (if needed), and Acoustic Society of America octave designation (e.g., C+4, E−3, A5). While it would be relatively easy to include a duration value, we have left it out of this program, as none of our analytical procedures requires this information.

4. The ability to save this melody for future use
5. The ability to read a melody created in either the Melody Player program (Chapter 6) or the Melody Maker program (previous example in this chapter). The implementation of this feature will necessitate storing the melodic information in a linked-list structure identical to that used in the above-mentioned programs.
6. The following analysis routines will be included:
   a. *Interval Succession* will generate a sequential list of numbers representing the distance in semitones between adjacent pitches in the melody.
   b. *Melodic Range* will find and display the highest and lowest pitches in the melody, as well as give the semitone distance between these two notes.
   c. *Conjunctivity Index* will take the sum of the absolute distance in semitones between all the adjacent pitches in the melody and divide that sum by the number of intervals in the melody.
   d. *Pitch Inventory* will generate a list of the total pitch content of a melody (excluding duplications).
   e. *Imbrication Search* will search a melody for a user-defined sequential pattern of pitches ranging from 3 to the total size of the melody (see Chapter 2 for a more detailed discussion of imbrication).

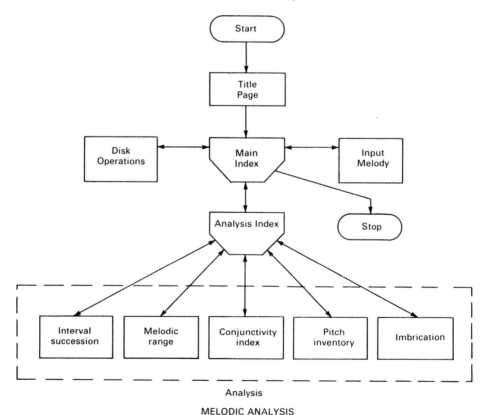

Analysis

MELODIC ANALYSIS
PROGRAM

Figure 7.3 Melodic Analysis Program

Second Stage: Diagramming Program Flow

Using this list of criteria, we next need to develop a diagram of the program flow in order to reinforce in our minds that the flow is simple, organized, and without dead-ends. Figure 7.3 on preceding page shows the structure of the proposed program flow.

As in all the previous examples the flow should move sequentially in one direction. Note in this diagram, however, that the inclusion of a second "nested" menu (arrived at through one of several choices in a previous "higher-level" menu) greatly increases the number of possible variations in program flow. It is for this reason that we must be very careful to diagram the flow in as straightforward a manner as possible. To avoid a "spaghetti-like" tangle of arrows, our program is designed so that every module still has only one entry and exit point. In this case, each module always returns to that module from which it was called.

Upon entering the program, we move to the main menu from which we may choose any one of five options: (1) input a new melody, (2) store a melody to disk, (3) load a melody from disk (both choices 2 and 3 are represented by one module in the diagram), (4) analyze a melody, and (5) exit the program. If we choose the fourth option (Analyze) we move to a second menu that also contains several options: (1) interval succession analysis, (2) melodic range analysis, (3) conjunctivity index analysis, (4) pitch inventory analysis, (5) imbrication search, and (6) return to the main menu (the menu that called this menu).

Third Stage: Developing
Specific Program Strategies

Finally, we must begin to develop the algorithms necessary to deal with each of the discrete units within the program. At this stage it is important to remember the phrase "divide and conquer." In other words, try to divide each module into as many discrete problems as possible. If one task seems complex or confusing, then try to divide it into several smaller tasks that can later be joined together to solve the larger problem. Let's examine each of the various programming tasks.

Title Page. The design of the title page is usually a single screen display and should present no programming problems. As in the previous program example, we will call the initialization routine from within this module. This allows for these preliminaries to be executed while the user is reading the title page and thus avoids a delay later on.

Main/Analysis Menus. These routines constitute a simple menu design that allows the user to choose among several program options. This type of routine represents one of the most important points in any program: "people-proofing." No matter how carefully a program is written, human nature tends to dictate that someone will inevitably press that one key that will cause the program to fail! For this reason all input in the program is accepted as character data instead of numeric data. This legalizes all keys on the computer keyboard and enables the program to choose which keys it will act upon while ignoring all the rest. The next three routines are all called from the main menu.

Load/Save a File. This module uses the same procedure for saving and loading a linked-list structure (to and from a sequential disk file) used in the Melody Maker example and developed as exercises in Chapter 4. In addition, the routine saves and reads a string variable (MEL$) that contains the literal string of pitch characters entered by the user.

Input Melody. Once again we can see the value of writing generic subroutines. For this module we are able, with very few changes, to utilize the input routine developed in Chapter 2 (Example 2.2) and used in the Melody Player program from Chapter 6. We have added several lines of code to enable us both to concatenate a string variable (MEL$) with each new input string, as well as call a local subroutine that will convert each input string to LTTR/ACC/OCT format and then insert it into the linked-list structure. The equations in this conversion routine (lines 4510 to 4530) are discussed in detail in Chapter 3.

The remaining five modules are called from the Analysis menu and represent the bulk of the program.

Interval Succession. This routine utilizes the principle of value swapping discussed in the section on imbrication in Chapter 2. The process is initiated by first setting CRNT so that it points to the first NODE of the melody and followed by a conversion of the LTTR/ACC/OCT code in this NODE to a numeric value (P2) representing the distance in semitones of that note from C0 (e.g., C4=48, C+4=49, D4=50, etc.). Converting all the pitches to this code allows for simple and fast comparisons between any two pitches. The main loop of the routine begins by swapping P2 with P1 and converting a new P2 from the next note. Comparison is made (P2−P1) and the difference is concatenated to form a string for later display. The routine ends when the NXT NODE is null.

Melodic Range. In this routine the linked-list is traversed in a manner similar to that in the previous routine. This time, however, the semi-tone value of the starting pitch is stored in two variables representing the highest (Temporary HIgh) and lowest (Temporary LOw) pitches of the melody. As each new note in the melody is converted, it is compared with both of these values. If the new note is found to be either higher than THI or lower than TLO its value replaces the value in the appropriate variable and the corresponding pointer (HI and LO) is updated so that it points to the new node (this is done to enable the actual LTTR/ACC/OCT codes to be retrieved for conversion and display at the end of the routine).

Conjunctivity Index. With several exceptions, this routine is quite similar to the interval succession routine discussed above. Instead of concatenating semitone intervals into a string, the absolute value of each interval is summed, and the total sum is divided by the total number of intervals in the melody. The variable CNT is initialized to 0 and incremented at the start of each traversal of the main loop, thereby counting the total number of pitches in the list.

Pitch Inventory. Once again we can utilize the same traversal procedures found in previous procedures. This routine utilizes an array (MTCH$()) to store the first appearance of each pitch in the melody. As each new note is read, it is matched against all the elements of MTCH$(). If a match is found the routine continues by reading the next note of the melody. On the other hand, if there is no match the new note is placed into the array. By the time the routine completes its traversal of the list, the array MTCH$() will contain the complete pitch inventory of the melody.

Imbrication Search. The imbrication routine is probably the most difficult to understand, as it uses a series of nested loops in which the starting value of the inner loop is based on the current value of the outer loop. More specifically, the outer loop represents the total length of the melody minus the size of the string to be compared. The inner loop begins at each successive note of the melody (as updated by the outer loop) and counts as far as the length of the string

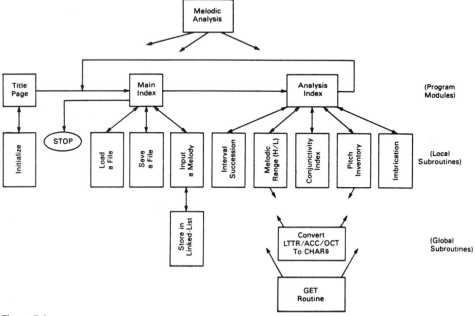

Figure 7.4

being compared. At each increment of the inner loop, each note of the comparison string (stored in the array N$()) is compared with each note of the melody (converted to character strings and stored in the array MTCH$()). If the inner loop completes its traversal and every comparison is matched, then the routine indicates to the user that a match of the imbrication pattern has been found.

As in the previous examples, it is highly recommended that a new (tree) diagram of the program be produced. This diagram should reflect all the refinements we have developed in the above discussions. Figure 7.4 on preceding page shows a completed tree diagram for this program.

The code for completed versions of this program appears at the end of this chapter. As in the previous examples, three versions are included, one for each of the three machines.

COMPLETE PROGRAMS

```
20  REM  ########################
21  REM  #----------------------#
22  REM  #-   Interval Drills   -#
23  REM  #-                     -#
24  REM  #-    Main Driver      -#
25  REM  #-                     -#
26  REM  #-      (IBM-PC)       -#
27  REM  #----------------------#
28  REM  ########################
29  :
100      WIDTH 40: SCREEN 1: KEY OFF
110  :
120      GOSUB 5000                        :REM title page
140      GOSUB 9000                        :REM initialization
160      GOSUB 5100                        :REM main index (NX)
170        IF NX=1 THEN GOSUB 6000: GOTO 160   :REM directions
180        IF NX=9 THEN GOSUB 7000: GOTO 480   :REM final stats / quit
200      GOSUB 5200                        :REM define lesson
220      GOSUB 5300                        :REM number of problems (PRBL)
240      GOSUB 500                         :REM main lesson loop
300      GOTO  160                         :REM return to index
479  :
480      WIDTH 80: SCREEN 0: KEY ON
490      END
498  :
499  :
500  REM  ************************
501  REM  * main lesson loop
502  REM  ************************
503  :
510      QFLG = 0
520      FOR  MAIN = 1 TO PRBL
540        GOSUB 1200                      :REM generate screen display
560        GOSUB 1600                      :REM generate interval
580          ON NX-1 GOSUB 1500, 3000      :REM visual/aural stimulus
600        GOSUB 2000                      :REM answer routine
620          IF QFLG = 1 THEN 910          :REM quit?
900      NEXT MAIN
910      CLS
989  :
990      RETURN
991  :
1200 REM     ========================
1201 REM     = setup screen
1202 REM     ========================
```

```
1203 :
1210            CLS
1220            NUM=2: X=40: Y=40
1230            GOSUB 1300                              :REM draw staff(s)
1289 :
1290            RETURN
1291 :
1300 REM       ------------------------
1301 REM       - draw staff(s)
1302 REM       ------------------------
1303 :
1305            FOR  J=1 TO NUM
1310              FOR  I=0 TO 24 STEP 6
1320                LINE (X,Y+I)-(X+214,Y+I)
1330              NEXT I
1340              IF J=1 THEN PRESET (X+FX,Y+FY): DRAW GC$  :REM draw G-clef
1350              IF J=2 THEN PRESET (X+FX,Y+FY): DRAW FC$  :REM draw F-clef
1360              Y = Y+36
1370            NEXT J
1389 :
1390            RETURN
1391 :
1500 REM       =========================
1501 REM       = draw note(s)
1502 REM       =========================
1503 :
1505            X = 100
1510            FOR  NN=1 TO 2
1515              X = X+35: Y = 154 - 3*( 7*NTE(NN,OCT)+NTE(NN,LTTR) )
1520              PRESET (X,Y): DRAW NTE$
1525              IF NTE(NN,ACC) <> 0 THEN GOSUB 1550    :REM draw accidental
1530              IF INT(Y/2) = Y/2   THEN GOSUB 1580    :REM draw ledger line
1535            NEXT NN
1539 :
1540            RETURN
1541 :
1550 REM       ------------------------
1551 REM       - draw accidental
1552 REM       ------------------------
1553 :
1555            ON NTE(NN,ACC)+3 GOTO 1557, 1560, 1570, 1562, 1565
1556 :
1557            PRESET (X-12,Y): DRAW DF$: GOTO 1570    :REM double flat
1560            PRESET (X-12,Y): DRAW F$:  GOTO 1570    :REM flat
1562            PRESET (X-12,Y): DRAW S$:  GOTO 1570    :REM sharp
1565            PRESET (X-12,Y): DRAW DS$: GOTO 1570    :REM double sharp
1569 :
1570            RETURN
1579 :
1580 REM       ------------------------
1581 REM       - draw ledger line(s)
1582 REM       ------------------------
1583 :
1585            LINE (X-8,Y)-(X+8,Y)
1587            IF Y<33 THEN LINE (X-8,33)-(X+8,33)
1589 :
1590            RETURN
1591 :
1600 REM       =========================
1601 REM       = generate interval
1602 REM       =========================
1603 :
1610            A2$="": FL=0
1620            GOSUB 1700                    :REM get note quality (NTVL)
1630            GOSUB 1850                    :REM get note #1
1640            GOSUB 1900                    :REM get note #2
1650            SZE = ABS( NTE(1,LTTR)-NTE(2,LTTR) )+1
```

```
1660            IF FL=1 THEN FL=0: SZE = 9-SZE   :REM invert
1670            IF NTVL>2 THEN GOSUB 1800        :REM mi/dim/Aug
1675            IF ( NTVL=4 AND SZE=1 ) OR ABS( NTE(2,ACC) )>2 THEN 1610
1676                                  :REM flag dim 1 & double acc.
1680            IF SZE=1 THEN SZE = 1+( 7*INT(RND(1)*2) )
1681                                  :REM unison or octave
1685          A2$ = A2$ + RIGHT$(STR$(SZE),1)
1689 :
1690          RETURN
1691 :
1700 REM      ------------------------
1701 REM      - get quality (NTVL)
1702 REM      ------------------------
1703 :
1710            NTVL = INT(RND(1)*5)+1: IF TYPE(NTVL)=0 THEN 1710
1720            ON NTVL GOSUB 1750, 1760, 1770, 1780, 1790
1740            RETURN
1741 :
1750              A2$ = "P"   :RETURN
1760              A2$ = "MA"  :RETURN
1770              A2$ = "MI"  :RETURN
1780              A2$ = "D"   :RETURN
1790              A2$ = "A"   :RETURN
1791 :
1800 REM      ------------------------
1801 REM      - mi / dim / Aug
1802 REM      ------------------------
1803 :
1810            IF NTVL=5 THEN NTE(2,ACC) = NTE(2,ACC)+1 :GOTO 1840
1820            IF NTVL=3 THEN NTE(2,ACC) = NTE(2,ACC)-1 :GOTO 1840
1830            NTE(2,ACC) = NTE(2,ACC)-1
1835            IF SZE=2 OR SZE=3 OR SZE=6 OR SZE=7 THEN NTE(2,ACC)=NTE(2,ACC)- 1
1839 :
1840            RETURN
1841 :
1850 REM      ------------------------
1851 REM      - get NTE #1
1852 REM      ------------------------
1853 :
1855            PNTR = INT(RND(1)*15)+1
1860            NTE(1,LTTR) = VAL( LEFT$(LT$(PNTR),1) )
1865            NTE(1,ACC)  = VAL( RIGHT$(LT$(PNTR),1) )-1
1870            NTE(1,OCT)  = INT(RND(1)*2)+3
1889 :
1890            RETURN
1891 :
1900 REM      ------------------------
1901 REM      - get NTE #2
1902 REM      ------------------------
1903 :
1910            IF NTVL=1 THEN P2NTR = INT(RND(1)*3)-1
1920            IF NTVL=2 OR NTVL=3 THEN P2NTR = INT(RND(1)*4)+2
1930            IF NTVL>3 THEN P2NTR = INT(RND(1)*7)-1
1939 :
1940            NTE(2,LTTR) = VAL( LEFT$(LT$(PNTR+P2NTR),1) )
1955            NTE(2,ACC)  = VAL( RIGHT$(LT$(PNTR+P2NTR),1) )-1
1960            NTE(2,OCT)  = NTE(1,OCT)
1970            IF NTE(2,LTTR) < NTE(1,LTTR) THEN NTE(2,OCT)=NTE(2,OCT)+1: FL=1
1989 :
1990            RETURN
1991 :
2000 REM      ========================
2001 REM      = answer routine
2002 REM      ========================
2003 :
2010          TR = 1: AN$=""
2020            IF NX=2 THEN  LOCATE 18,1: PRINT "What INTERVAL do you see ?";
```

```
2030          IF NX=3 THEN  LOCATE 18,1: PRINT "What INTERVAL do you hear?";
2040        GOSUB 2500                              :REM get answer (AN$)
2045         IF AN$ = "Q" THEN QFLG=1: GOTO 2090
2050         IF ER  = 1    THEN 2020                :REM next guess
2055         IF AN$ = A2$ THEN GOSUB 2400: GOTO 2075  :REM correct!
2060        ON TR GOSUB 2200, 2300                  :REM try #1/#2
2070         IF TR < 3      THEN 2020
2075         IF NX-1=2 THEN GOSUB 1500
2080        GOSUB 4100
2089 :
2090        RETURN
2091 :
2200 REM    ------------------------
2201 REM    - wrong try #1
2202 REM    ------------------------
2203 :
2210        LOCATE  19,1: PRINT "SORRY...try again"
2220        LOCATE 18,27: PRINT "        "          :REM erase answer
2230        TTR = TTR+1: TR = TR+1                  :REM update scores
2289 :
2290        RETURN
2291 :
2300 REM    ------------------------
2301 REM    - wrong try #2
2302 REM    ------------------------
2303 :
2310        LOCATE 19,1: PRINT "SORRY...the answer is: "; A2$
2320        TTR = TTR+1: TR = TR+1: NW = NW+1
2389 :
2390        RETURN
2391 :
2400 REM    ------------------------
2401 REM    - correct!
2402 REM    ------------------------
2403 :
2410        LOCATE 19,1: PRINT "CORRECT!          "
2420        TTR = TTR+1: NR = NR+1
2489 :
2490        RETURN
2491 :
2500 REM    ------------------------
2501 REM    - input AN$
2502 REM    ------------------------
2503 :
2510        ER=0: SZE$="": QUAL$=""
2520        INPUT AN$
2530         IF LEN(AN$)<2 OR LEN(AN$)>3 THEN ER=1: GOTO 2590
2540        GOSUB 2600                              :REM validate QUAL$
2550        GOSUB 2700                              :REM validate SZE$
2589 :
2590        RETURN
2591 :
2600 REM    ::::::::::::::::::::::::
2601 REM    : validate QUAL$
2602 REM    ::::::::::::::::::::::::
2603 :
2610         QUAL$ = LEFT$(AN$,LEN(AN$)-1)
2620          IF QUAL$="P" OR QUAL$="MA" OR QUAL$="MI" THEN 2690
2630          IF QUAL$="D" OR QUAL$="A" THEN 2690
2640         ER = 1
2689 :
2690         RETURN
2691 :
2700 REM    ::::::::::::::::::::::::
2701 REM    : validate SZE$
2702 REM    ::::::::::::::::::::::::
2703 :
```

```
2710              SZE$ = RIGHT$(AN$,1)
2720              IF SZE$<"1" OR SZE$>"8" THEN ER=1
2789 :
2790           RETURN
2791 :
2792 REM   =====================
2798 :
3000 REM   =====================
3001 REM   = play interval
3002 REM   =====================
3003 :
3005       M$  = ""
3010       FOR  Z=1 TO 2
3020         GOSUB 3400
3030         O$  = STR$(VAL(O$)-1)
3040         O$  = "O"+O$
3050         M$  = M$+O$+L$+A$+"4"
3060       NEXT Z
3099 :
3100       M$  = "T60 "+M$
3110       PLAY M$
3389 :
3390       RETURN
3391 :
3400 REM    -- translate --
3409 :
3410           IF NTE(Z,LTTR)<5 THEN L$=CHR$(NTE(Z,LTTR)+67)
3420           IF NTE(Z,LTTR)>4 THEN L$=CHR$(NTE(Z,LTTR)+60)
3430           IF NTE(Z,ACC)=0 THEN A$="" :GOTO 3450
3440           A$ = CHR$(44-NTE(Z,ACC))
3450           O$ = STR$(NTE(Z,OCT))
3489 :
3490           RETURN
3491 :
4000 REM   =====================
4001 REM   = INPUT routine
4002 REM   =====================
4003 :
4010       QFLG=0: ER=0: TEMP$=""              :REM clear/define all variables
4020       INPUT TEMP$
4030       IF LEFT$(TEMP$,1)="Q" THEN QFLG=1: GOTO 4090
4040       IF ( TEMP$<LW$ OR TEMP$>HG$ ) AND TEMP$<>ODD$ THEN ER=1
4089 :
4090           RETURN
4091 :
4092 REM   =====================
4098 :
4100 REM   =====================
4101 REM   = INKEY$ routine
4102 REM   =====================
4103 :
4110       QFLG=0: Q$=""
4120       LOCATE 23,5: PRINT "<PRESS SPACE BAR TO CONTINUE>"
4130       Q$=INKEY$: IF Q$="" THEN 4130
4140       CLS: IF Q$ = "Q" THEN QFLG=1
4189 :
4190           RETURN
4191 :
5000 REM ***********************
5001 REM * title page
5002 REM ***********************
5003 :
5010       CLS
5020       LOCATE  8,9: PRINT "***********************"
5030       LOCATE  9,9: PRINT "*   INTERVAL   DRILLS   *"
5040       LOCATE 10,9: PRINT "***********************"
5050       GOSUB 4100
```

```
5089 :
5090        RETURN
5091 :
5099 :
5100 REM ************************
5101 REM * main index
5102 REM ************************
5103 :
5105        CLS
5110        LOCATE  3,2: PRINT "WHAT WOULD YOU LIKE..."
5115        LOCATE  8,7: PRINT "1. Directions"
5120        LOCATE 10,7: PRINT "2. Visual Drills"
5125        LOCATE 12,7: PRINT "3. Aural Drills"
5130        LOCATE 15,7: PRINT "9. <QUIT>"
5150        LOCATE 21,2: PRINT "CHOOSE A NUMBER...";
5155 :
5160        LW$="1": HG$="3": ODD$="9": GOSUB 4000: NX$=TEMP$
5170         IF ER=1 THEN ER=0: GOTO 5150
5180        NX = VAL(NX$)
5189 :
5190        RETURN
5191 :
5200 REM ************************
5201 REM * define lesson
5202 REM ************************
5203 :
5205        CLS: FL=0
5210        FOR I=1 TO 5: TYPE(I)=0: NEXT       :REM clear 5 flags
5215 :
5220        LOCATE  2,2: PRINT "WHICH TYPE(S) WOULD YOU LIKE..."
5230        LOCATE  6,7: PRINT "1. Perfect"
5235        LOCATE  8,7: PRINT "2. Major"
5240        LOCATE 10,7: PRINT "3. Minor"
5245        LOCATE 12,7: PRINT "4. Diminished"
5250        LOCATE 14,7: PRINT "5. Augmented"
5255        LOCATE 17,7: PRINT "9. <DONE>"
5260        LOCATE 22,2: PRINT "CHOOSE NUMBER(S)...";
5263 :
5265        LW$="1": HG$="5": ODD$="9": GOSUB 4000
5270         IF ER=1 THEN ER=0: GOTO 5220
5275         IF TEMP$ = "9" THEN 5285
5280        TEMP = VAL(TEMP$): TYPE(TEMP)=1: FL=1
5282        LOCATE 2*TEMP+4,2: PRINT "*": GOTO 5260
5285         IF FL=0 THEN FOR I=1 TO 5: TYPE(I)=1: NEXT    :REM default settings
5289 :
5290        RETURN
5291 :
5300 REM ************************
5301 REM * NUM of problems
5302 REM ************************
5303 :
5310        CLS: ER=0
5320        LOCATE 10,1: PRINT "How many problems do you want (1-99)"
5330        LW$="1": HG$="99": ODD$="0": GOSUB 4000: PRBL$=TEMP$
5340         IF ER=1 THEN ER=0: GOTO 5320
5350        PRBL = VAL(PRBL$)
5389 :
5390        RETURN
5391 :
6000 REM ************************
6001 REM * directions
6002 REM ************************
6003 :
6010        CLS
6020        LOCATE 10,2: PRINT "(to be added later)"
6030        GOSUB 4100
6089 :
```

```
6090        RETURN
6091 :
6099 :
7000 REM **************************
7001 REM * final statistics
7002 REM **************************
7003 :
7005        CLS
7010        LOCATE  3,2: PRINT "HERE ARE YOUR RESULTS..."
7020        LOCATE  4,1: PRINT "====================================="
7030        LOCATE  6,7: PRINT "Total Correct:   "; NR
7040        LOCATE  8,7: PRINT "Total Wrong:     "; NW
7050        LOCATE 10,7: PRINT "Total Attempts: "; TTR
7060        LOCATE 12,7: PRINT "====================================="
7065         IF TTR = 0 THEN 7080          :REM avoid div-by-zero error
7070        LOCATE 15,7: PRINT "Final Score:     "; INT( NR/(NR+NW)*100 );" %"
7080        GOSUB 4100
7089 :
7090        RETURN
7091 :
9000 REM **************************
9001 REM * initialization
9002 REM **************************
9003 :
9010        NTE=4: FX=10: FY=24
9015        LTTR=1: ACC=2: OCT=3: LNTH=4
9020        FCTR=(-1): NUM=2: CLF(1)=1: CLF(2)=2
9030        DIM NTE(2,4), TYPE(5), LT$(20)
9039 :
9040 REM    --- DEF FN ---
9045        DEF FN MOD7(Z) = INT( (Z/7-INT(Z/7))*7 + .05 )
9049 :
9050 REM    --- LT$() Data ---
9060        FOR I=0 TO 20: READ LT$(I): NEXT
9061 :
9065         DATA 30,00,40,10,50,20,60
9070         DATA 31,01,41,11,51,21,61
9075         DATA 32,02,42,12,52,22,62
9099 :
9100 REM    --- define SHAPES ---
9103 :
9110        GC$ =       "C3BUBD6RULULDLDRDR5URU9LU3LU4LU4LU3LU3LU3LURURULU2BDRU"
9111        GC$ = GC$ + "3BDRU2BDRU2BDRU2RDRDRDRD6LDLDLDLDLDL2DLDLDLDLDLD2LDLD6"
9112        GC$ = GC$ + "RBLDRDRDRDR2DRDR8UR2URURU2RU3LULBRUL2BRUL2ULDLULDLUL"
9113        GC$ = GC$ + "L2DLUBDDLUBDDLUBDDLDRDLBRD2RDBL3BU4BL2LU4RURURULBRRU"
9114        GC$ = GC$ + "LBRRULBRRULBRRURUUBDRURURU"
9119 :
9120        FC$ =       "C3BL2BU2R2UR2UR2UR2URURURURURU2RU2BR4RULDBL4U5LUBR5"
9121        FC$ = FC$ + "RDLUBL5LULUL2UL5L5DL2DLDLDLD4RDRDR6U2BDRU2LURULULD5"
9122        FC$ = FC$ + "LU5LD5LU5LD5BULULURULBRU2R2URURBR6R2DR3DL3BRDR4DL4DR4"
9123        FC$ = FC$ + "DL4DR4DL4DR4DL4DR4DL4DR2DL2DBULD2LDLDL"
9199 :
9200        NTE$ =      "C3BL4DRDR5URDRURU2LUL5DLULDLD"
9299 :
9300        F$  =       "C3DLDL2U6U6BD8R2URDRUBDRDLD"
9310        DF$ = F$ + "BL8" + F$
9320        S$  =       "C3BD8BL2U4L2UR2U4L2UR2U5BD4R4U5BD4R2DL2DL3BR3D3R2D"
9325        S$  = S$ + "L5DR3D3"
9330        DS$ =       "C3BL4BD2R2UR2UR2UR2UR2BD4L2UL2UL2UL2UL2"
9489 :
9490        RETURN
9989 :
9990 REM    **************************
9991 :
9997 REM    #########################
```

```
20 REM ########################
21 REM #---------------------#
22 REM #-  Interval Drills  -#
23 REM #-                    -#
24 REM #-     Main Driver    -#
25 REM #-                    -#
26 REM #-       (C-64)       -#
27 REM #---------------------#
28 REM ########################
29 :
100     COLOUR 1,1
110 :
120     GOSUB 5000                          :REM title page
140     GOSUB 9000                          :REM initialization
160     GOSUB 5100                          :REM main index (NX)
170       IF NX=1 THEN GOSUB 6000: GOTO 160 :REM directions
180       IF NX=9 THEN GOSUB 7000: GOTO 480 :REM final stats / quit
200     GOSUB 5200                          :REM define lesson
220     GOSUB 5300                          :REM number of problems (PRBL)
240     GOSUB 500                           :REM main lesson loop
300     GOTO  160                           :REM return to index
479 :
490     END
498 :
499 :
500 REM  ************************
501 REM  * main lesson loop
502 REM  ************************
503 :
510     QFLG = 0
520     FOR  MAIN = 1 TO PRBL
540       GOSUB 1200                        :REM generate screen display
560       GOSUB 1600                        :REM generate interval
580        ON NX-1 GOSUB 1500, 3000         :REM visual/aural stimulus
600       GOSUB 2000                        :REM answer routine
620        IF QFLG = 1 THEN 910             :REM quit?
900     NEXT MAIN
910     PRINT HOME$: NRM
989 :
990     RETURN
991 :
1200 REM    =======================
1201 REM    = setup screen
1202 REM    =======================
1203 :
1210      HIRES 0,1: ROT 0,1
1220      NUM=2: X=40: Y=40
1230      GOSUB 1300                        :REM draw staff(s)
1289 :
1290      RETURN
1291 :
1300 REM    ---------------------
1301 REM    - draw staff(s)
1302 REM    ---------------------
1303 :
1305      FOR  J=1 TO NUM
1310        FOR  I=0 TO 24 STEP 6
1320          LINE X,Y+I,X+214,Y+I,1
1330        NEXT I
1340        IF J=1 THEN DRAW GC$,X+FX,Y+FY,1         :REM draw G-clef
1350        IF J=2 THEN DRAW FC$,X+FX,Y+FY,1         :REM draw F-clef
1360        Y = Y+36
1370      NEXT J
1389 :
1390        RETURN
```

```
1391 :
1500 REM    ========================
1501 REM    = draw note(s)
1502 REM    ========================
1503 :
1505        X = 100
1510        FOR  NN=1 TO 2
1515        X = X+35: Y = 154 - 3*( 7*NTE(NN,OCT)+NTE(NN,LTTR) )
1520          DRAW NTE$,X,Y,1
1525            IF NTE(NN,ACC) <> 0 THEN GOSUB 1550    :REM draw accidental
1530            IF INT(Y/2) = Y/2   THEN GOSUB 1580    :REM draw ledger line
1535        NEXT NN
1539 :
1540        RETURN
1541 :
1550 REM    ---------------------
1551 REM    - draw accidental
1552 REM    ---------------------
1553 :
1555        ON NTE(NN,ACC)+3 GOTO 1557, 1560, 1570, 1562, 1565
1556 :
1557          DRAW DF$,X-12,Y,1: GOTO 1570          :REM double flat
1560          DRAW F$ ,X-12,Y,1: GOTO 1570          :REM flat
1562          DRAW S$ ,X-12,Y,1: GOTO 1570          :REM sharp
1565          DRAW DS$,X-12,Y,1: GOTO 1570          :REM double sharp
1569 :
1570        RETURN
1579 :
1580 REM    ---------------------
1581 REM    - draw ledger line(s)
1582 REM    ---------------------
1583 :
1585        LINE  X-8,Y,X+8,Y,1
1587          IF Y<33 THEN LINE X-8,33,X+8,33,1
1589 :
1590        RETURN
1591 :
1600 REM    ========================
1601 REM    = generate interval
1602 REM    ========================
1603 :
1610        A2$="": FL=0
1620        GOSUB 1700                       :REM get note quality (NTVL)
1630        GOSUB 1850                       :REM get note #1
1640        GOSUB 1900                       :REM get note #2
1650        SZE = ABS( NTE(1,LTTR)-NTE(2,LTTR) )+1
1660        IF FL=1 THEN FL=0: SZE = 9-SZE   :REM invert
1670        IF NTVL>2 THEN GOSUB 1800        :REM mi/dim/Aug
1675        IF ( NTVL=4 AND SZE=1 ) OR ABS( NTE(2,ACC) )>2 THEN 1610
1676                                  :REM flag dim 1 & double acc.
1680        IF SZE=1 THEN SZE = 1+( 7*INT(RND(1)*2) )
1681                                  :REM unison or octave
1685        A2$ = A2$ + RIGHT$(STR$(SZE),1)
1689 :
1690        RETURN
1691 :
1700 REM    ---------------------
1701 REM    - get quality (NTVL)
1702 REM    ---------------------
1703 :
1710        NTVL = INT(RND(1)*5)+1: IF TYPE(NTVL)=0 THEN 1710
1720        ON NTVL GOSUB 1750, 1760, 1770, 1780, 1790
1740        RETURN
1741 :
1750          A2$ = "P"  :RETURN
1760          A2$ = "MA" :RETURN
1770          A2$ = "MI" :RETURN
```

```
1780              A2$ = "D"    :RETURN
1790              A2$ = "A"    :RETURN
1791 :
1800 REM      ------------------------
1801 REM      - mi / dim / Aug
1802 REM      ------------------------
1803 :
1810          IF NTVL=5 THEN NTE(2,ACC) = NTE(2,ACC)+1 :GOTO 1840
1820          IF NTVL=3 THEN NTE(2,ACC) = NTE(2,ACC)-1 :GOTO 1840
1830          NTE(2,ACC) = NTE(2,ACC)-1
1835          IF SZE=2 OR SZE=3 OR SZE=6 OR SZE=7 THEN NTE(2,ACC)=NTE(2,ACC)-1
1839 :
1840          RETURN
1841 :
1850 REM      ------------------------
1851 REM      - get NTE #1
1852 REM      ------------------------
1853 :
1855          PNTR = INT(RND(1)*15)+1
1860          NTE(1,LTTR) = VAL( LEFT$(LT$(PNTR),1) )
1865          NTE(1,ACC)  = VAL( RIGHT$(LT$(PNTR),1) )-1
1870          NTE(1,OCT)  = INT(RND(1)*2)+3
1889 :
1890          RETURN
1891 :
1900 REM      ------------------------
1901 REM      - get NTE #2
1902 REM      ------------------------
1903 :
1910          IF NTVL=1 THEN P2NTR = INT(RND(1)*3)-1
1920          IF NTVL=2 OR NTVL=3 THEN P2NTR = INT(RND(1)*4)+2
1930          IF NTVL>3 THEN P2NTR = INT(RND(1)*7)-1
1939 :
1940          NTE(2,LTTR) = VAL( LEFT$(LT$(PNTR+P2NTR),1) )
1955          NTE(2,ACC)  = VAL( RIGHT$(LT$(PNTR+P2NTR),1) )-1
1960          NTE(2,OCT)  = NTE(1,OCT)
1970          IF NTE(2,LTTR) < NTE(1,LTTR) THEN NTE(2,OCT)=NTE(2,OCT)+1: FL=1
1989 :
1990          RETURN
1991 :
2000 REM      ========================
2001 REM      = answer routine
2002 REM      ========================
2003 :
2010          TR = 1: AN$=""
2020          IF NX=2 THEN   TEXT 1,156,"What INTERVAL do you see ?",1,1,8
2030          IF NX=3 THEN   TEXT 1,156,"What INTERVAL do you hear?",1,1,8
2040          GOSUB 2500                        :REM get answer (AN$)
2045          IF AN$ = "Q" THEN QFLG=1: GOTO 2090
2050          IF ER  = 1   THEN 2020            :REM next guess
2055          IF AN$ = A2$ THEN GOSUB 2400: GOTO 2075   :REM correct!
2060          ON TR GOSUB 2200, 2300            :REM try #1/#2
2070          IF TR < 3    THEN 2020
2075          IF NX-1=2 THEN GOSUB 1500
2080          TEXT 1,180,"<PRESS SPACE BAR TO CONTINUE>",1,1,8
2085          GET Q$: IF Q$="" THEN 2085
2087          IF Q$ = "Q" THEN QFLG=1
2089 :
2090          RETURN
2091 :
2200 REM      ------------------------
2201 REM      - wrong try #1
2202 REM      ------------------------
2203 :
2210          TEXT 1,164,"SORRY...try again",1,1,8
2220          TEXT 220,164,""+AN$,2,1,8                :REM erase answer
2230          TTR = TTR+1: TR = TR+1                   :REM update scores
```

```
2289 :
2290          RETURN
2291 :
2300 REM      --------------------
2301 REM      - wrong try #2
2302 REM      --------------------
2303 :
2310          TEXT 1,164,"SORRY...try again",2,1,8
2320          TEXT 1,164,"SORRY...the answer is: "+A2$,1,1,8
2330          TTR = TTR+1: TR = TR+1: NW = NW+1
2389 :
2390          RETURN
2391 :
2400 REM      --------------------
2401 REM      - correct!
2402 REM      --------------------
2403 :
2410          IF TR=2 THEN TEXT 1,164,"SORRY...try again",2,1,8
2420          TEXT 1,164,"CORRECT!",1,1,8
2430          TTR = TTR+1: NR = NR+1
2489 :
2490          RETURN
2491 :
2500 REM      --------------------
2501 REM      - input AN$
2502 REM      --------------------
2503 :
2510          ER=0: SZE$="": QUAL$=""
2520          GOSUB 4200                         :REM HIRES input
2530          IF LEN(AN$)<2 OR LEN(AN$)>3 THEN ER=1: GOTO 2590
2540          GOSUB 2600                         :REM validate QUAL$
2550          GOSUB 2700                         :REM validate SZE$
2589 :
2590          RETURN
2591 :
2600 REM      :::::::::::::::::::::::
2601 REM      : validate QUAL$
2602 REM      :::::::::::::::::::::::
2603 :
2610          QUAL$ = LEFT$(AN$,LEN(AN$)-1)
2620          IF QUAL$="P" OR QUAL$="MA" OR QUAL$="MI" THEN 2690
2630          IF QUAL$="D" OR QUAL$="A" THEN 2690
2640          ER = 1
2689 :
2690          RETURN
2691 :
2700 REM      :::::::::::::::::::::::
2701 REM      : validate SZE$
2702 REM      :::::::::::::::::::::::
2703 :
2710          SZE$ = RIGHT$(AN$,1)
2720          IF SZE$<"1" OR SZE$>"8" THEN ER=1
2789 :
2790          RETURN
2791 :
2792 REM   =====================
2798 :
3000 REM   =====================
3001 REM   = convert & play interval
3002 REM   =====================
3003 :
3005          M$="" :VOL 10 :ENVELOPE 1,6,2,11,9 :WAVE 1,100000!
3010          FOR  Z=1 TO 2
3020            GOSUB 3400
3030            LF(Z) = ASC(L$)-128*INT(ASC(L$)/128)
3035            IF A$="" THEN 3060
3040            IF A$="+" THEN LF(Z)=LF(Z)+128 :GOTO 3060
```

```
3045            LF(Z) = LF(Z)+127
3050             IF LF(Z)=192 THEN LF(Z)=199
3055             IF LF(Z)=194 OR LF(Z)=197 THEN LF(Z)=LF(Z)-128
3060            L$ = CHR$(LF(Z))
3070            M$ = M$+L$+RIGHT$(O$,1)+CHR$(136)
3080         NEXT Z
3099 :
3100 REM    -- play interval --
3109 :
3110            M$ = CHR$(147)+"1"+M$+CHR$(147)+CHR$(199)
3120            MUSIC 15,M$
3130            PLAY 1
3189 :
3190            RETURN
3191 :
3400 REM    -- translate --
3409 :
3410             IF NTE(Z,LTTR)<5 THEN L$=CHR$(NTE(Z,LTTR)+67)
3420             IF NTE(Z,LTTR)>4 THEN L$=CHR$(NTE(Z,LTTR)+60)
3430             IF NTE(Z,ACC)=0 THEN A$="" :GOTO 3450
3440            A$ = CHR$(44-NTE(Z,ACC))
3450            O$ = STR$(NTE(Z,OCT))
3489 :
3490            RETURN
3491 :
3497 REM ************************
3498 :
4000 REM    ======================
4001 REM    = INPUT routine
4002 REM    ======================
4003 :
4010        QFLG=0: ER=0: TEMP$=""                :REM clear/define all variables
4020        INPUT TEMP$
4030         IF LEFT$(TEMP$,1)="Q" THEN QFLG=1: GOTO 4090
4040         IF ( TEMP$<LW$ OR TEMP$>HG$ ) AND TEMP$<>ODD$ THEN ER=1
4089 :
4090            RETURN
4091 :
4092 REM    ======================
4098 :
4100 REM    ======================
4101 REM    = GET routine
4102 REM    ======================
4103 :
4110        QFLG=0: Q$=""
4120        PRINT AT (5,23) "<PRESS SPACE BAR TO CONTINUE>"
4130        GET Q$: IF Q$="" THEN 4130
4140        PRINT HOME$: IF Q$ = "Q" THEN QFLG=1
4189 :
4190            RETURN
4191 :
4200 REM    ======================
4201 REM    = HIRES input
4202 REM    ======================
4203 :
4210        Q$="": AN$="": XC=220: YC=156
4220        GET Q$: IF Q$="" THEN 4220
4230         IF Q$=CHR$(20) OR Q$=CHR$(157) THEN GOSUB 4300: GOTO 4220
4240         IF Q$=CHR$(13) THEN 4290              :REM carriage return
4244 :
4245         IF Q$<"A" OR Q$>"Z" THEN 4260
4250            CHAR XC,YX,ASC(Q$)-64,1,1: XC = XC+8
4255            AN$ = AN$+Q$: GOTO 4280
4259 :
4260         IF Q$<"0" OR Q$>"9" THEN 4280
4270            CHAR XC,YC,ASC(Q$),1,1: XC = XC+8
4275            AN$ = AN$+Q$
```

```
4279 :
4280          GOTO 4220
4290          RETURN
4291 :
4300 REM      ------------------------
4301 REM      - move cursor left
4302 REM      ------------------------
4303 :
4310          IF AN$ = "" THEN 4390
4320          C = ASC( RIGHT$(AN$,1) )
4330          IF C >= 65 THEN C = C-64
4340          XC = XC-8: CHAR XC,YC,C,2,1      :REM erase last char
4350          AN$ = LEFT$(AN$,LEN(AN$)-1)
4389 :
4390          RETURN
4489 :
4490 REM      ========================
4498 :
5000 REM ************************
5001 REM * title page
5002 REM ************************
5003 :
5010          PRINT HOME$
5020          PRINT AT (9,8) "**********************"
5030          PRINT AT (9,9) "*  INTERVAL  DRILLS  *"
5040          PRINT AT (9,10) "**********************"
5050          GOSUB 4100
5089 :
5090          RETURN
5091 :
5099 :
5100 REM ************************
5101 REM * main index
5102 REM ************************
5103 :
5105          PRINT HOME$
5110          PRINT AT (2,3) "WHAT WOULD YOU LIKE..."
5115          PRINT AT (7,8) "1. Directions"
5120          PRINT AT (7,10) "2. Visual Drills"
5125          PRINT AT (7,12) "3. Aural Drills"
5130          PRINT AT (7,15) "9. <QUIT>"
5150          PRINT AT (2,21) "CHOOSE A NUMBER...";
5155 :
5160          LW$="1": HG$="3": ODD$="9": GOSUB 4000: NX$=TEMP$
5170          IF ER=1 THEN ER=0: GOTO 5150
5180          NX = VAL(NX$)
5189 :
5190          RETURN
5191 :
5199 :
5200 REM ************************
5201 REM * define lesson
5202 REM ************************
5203 :
5205          PRINT HOME$: FL=0
5210          FOR I=1 TO 5: TYPE(I)=0: NEXT          :REM clear 5 flags
5215 :
5220          PRINT AT (2,2) "WHICH TYPE(S) WOULD YOU LIKE..."
5230          PRINT AT (7,6) "1. Perfect"
5235          PRINT AT (7,8) "2. Major"
5240          PRINT AT (7,10) "3. Minor"
5245          PRINT AT (7,12) "4. Diminished"
5250          PRINT AT (7,14) "5. Augmented"
5255          PRINT AT (7,17) "9. <DONE>"
5260          PRINT AT (2,22) "CHOOSE NUMBER(S)...";
5263 :
5265          LW$="1": HG$="5": ODD$="9": GOSUB 4000
```

```
5270        IF ER=1 THEN ER=0: GOTO 5220
5275        IF TEMP$ = "9" THEN 5285
5280        TEMP = VAL(TEMP$): TYPE(TEMP)=1: FL=1
5282        PRINT AT (2,2*TEMP+4) "*": GOTO 5260
5285        IF FL=0 THEN FOR I=1 TO 5: TYPE(I)=1: NEXT    :REM default settings
5289 :
5290        RETURN
5291 :
5299 :
5300 REM ************************
5301 REM * NUM of problems
5302 REM ************************
5303 :
5310        PRINT HOME$: ER=0
5320        PRINT AT (10,0) "How many problems do you want (1-99)"
5330        LW$="1": HG$="99": ODD$="Q": GOSUB 4000: PRBL$=TEMP$
5340        IF ER=1 THEN ER=0: GOTO 5320
5350        PRBL = VAL(PRBL$)
5389 :
5390        RETURN
5391 :
5399 :
6000 REM ************************
6001 REM * directions
6002 REM ************************
6003 :
6010        PRINT HOME$
6020        PRINT AT (2,10) "(to be added later)"
6030        GOSUB 4100
6089 :
6090        RETURN
6091 :
7000 REM ************************
7001 REM * final statistics
7002 REM ************************
7003 :
7005        PRINT HOME$
7010        PRINT AT  (2,3) "HERE ARE YOUR RESULTS..."
7020        PRINT AT  (1,4) "===================================="
7030        PRINT AT  (7,6) "Total Correct:   "; NR
7040        PRINT AT  (7,8) "Total Wrong:     "; NW
7050        PRINT AT  (7,10) "Total Attempts: "; TTR
7060        PRINT AT (7,12) "===================================="
7065        IF TTR = 0 THEN 7080                  :REM avoid div-by-zero error
7070        PRINT AT (7,15) "Final Score:     "; INT( NR/(NR+NW)*100 );" %"
7080        GOSUB 4100
7089 :
7090        RETURN
7091 :
9000 REM ************************
9001 REM * initialization
9002 REM ************************
9003 :
9010        NTE=4: FX=10: FY=24
9015        LTTR=1: ACC=2: OCT=3: LNTH=4
9020        FCTR=(-1): NUM=2: CLF(1)=1: CLF(2)=2
9025        HOME$=CHR$(147)
9030        DIM NTE(2,4), TYPE(5), LT$(20)
9039 :
9040 REM   --- DEF FN ---
9045        DEF FN MD7(Z) = INT( (Z/7-INT(Z/7))*7 + .05 )
9049 :
9050 REM   --- LT$() Data ---
9060        FOR I=0 TO 20: READ LT$(I): NEXT
9061 :
9065        DATA 30,00,40,10,50,20,60
9070        DATA 31,01,41,11,51,21,61
```

```
9075        DATA 32,02,42,12,52,22,62
9099 :
9100 REM  --- define SHAPES ---
9103 :
9110       GC$ =        "12222225686878757555565666666686668666866668666"
9111       GC$ = GC$ +  "8666866686568662566625662566256665757577777878787B"
9112       GC$ = GC$ +  "78788787878787787878777775375757575755757555555655656"
9113       GC$ = GC$ +  "566566686806880688687868786688786278627862787578077757"
9114       GC$ = GC$ +  "333111133866666565680568056805680565662565656569"
9119 :
9120       FC$ =        "331155655655655655655655655665566000056873333666686"
9121       FC$ = FC$ +  "000005786333333868688688888888888788787878877775757"
9122       FC$ = FC$ +  "55555566256686568686877778666668777786666687777718 68"
9123       FC$ = FC$ +  "656806655656565000000557555788807555578888755 5578888"
9124       FC$ = FC$ +  "7555578888755557888875555788887557887187787 8789"
9199 :
9200       NTE$ =       "33337575555565756566868888878687879"
9299 :
9300       F$  =        "78788666666666666622222222556575625787"
9310       DF$ = F$ + "33333333" + F$ + "9"
9320       S$  =        "2222222233666688656666886566666222255556 66662222"
9325       S$  = S$ + "5578878880007775578888875557779"
9330       DS$ =        "3333225565565565655652222886886886886889"
9489 :
9490       RETURN
9591 :
9990 REM  ************************
9991 :
9997 REM  ########################


20 REM ########################
21 REM #---------------------#
22 REM #-   Interval Drills   -#
23 REM #-                     -#
24 REM #-     Main Driver     -#
25 REM #-                     -#
26 REM #-       (APPLE)       -#
27 REM #---------------------#
28 REM ########################
29 :
100       HOME
110 :
120       GOSUB 5000                        :REM title page
140       GOSUB 9000                        :REM initialization
160       GOSUB 5100                        :REM main index (NX)
170         IF NX=1 THEN GOSUB 6000: GOTO 160 :REM directions
180         IF NX=9 THEN GOSUB 7000: GOTO 480 :REM final stats / quit
200       GOSUB 5200                        :REM define lesson
220       GOSUB 5300                        :REM number of problems (PRBL)
240       GOSUB 500                         :REM main lesson loop
300       GOTO  160                         :REM return to index
479 :
480       HOME
490       END
498 :
499 :
500 REM   ************************
501 REM   * main lesson loop
502 REM   ************************
503 :
510       QFLG = 0
520       FOR  MAIN = 1 TO PRBL
540         GOSUB 1200                      :REM generate screen display
560         GOSUB 1600                      :REM generate interval
580           ON NX-1 GOSUB 1500, 3000      :REM visual/aural stimulus
600         GOSUB 2000                      :REM answer routine
```

```
620            IF QFLG = 1 THEN 910              :REM quit?
900        NEXT MAIN
910        HOME
989 :
990        RETURN
991 :
1200 REM   ========================
1201 REM   = setup screen
1202 REM   ========================
1203 :
1210       HOME :HGR :SCALE=1 :ROT=0
1220       NUM=2: X=20: Y=40
1230       GOSUB 1300                            :REM draw staff(s)
1289 :
1290       RETURN
1291 :
1300 REM   ------------------------
1301 REM   - draw staff(s)
1302 REM   ------------------------
1303 :
1305       FOR  J=1 TO NUM
1310         FOR I=0 TO 24 STEP 6
1320           HPLOT X,Y+I TO X+194,Y+I
1330         NEXT I
1340         IF J=1 THEN DRAW GC AT X+FX,Y+FY     :REM draw G-clef
1350         IF J=2 THEN DRAW FC AT X+FX,Y+FY     :REM draw F-clef
1360         Y = Y+36
1370       NEXT J
1389 :
1390       RETURN
1391 :
1500 REM   ========================
1501 REM   = draw note(s)
1502 REM   ========================
1503 :
1505       X = 100
1510       FOR  NN=1 TO 2
1515         X = X+35: Y = 154 - 3*( 7*NTE(NN,OCT)+NTE(NN,LTTR) )
1520         DRAW NTE AT X,Y
1525         IF NTE(NN,ACC) <> O THEN GOSUB 1550   :REM draw accidental
1530         IF INT(Y/2) = Y/2   THEN GOSUB 1580   :REM draw ledger line
1535       NEXT NN
1539 :
1540       RETURN
1541 :
1550 REM   ------------------------
1551 REM   - draw accidental
1552 REM   ------------------------
1553 :
1555       ON NTE(NN,ACC)+3 GOTO 1557, 1560, 1570, 1562, 1565
1556 :
1557         DRAW DF AT X-12,Y: GOTO 1570      :REM double flat
1560         DRAW F  AT X-12,Y: GOTO 1570      :REM flat
1562         DRAW S  AT X-12,Y: GOTO 1570      :REM sharp
1565         DRAW DS AT X-12,Y: GOTO 1570      :REM double sharp
1569 :
1570       RETURN
1579 :
1580 REM   ------------------------
1581 REM   - draw ledger line(s)
1582 REM   ------------------------
1583 :
1585         HPLOT X-8,Y TO X+8,Y
1587         IF Y<33 THEN HPLOT X-8,33 TO X+8,33
1589 :
1590       RETURN
1591 :
```

```
1600 REM    =======================
1601 REM    = generate interval
1602 REM    =======================
1603 :
1610        A2$="": FL=0
1620        GOSUB 1700                           :REM get note quality (NTVL)
1630        GOSUB 1850                           :REM get note #1
1640        GOSUB 1900                           :REM get note #2
1650        SZE = ABS( NTE(1,LTTR)-NTE(2,LTTR) )+1
1660         IF FL=1 THEN FL=0: SZE = 9-SZE   :REM invert
1670         IF NTVL>2 THEN GOSUB 1800         :REM mi/dim/Aug
1675         IF ( NTVL=4 AND SZE=1 ) OR ABS( NTE(2,ACC) )>2 THEN 1610
1676                               :REM flag dim 1 & double acc.
1680         IF SZE=1 THEN SZE = 1+( 7*INT(RND(1)*2) )
1681                                 :REM unison or octave
1685        A2$ = A2$ + RIGHT$(STR$(SZE),1)
1689 :
1690        RETURN
1691 :
1700 REM    ------------------------
1701 REM    - get quality (NTVL)
1702 REM    ------------------------
1703 :
1710        NTVL = INT(RND(1)*5)+1: IF TYPE(NTVL)=0 THEN 1710
1720        ON NTVL GOSUB 1750, 1760, 1770, 1780, 1790
1740        RETURN
1741 :
1750        A2$ = "P"    :RETURN
1760        A2$ = "MA"   :RETURN
1770        A2$ = "MI"   :RETURN
1780        A2$ = "D"    :RETURN
1790        A2$ = "A"    :RETURN
1791 :
1800 REM    ------------------------
1801 REM    - mi / dim / Aug
1802 REM    ------------------------
1803 :
1810        IF NTVL=5 THEN NTE(2,ACC) = NTE(2,ACC)+1 :GOTO 1840
1820        IF NTVL=3 THEN NTE(2,ACC) = NTE(2,ACC)-1 :GOTO 1840
1830        NTE(2,ACC) = NTE(2,ACC)-1
1835        IF SZE=2 OR SZE=3 OR SZE=6 OR SZE=7 THEN NTE(2,ACC)=NTE(2,ACC)-1
1839 :
1840        RETURN
1841 :
1850 REM    ------------------------
1851 REM    - get NTE #1
1852 REM    ------------------------
1853 :
1855        PNTR = INT(RND(1)*15)+1
1860        NTE(1,LTTR) = VAL( LEFT$(LT$(PNTR),1) )
1865        NTE(1,ACC)  = VAL( RIGHT$(LT$(PNTR),1) )-1
1870        NTE(1,OCT)  = INT(RND(1)*2)+3
1889 :
1890        RETURN
1891 :
1900 REM    ------------------------
1901 REM    - get NTE #2
1902 REM    ------------------------
1903 :
1910        IF NTVL=1 THEN P2NTR = INT(RND(1)*3)-1
1920        IF NTVL=2 OR NTVL=3 THEN P2NTR = INT(RND(1)*4)+2
1930        IF NTVL>3 THEN P2NTR = INT(RND(1)*7)-1
1939 :
1940        NTE(2,LTTR) = VAL( LEFT$(LT$(PNTR+P2NTR),1) )
1955        NTE(2,ACC)  = VAL( RIGHT$(LT$(PNTR+P2NTR),1) )-1
1960        NTE(2,OCT)  = NTE(1,OCT)
1970         IF NTE(2,LTTR) < NTE(1,LTTR) THEN NTE(2,OCT)=NTE(2,OCT)+1: FL=1
1989 :
```

```
1990            RETURN
1991 :
2000 REM    ======================
2001 REM    = answer routine
2002 REM    ======================
2003 :
2010            TR = 1: AN$=""
2020             IF NX=2 THEN  VTAB 18: PRINT " What INTERVAL do you see ?";
2030             IF NX=3 THEN  VTAB 18: PRINT " What INTERVAL do you hear?";
2040            GOSUB 2500                        :REM get answer (AN$)
2045             IF AN$ = "Q" THEN QFLG=1: GOTO 2090
2050             IF ER  = 1   THEN 2020           :REM next guess
2055             IF AN$ = A2$ THEN GOSUB 2400: GOTO 2075   :REM correct!
2060            ON TR GOSUB 2200, 2300           :REM try #1/#2
2070             IF TR < 3    THEN 2020
2075             IF NX-1=2 THEN GOSUB 1500
2080            GOSUB 4100
2089 :
2090            RETURN
2091 :
2200 REM       -------------------------
2201 REM       - wrong try #1
2202 REM       -------------------------
2203 :
2210            VTAB 19: PRINT " SORRY...try again"
2220            VTAB 18:HTAB 27: PRINT "        "          :REM erase answer
2230            TTR = TTR+1: TR = TR+1                      :REM update scores
2289 :
2290            RETURN
2291 :
2300 REM       -------------------------
2301 REM       - wrong try #2
2302 REM       -------------------------
2303 :
2310            VTAB 19: PRINT " SORRY...the answer is: "; A2$
2320            TTR = TTR+1: TR = TR+1: NW = NW+1
2389 :
2390            RETURN
2391 :
2400 REM       -------------------------
2401 REM       - correct!
2402 REM       -------------------------
2403 :
2410            VTAB 19: PRINT " CORRECT!          "
2420            TTR = TTR+1: NR = NR+1
2489 :
2490            RETURN
2491 :
2500 REM       -------------------------
2501 REM       - input AN$
2502 REM       -------------------------
2503 :
2510            ER=0: SZE$="": QUAL$=""
2520            INPUT AN$
2530             IF LEN(AN$)<2 OR LEN(AN$)>3 THEN ER=1: GOTO 2590
2540            GOSUB 2600                        :REM validate QUAL$
2550            GOSUB 2700                        :REM validate SZE$
2589 :
2590            RETURN
2591 :
2600 REM       ::::::::::::::::::::::::
2601 REM       : validate QUAL$
2602 REM       ::::::::::::::::::::::::
2603 :
2610             QUAL$ = LEFT$(AN$,LEN(AN$)-1)
2620              IF QUAL$="P" OR QUAL$="MA" OR QUAL$="MI" THEN 2690
2630              IF QUAL$="D" OR QUAL$="A" THEN 2690
```

```
2640              ER = 1
2689 :
2690              RETURN
2691 :
2700 REM      ::::::::::::::::::::::::
2701 REM      : validate SZE$
2702 REM      ::::::::::::::::::::::::
2703 :
2710              SZE$ = RIGHT$(AN$,1)
2720               IF SZE$<"1" OR SZE$>"8" THEN ER=1
2789 :
2790              RETURN
2791 :
3000 REM     =======================
3001 REM     = play interval
3002 REM     =======================
3003 :
3010         FOR  Z=1 TO 2
3020           LF = INT(NTE(Z,LTTR)*1.8+.5)
3030           HS = LF + NTE(Z,ACC)+NTE(Z,OCT)*12
3040           TRANS(Z,PLOW)  = SND(HS,PLOW)
3050           TRANS(Z,PHIGH) = SND(HS,PHIGH)
3060           TRANS(Z,DURTN) = SND(HS,DURTN)+256
3070         NEXT Z
3099 :
3100 REM      -- play --
3109 :
3110           FOR  Z=1 TO 2
3120            P1 = TRANS(Z,PLOW)
3130            P2 = TRANS(Z,PHIGH)
3140            R  = TRANS(Z,DURTN)
3149 :
3150             POKE 0,P1 :POKE 1,P2
3160             R2 = INT(R/256) :R1 = R-(R2*256)
3170             POKE 2,R1 :POKE 3,R2
3180             CALL 768
3189 :
3190           NEXT Z
3489 :
3490         RETURN
3491 :
4000 REM     =======================
4001 REM     = INPUT routine
4002 REM     =======================
4003 :
4010         QFLG=0: ER=0: TEMP$=""          :REM clear/define all variables
4020         INPUT TEMP$
4030          IF LEFT$(TEMP$,1)="Q" THEN QFLG=1: GOTO 4090
4040          IF ( TEMP$<LW$ OR TEMP$>HG$ ) AND TEMP$<>ODD$ THEN ER=1
4089 :
4090         RETURN
4091 :
4100 REM     =======================
4101 REM     = GET routine
4102 REM     =======================
4103 :
4110         QFLG=0: Q$=""
4120         VTAB 23 :PRINT "     <PRESS SPACE BAR TO CONTINUE>"
4130         GET Q$
4140         HOME: IF Q$ = "Q" THEN QFLG=1
4189 :
4190         RETURN
4191 :
5000 REM ***********************
5001 REM * title page
5002 REM ***********************
5003 :
```

```
5010        HOME
5020        VTAB   8: HTAB 9: PRINT "************************"
5030        VTAB   9: HTAB 9: PRINT "*   INTERVAL   DRILLS   *"
5040        VTAB 10: HTAB 9: PRINT "************************"
5050        GOSUB 4100
5089 :
5090        RETURN
5091 :
5100 REM ************************
5101 REM * main index
5102 REM ************************
5103 :
5105        HOME
5110        VTAB   3: HTAB 2: PRINT "WHAT WOULD YOU LIKE..."
5115        VTAB   8: HTAB 7: PRINT "1. Directions"
5120        VTAB 10: HTAB 7: PRINT "2. Visual Drills"
5125        VTAB 12: HTAB 7: PRINT "3. Aural Drills"
5130        VTAB 15: HTAB 7: PRINT "9. <QUIT>"
5150        VTAB 21: HTAB 2: PRINT "CHOOSE A NUMBER...";
5155 :
5160        LW$="1": HG$="3": ODD$="9": GOSUB 4000: NX$=TEMP$
5170         IF ER=1 THEN ER=0: GOTO 5150
5180        NX = VAL(NX$)
5189 :
5190        RETURN
5191 :
5199 :
5200 REM ************************
5201 REM * define lesson
5202 REM ************************
5203 :
5205        HOME: FL=0
5210        FOR I=1 TO 5: TYPE(I)=0: NEXT          :REM clear 5 flags
5215 :
5220        VTAB   2: HTAB 2: PRINT "WHICH TYPE(S) WOULD YOU LIKE..."
5230        VTAB   6: HTAB 7: PRINT "1. Perfect"
5235        VTAB   8: HTAB 7: PRINT "2. Major"
5240        VTAB 10: HTAB 7: PRINT "3. Minor"
5245        VTAB 12: HTAB 7: PRINT "4. Diminished"
5250        VTAB 14: HTAB 7: PRINT "5. Augmented"
5255        VTAB 17: HTAB 7: PRINT "9. <DONE>"
5260        VTAB 22: HTAB 2: PRINT "CHOOSE NUMBER(S)...";
5263 :
5265        LW$="1": HG$="5": ODD$="9": GOSUB 4000
5270         IF ER=1 THEN ER=0: GOTO 5220
5275         IF TEMP$ = "9" THEN 5285
5280        TEMP = VAL(TEMP$): TYPE(TEMP)=1: FL=1
5282        VTAB 2*TEMP+4: PRINT "  *": GOTO 5260
5285         IF FL=0 THEN FOR I=1 TO 5: TYPE(I)=1: NEXT    :REM default settings
5289 :
5290        RETURN
5291 :
5300 REM ************************
5301 REM * NUM of problems
5302 REM ************************
5303 :
5310        HOME: ER=0
5320        VTAB 10: PRINT " How many problems do you want (1-99)"
5330        LW$="1": HG$="99": ODD$="Q": GOSUB 4000: PRBL$=TEMP$
5340         IF ER=1 THEN ER=0: GOTO 5320
5350        PRBL = VAL(PRBL$)
5389 :
5390        RETURN
5391 :
6000 REM ************************
6001 REM * directions
6002 REM ************************
```

```
6003 :
6010          HOME
6020          VTAB 10: PRINT "  (to be added later)"
6030          GOSUB 4100
6089 :
6090          RETURN
6091 :
7000 REM **************************
7001 REM * final statistics
7002 REM **************************
7003 :
7005          HOME
7010          VTAB  3: HTAB 2: PRINT "HERE ARE YOUR RESULTS..."
7020          VTAB  4: HTAB 1: PRINT "===================================="
7030          VTAB  6: HTAB 7: PRINT "Total Correct:   "; NR
7040          VTAB  8: HTAB 7: PRINT "Total Wrong:     "; NW
7050          VTAB 10: HTAB 7: PRINT "Total Attempts: "; TTR
7060          VTAB 12: HTAB 7: PRINT "===================================="
7065           IF TTR = 0 THEN 7080               :REM avoid div-by-zero error
7070          VTAB15: HTAB7: PRINT "Final Score:     "; INT( NR/(NR+NW)*100 );"%"
7080          GOSUB 4100
7089 :
7090          RETURN
7091 :
9000 REM **************************
9001 REM * initialization
9002 REM **************************
9003 :
9005          GC=1: FC=2: NTE=3: DF=4: F=5: S=6: DS=7
9010          FX=10: FY=24
9015          LTTR=1: ACC=2: OCT=3: LNTH=4
9020          FCTR=(-1): NUM=2: CLF(1)=1: CLF(2)=2
9030          DIM NTE(2,4), TYPE(5), LT$(20)
9039 :
9040 REM   --- DEF FN ---
9045          DEF FN MOD7(Z) = INT( (Z/7-INT(Z/7))*7 + .05 )
9049 :
9050 REM   --- LT$() Data ---
9060          FOR I=0 TO 20: READ LT$(I): NEXT
9061 :
9065           DATA 30,00,40,10,50,20,60
9070           DATA 31,01,41,11,51,21,61
9075           DATA 32,02,42,12,52,22,62
9099 :
9100 REM   --- load SHAPES ---
9103 :
9110          PRINT CHR$(4) "BLOAD shape table, A$1000" :REM addr=4096
9120          POKE 232,0: POKE 233,16                  :REM point to shape table
9479 :
9480 REM   --- init sound ---
9485          GOSUB 9500                               :REM setup sound
9489 :
9490          RETURN
9498 :
9499 :
9500 REM   ========================
9501 REM   = initialize sound
9502 REM   ========================
9503 :
9510           PRINT CHR$(4);"BLOAD MUSE"
9519 :
9520           DIM TRANS(2,3), SND(51,3)
9530           PLOW=1 :PHIGH=2 :DURTN=3
9539 :
9540           FOR  J=0 TO 51
9545             FOR  K=PLOW TO DURTN
9550               READ SND(I,J)
```

```
9555          NEXT K
9560        NEXT J
9569 :
9570          REM: take data from table 6.2
9589 :
9590        RETURN
9591 :
9990 REM   ***********************

10 REM  ***********************
15 REM  *=====================*
20 REM  *=                   =*
25 REM  *=    MELODY MAKER    =*
30 REM  *=                   =*
35 REM  *=      (IBM-PC)      =*
40 REM  *=                   =*
45 REM  *=====================*
50 REM  ***********************
100 :
110       WIDTH 40
120       GOSUB 5000                              :REM title page
140       GOSUB 5100                              :REM main index
160        IF NX$ = "1" THEN GOSUB 4000 :GOTO 140    :REM load
180        IF NX$ = "3" THEN GOSUB 4200 :GOTO 140    :REM save
200        IF NX$ = "9" THEN GOTO  490            :REM quit
220       GOSUB 3000                              :REM generate screen
240       GOSUB 500                               :REM editor
400       GOTO 140
489 :
490       END
491 :
492 :
500 REM ****************
501 REM * editor (calls)
502 REM ****************
503 :
550       NPT$=INKEY$ :IF NPT$="" THEN 550
555 :
570        IF NPT$ = "F" THEN GOSUB 1200 :GOTO 550         :REM left
590        IF NPT$ = "H" THEN GOSUB 1300 :GOTO 550         :REM right
610        IF NPT$ = "T" THEN GOSUB 1400 :GOTO 550         :REM up
630        IF NPT$ = "B" THEN GOSUB 1500 :GOTO 550         :REM down
650        IF NPT$ = "I" THEN GOSUB 1000 :GOTO 550         :REM insert
670        IF NPT$ = "D" THEN GOSUB 1100 :GOTO 550         :REM delete
690        IF NPT$ = "W" THEN DR=48 :GOSUB 1900 :GOTO 550
700            :REM whole note
710        IF NPT$ = "H" THEN DR=24 :GOSUB 1900 :GOTO 550
720            :REM half note
730        IF NPT$ = "Q" THEN DR=12 :GOSUB 1900 :GOTO 550
740            :REM quarter note
750        IF NPT$ = "+" THEN GOSUB 1700 :GOTO 550         :REM sharp
770        IF NPT$ = "-" THEN GOSUB 1800 :GOTO 550         :REM flat
900        IF NPT$ <>"X" THEN 550
989 :
990       SCREEN 0 :RETURN
991 :
1000 REM  ================
1001 REM  = insert (after)
1002 REM  ================
1003 :
1010       TEMP = NTE(NXT,RL)
1020       NTE(NXT,RL)  = NTE(CRNT,RL)
1030       NTE(CRNT,RL) = NXT
1040       NTE(NXT,LL)  = CRNT
1050       NTE(NTE(NXT,RL),LL) = NXT
1060       CRNT = NXT
1070       NXT  = TEMP
```

```
1080        GOSUB 1600                            :REM record/display note
1089 :
1090        RETURN
1091 :
1100 REM  ===============
1101 REM  = delete (after)
1102 REM  ===============
1103 :
1110        IF CRNT = 0 THEN 1190
1115        LUMN=0 :GOSUB 3500 :LUMN=1           :REM erase note
1120        GOSUB 2000                           :REM draw cursor
1124 :
1125        NTE(NTE(CRNT,LL),RL) = NTE(CRNT,RL)
1130        NTE(NTE(CRNT,RL),LL) = NTE(CRNT,LL)
1140        NTE(CRNT,RL) = NXT
1150        NXT = CRNT
1160        CRNT = NTE(CRNT,LL)
1170        NTE(NXT,LTTR)=0:NTE(NXT,ACC)=0:NTE(NXT,OCT)=0:NTE(NXT,LNTH)=0
1189 :
1190        RETURN
1191 :
1200 REM  ===============
1201 REM  = move left
1202 REM  ===============
1203 :
1210        IF (XX=LFT) AND (XOF=0) THEN 1290
1220        LUMN=0 :GOSUB 2000 :LUMN=1           :REM erase cursor
1225        IF NTE(CRNT,XPNTR)=XX THEN GOSUB 3500 :REM redraw note
1230        XX = XX-MVE
1240        IF XX < (LFT+XOF) THEN GOSUB 2100    :REM scroll right
1250        GOSUB 2000                           :REM draw cursor
1260        IF (NTE(CRNT,XPNTR)>XX) THEN CRNT = NTE(CRNT,LL)
1270        IF XX = NTE(CRNT,XPNTR) THEN GOSUB 3500 :REM draw note
1289 :
1290        RETURN
1291 :
1300 REM  ===============
1301 REM  = move right
1302 REM  ===============
1303 :
1310        IF CRNT = MAX THEN 1390
1320        LUMN=0 :GOSUB 2000 :LUMN=1           :REM erase cursor
1325        IF NTE(CRNT,XPNTR)=XX THEN GOSUB 3500 :REM redraw note
1330        XX = XX+MVE
1340        IF XX > (RHT+XOF) THEN GOSUB 2200    :REM scroll left
1350        GOSUB 2000                           :REM draw cursor
1360        IF XX>=NTE(NTE(CRNT,RL),XPNTR) AND NTE(CRNT,RL)<>0
                    THEN CRNT=NTE(CRNT,RL)
1370        IF XX = NTE(CRNT,XPNTR) THEN GOSUB 3500 :REM draw note
1389 :
1390        RETURN
1391 :
1400 REM  ===============
1401 REM  = move up
1402 REM  ===============
1403 :
1410        LUMN=0 :GOSUB 2000 :LUMN=1           :REM erase cursor
1420        IF NTE(CRNT,XPNTR)=XX THEN GOSUB 3500 :REM redraw note
1430        YY = YY-3
1435        IF YY<TP THEN YY=BTM
1440        GOSUB 2000                           :REM draw cursor
1489 :
1490        RETURN
1491 :
1500 REM  ===============
1501 REM  = move down
1502 REM  ===============
```

```
1503 :
1510          LUMN=0 :GOSUB 2000 :LUMN=1                      :REM erase cursor
1520          IF NTE(CRNT,XPNTR)=XX THEN GOSUB 3500    :REM redraw note
1530          YY = YY+3
1535          IF YY>BTM THEN YY=TP
1540          GOSUB 2000                                     :REM draw cursor
1589 :
1590          RETURN
1591 :
1600 REM    ===============
1601 REM    = record note
1602 REM    ===============
1603 :
1610          IF CRNT = 0 THEN 1690
1620          NTE(CRNT,LTTR)   = FN MD7((154-YY)/3)
1625          NTE(CRNT,OCT)    = INT((154-YY)/21)
1630          NTE(CRNT,ACC)    = 0
1635          NTE(CRNT,LNTH)   = DR
1640          NTE(CRNT,XPNTR)  = XX
1650          GOSUB 3500                                     :REM draw note
1689 :
1690          RETURN
1691 :
1700 REM    ===============
1701 REM    = add a sharp
1702 REM    ===============
1703 :
1710          IF CRNT = 0 THEN 1790
1720          NTE(CRNT,ACC) = 1
1730          GOSUB 3500                                     :REM draw accidental
1789 :
1790          RETURN
1791 :
1800 REM    ===============
1801 REM    = add a flat
1802 REM    ===============
1803 :
1810          IF CRNT = 0 THEN 1890
1820          NTE(CRNT,ACC) = -1
1830          GOSUB 3500
1889 :
1890          RETURN
1891 :
1900 REM    ===============
1901 REM    = change note value
1902 REM    ===============
1903 :
1910          IF CRNT = 0 THEN 1990
1920          IF NTE(CRNT,XPNTR)-XOF < LFT THEN 1990
1930          LUMN=0 :GOSUB 3500 :LUMN=1
1940          NTE(CRNT,LNTH)=DR
1950          GOSUB 3500
1989 :
1990          RETURN
1991 :
2000 REM    ------------------
2001 REM    - draw/erase cursor
2002 REM    ------------------
2003 :
2010          PSET (XX-XOF,YY):A$="C=LUMN;"+CRSR$
2020          DRAW A$
2089 :
2090          RETURN
2091 :
2100 REM    ------------------
2101 REM    - scroll right
2102 REM    ------------------
```

```
2103 :
2120          GET (LFT-MVE,20)-(RHT-MVE,114),A%
2130          PUT (LFT,20),A%,PSET
2189 :
2190          RETURN
2191 :
2200 REM     -----------------
2201 REM     - scroll left
2202 REM     -----------------
2203 :
2220          GET (LFT+MVE,20)-(RHT+MVE,114),A%
2230          PUT (LFT,20),A%,PSET
2289 :
2290          RETURN
2291 :
2292 REM  ===============
2293 :
3000 REM  ================
3001 REM  = setup screen
3002 REM  ================
3003 :
3005          CLS
3010          SCREEN 1
3020          NUM=2:X=8:Y=40:XX=LFT:YY=70
3030          LUMN=1 :GOSUB 3200                        :REM draw staff
3035          LUMN=1 :GOSUB 3300                        :REM draw melody
3040          LUMN=1 :GOSUB 2000                        :REM draw cursor
3099 :
3100          LOCATE 20,3 :PRINT "Use: T, B, F, & H to move: U,D,L,R"
3110          LOCATE 21,3 :PRINT "I:Inserts a note  D:Deletes a note"
3120          LOCATE 22,8 :PRINT "+:sharp          -:flat"
3130          LOCATE 23,3 :PRINT "W:Whole  H:Half  Q:Quarter  X:Exit"
3189 :
3190          RETURN
3191 :
3200 REM     -----------------
3201 REM     - draw staff(s)  .
3202 REM     -----------------
3203 :
3205        FOR  J=1 TO NUM
3210          FOR  I=0 TO 24 STEP 6
3220            LINE (X,Y+I)-(X+295,Y+I)
3230          NEXT I
3240            IF J=1 THEN PSET X+FX,Y+FY :DRAW GC$
3250            IF J=2 THEN PSET X+FX,Y+FY :DRAW FC$
3260          Y=Y+36
3270        NEXT J
3289 :
3290          RETURN
3291 :
3300 REM     -----------------
3301 REM     - draw melody
3302 REM     -----------------
3303 :
3310          CRNT = NTE(0,RL)
3319 :
3320           IF NTE(CRNT,XPNT)>RHT OR CRNT=0 THEN 3380
3330          GOSUB 3500                               :REM draw note
3340          CRNT = NTE(CRNT,RL)
3350          GOTO 3320
3379 :
3380          CRNT = 0
3385           IF NTE(NTE(CRNT,RL),XPNTR) <= XX THEN CRNT = NTE(CRNT,RL)
3389 :
3390          RETURN
3391 :
3392 REM  ===============
3393 :
```

```
3500 REM   ================
3501 REM   = draw note
3502 REM   ================
3503 :
3520        XDRW = NTE(CRNT,XPNTR)-XOF
3530        YDRW = 154 - 3*( 7*NTE(CRNT,OCT)+NTE(CRNT,LTTR) )
3540        A$="C=LUMN"+NTE$(INT(NTE(CRNT,LNTH)/24)+1)
3545        PSET XDRW,YDRW :DRAW A$
3550        IF YDRW = 70 THEN GOSUB 3700          :REM ledger lines
3560        IF NTE(CRNT,ACC) <> 0 THEN GOSUB 3600  :REM accidentals
3589 :
3590        RETURN
3591 :
3600 REM   ----------------
3601 REM   - draw accidentals
3602 REM   ----------------
3603 :
3610         ON NTE(CRNT,ACC)+2 GOSUB 3660, 3670, 3680
3639 :
3640        RETURN
3641 :
3660         PSET XDRW-12,YDRW :A$="C=LUMN"+F$ :DRAW A$ :RETURN
3670         RETURN
3680         PSET XDRW-12,YDRW :A$="C=LUMN"+S$ :DRAW A$ :RETURN
3691 :
3700 REM   ----------------
3701 REM   - ledger lines
3702 REM   ----------------
3703 :
3710        LINE (XDRW-7,YDRW)-(XDRW+7,YDRW)
2789 :
3790        RETURN
3791 :
3790 REM   ===============
3792 :
3793 REM***************
3794 :
3795 :
4000 REM***************
4001 REM* load a file
4002 REM***************
4003 :
4010    CLS
4020    LOCATE 23,2 :PRINT "FILE NAME: ";
4030    INPUT FLNM$
4049 :
4050    OPEN FLNM$ FOR INPUT AS #1
4060    PNTR = 0
4069 :
4080      INPUT #1, NTE(CRNT,LTTR)
4082      INPUT #1, NTE(CRNT,ACC)
4084      INPUT #1, NTE(CRNT,OCT)
4086      INPUT #1, NTE(CRNT,LNTH)
4088      INPUT #1, NTE(CRNT,LL)
4090      INPUT #1, NTE(CRNT,RL)
4092      INPUT #1, NTE(CRNT,XPNTR)
4100       IF NTE(CRNT,RL) = 0 THEN 4180
4110         CRNT = NTE(CRNT,RL)
4120    GOTO 4080
4179 :
4180    CLOSE #1
4189 :
4190    RETURN
4191 :
4200 REM***************
4201 REM* save a file
4202 REM***************
4203 :
```

```
4210      PRINT HOME$
4220      LOCATE 21,2 :PRINT "FILE NAME: ";
4225      INPUT FLNM$
4249 :
4250      OPEN FLNM$ FOR OUTPUT AS #1
4270      CRNT = 0
4279 :
4280        WRITE #1, NTE(CRNT,LTTR)
4282        WRITE #1, NTE(CRNT,ACC)
4284        WRITE #1, NTE(CRNT,OCT)
4286        WRITE #1, NTE(CRNT,LNTH)
4288        WRITE #1, NTE(CRNT,LL)
4290        WRITE #1, NTE(CRNT,RL)
4292        WRITE #1, NTE(CRNT,XPNTR)
4300          IF NTE(CRNT,RL)=0 THEN 4380
4310            CRNT = NTE(CRNT,RL)
4320      GOTO 4280
4369 :
4380      CLOSE #1
4389 :
4390      RETURN
4391 :
5000 REM****************
5001 REM* title page
5002 REM****************
5003 :
5010      CLS
5020      LOCATE  8,12 :PRINT "****************"
5030      LOCATE  9,12 :PRINT "* MELODY MAKER *"
5040      LOCATE 10,12 :PRINT "****************"
5050      GOSUB 9000                              :REM initialize
5060      LOCATE 23,6 :PRINT  "<PRESS ANY KEY TO CONTINUE>"
5080      Q$=INKEY$ :IF Q$="" THEN 5060
5089 :
5090      RETURN
5091 :
5100 REM****************
5101 REM* main index
5102 REM****************
5103 :
5110      CLS
5120      LOCATE  4,2 :PRINT "WHAT WOULD YOU LIKE TO DO..."
5130      LOCATE  8,7 :PRINT "1. LOAD A MELODY"
5140      LOCATE 10,7 :PRINT "2. EDIT A MELODY"
5150      LOCATE 12,7 :PRINT "3. SAVE A MELODY"
5160      LOCATE 16,7 :PRINT "9. EXIT"
5170      LOCATE 21,2 :PRINT "CHOOSE A NUMBER...";
5175      INPUT NX$
5177       IF NX$<"1" OR (NX$>"3" AND NX$<>"9") THEN 5170
5180      NX = VAL(NX$)
5189 :
5190      RETURN
5191 :
9000 REM****************
9001 REM* init variables
9002 REM****************
9003 :
9005      DR=48 :FX=10 :FY=24 :TP=37 :BTM=103 :LUMN=1
9010      LTTR=0 :ACC=1 :OCT=2 :LNTH=3 :LL=4 :RL=5 :XPNTR=6
9015      MAX=60 :LFT=71 :RHT=279 :MVE=24
9020      FCTR=(-1)
9029 :
9030      DIM A%(4892)                     :REM for HIRES scroller
9034 :
9035      GOSUB 9100                              :REM define shapes
9040      GOSUB 9500                              :REM setup nte()
9045      GOSUB 9600                              :REM load scroller
```

```
9049 :
9055      DEF FN MD7(Z) = INT((Z/7-INT(Z/7))*7+.05)
9089 :
9090      RETURN
9091 :
9100 REM  ================
9101 REM  = define shapes
9102 REM  ================
9103 :
9105 REM  --- CLEFS ---
9110      GC$ =  (copy code from interval drill program)
9120      FC$ =  (copy code from interval drill program)
9199 :
9200 REM  --- NOTES ---
9210      DIM NTE$(5)
9220      NTE$(3) =        "BL4DRDR5URDRURU2LUL5DLULDLD"    :REM whole
9230      NTE$(2) =        "BR4ULUL5DLULDLD2RDR5URDRURU8U8":REM half
9240      NTE$(1) =        "BR4ULUL5DLULDLD2RDR5URDRURUL4" :REM quarter
9245      NTE$(1) = NTE$(1)+"DL3ULBRR2UR3BR2U7U7"
9299 :
9300 REM  --- ACCIDENTALS ---
9330      F$ = (copy code from interval drill program)
9350      S$ = (copy code from interval drill program)
9399 :
9400 REM  --- CURSOR ---
9410      CRSR$ = "BL4U2BR3U2BR2RDBDD2BL3L2BL2LUBU"
9489 :
9490      RETURN
9491 :
9500 REM  ================
9501 REM  = setup nte()
9502 REM  ================
9503 :
9510      DIM NTE(MAX,6)
9520      FOR  I=1 TO MAX
9530        NTE(I-1,RL)=I
9540      NEXT I
9545      NTE(MAX,RL)=0 :NTE(0,RL)=0
9550      CRNT=0 :NXT=1 :XOF=0
9589 :
9590      RETURN
9591 :
9592 REM************************


10 REM ***********************
15 REM *=====================*
20 REM *=                   =*
25 REM *=    MELODY MAKER    =*
30 REM *=                   =*
35 REM *=       (C-64)       =*
40 REM *=                   =*
45 REM *=====================*
50 REM ***********************
100 :
120      GOSUB 5000                              :REM title page
140      GOSUB 5100                              :REM main index
160      IF NX$ = "1" THEN GOSUB 4000 :GOTO 140  :REM load
180      IF NX$ = "3" THEN GOSUB 4200 :GOTO 140  :REM save
200      IF NX$ = "9" THEN GOTO  490             :REM quit
220      GOSUB 3000                              :REM generate screen
240      GOSUB 500                               :REM editor
400      GOTO 140
489 :
490      END
491 :
492 :
```

```
500 REM ****************
501 REM * editor (calls)
502 REM ****************
503 :
550       GET NPT$ :IF NPT$="" THEN 550
555 :
570       IF NPT$ = CHR$(157) THEN GOSUB 1200 :GOTO 550    :REM left
590       IF NPT$ = CHR$(29)  THEN GOSUB 1300 :GOTO 550    :REM right
610       IF NPT$ = CHR$(145) THEN GOSUB 1400 :GOTO 550    :REM up
630       IF NPT$ = CHR$(17)  THEN GOSUB 1500 :GOTO 550    :REM down
650       IF NPT$ = "I" THEN GOSUB 1000 :GOTO 550          :REM insert
670       IF NPT$ = "D" THEN GOSUB 1100 :GOTO 550          :REM delete
690       IF NPT$ = "W" THEN DR=48 :GOSUB 1900 :GOTO 550
700            :REM whole note
710       IF NPT$ = "H" THEN DR=24 :GOSUB 1900 :GOTO 550
720              :REM half note
730       IF NPT$ = "Q" THEN DR=12 :GOSUB 1900 :GOTO 550
740              :REM quarter note
750       IF NPT$ = "+" THEN GOSUB 1700 :GOTO 550          :REM sharp
770       IF NPT$ = "-" THEN GOSUB 1800 :GOTO 550          :REM flat
900       IF NPT$ <>"X" THEN 550
989 :
990       NRM :RETURN
991 :
1000 REM  =================
1001 REM  = insert (after)
1002 REM  =================
1003 :
1010      TEMP = NTE(NXT,RL)
1020      NTE(NXT,RL)  = NTE(CRNT,RL)
1030      NTE(CRNT,RL) = NXT
1040      NTE(NXT,LL)  = CRNT
1050      NTE(NTE(NXT,RL),LL) = NXT
1060      CRNT = NXT
1070      NXT  = TEMP
1080      GOSUB 1600                           :REM record/display note
1089 :
1090      RETURN
1091 :
1100 REM  =================
1101 REM  = delete (after)
1102 REM  =================
1103 :
1110      IF CRNT = 0 THEN 1190
1115      LUMN=0 :GOSUB 3500 :LUMN=1           :REM erase note
1120      GOSUB 2000                           :REM draw cursor
1124 :
1125      NTE(NTE(CRNT,LL),RL) = NTE(CRNT,RL)
1130      NTE(NTE(CRNT,RL),LL) = NTE(CRNT,LL)
1140      NTE(CRNT,RL) = NXT
1150      NXT = CRNT
1160      CRNT = NTE(CRNT,LL)
1170      NTE(NXT,LTTR)=0:NTE(NXT,ACC)=0:NTE(NXT,OCT)=0:NTE(NXT,LNTH)=0
1189 :
1190      RETURN
1191 :
1200 REM  =================
1201 REM  = move left
1202 REM  =================
1203 :
1210      IF (XX=LFT) AND (XOF=0) THEN 1290
1220      LUMN=0 :GOSUB 2000                    :REM erase cursor
1225      IF NTE(CRNT,XPNTR)=XX THEN GOSUB 3500 :REM redraw note
1230      XX = XX-MVE
1240      IF XX < (LFT+XOF) THEN GOSUB 2100     :REM scroll right
1250      GOSUB 2000                            :REM draw cursor
1260      IF (NTE(CRNT,XPNTR)>XX) THEN CRNT = NTE(CRNT,LL)
```

```
1270          IF XX = NTE(CRNT,XPNTR) THEN GOSUB 3500 :REM draw note
1289 :
1290          RETURN
1291 :
1300 REM   ===============
1301 REM   = move right
1302 REM   ===============
1303 :
1310          IF CRNT = MAX THEN 1390
1320          LUMN=0 :GOSUB 2000 :LUMN=1                    :REM erase cursor
1325          IF NTE(CRNT,XPNTR)=XX THEN GOSUB 3500    :REM redraw note
1330          XX = XX+MVE
1340          IF XX > (RHT+XOF) THEN GOSUB 2200        :REM scroll left
1350          GOSUB 2000                               :REM draw cursor
1360          IF XX>=NTE(NTE(CRNT,RL),XPNTR) AND NTE(CRNT,RL)<>0
                      THEN CRNT=NTE(CRNT,RL)
1370          IF XX = NTE(CRNT,XPNTR) THEN GOSUB 3500 :REM draw note
1389 :
1390          RETURN
1391 :
1400 REM   ===============
1401 REM   = move up
1402 REM   ===============
1403 :
1410          LUMN=0 :GOSUB 2000 :LUMN=1                    :REM erase cursor
1420          IF NTE(CRNT,XPNTR)=XX THEN GOSUB 3500    :REM redraw note
1430          YY = YY-3
1435          IF YY<TP THEN YY=BTM
1440          GOSUB 2000                               :REM draw cursor
1489 :
1490          RETURN
1491 :
1500 REM   ===============
1501 REM   = move down
1502 REM   ===============
1503 :
1510          LUMN=0 :GOSUB 2000 :LUMN=1                    :REM erase cursor
1520          IF NTE(CRNT,XPNTR)=XX THEN GOSUB 3500    :REM redraw note
1530          YY = YY+3
1535          IF YY>BTM THEN YY=TP
1540          GOSUB 2000                               :REM draw cursor
1589 :
1590          RETURN
1591 :
1600 REM   ===============
1601 REM   = record note
1602 REM   ===============
1603 :
1610          IF CRNT = 0 THEN 1690
1620          NTE(CRNT,LTTR)   = FN MD7((154-YY)/3)
1625          NTE(CRNT,OCT)    = INT((154-YY)/21)
1630          NTE(CRNT,ACC)    = 0
1635          NTE(CRNT,LNTH)   = DR
1640          NTE(CRNT,XPNTR) = XX
1650          GOSUB 3500                                        :REM draw note
1689 :
1690          RETURN
1691 :
1700 REM   ===============
1701 REM   = add a sharp
1702 REM   ===============
1703 :
1710          IF CRNT = 0 THEN 1790
1720          NTE(CRNT,ACC) = 1
1730          GOSUB 3500                               :REM draw accidental
1789 :
1790          RETURN
```

```
1791 :
1800 REM   ===============
1801 REM   = add a flat
1802 REM   ===============
1803 :
1810         IF CRNT = 0 THEN 1890
1820         NTE(CRNT,ACC) = -1
1830         GOSUB 3500
1889 :
1890         RETURN
1891 :
1900 REM   ===============
1901 REM   = change note value
1902 REM   ===============
1903 :
1910         IF CRNT = 0 THEN 1990
1920         IF NTE(CRNT,XPNTR)-XOF < LFT THEN 1990
1930         LUMN=0 :GOSUB 3500 :LUMN=1
1940         NTE(CRNT,LNTH)=DR
1950         GOSUB 3500
1989 :
1990         RETURN
1991 :
2000 REM   ---------------
2001 REM   - draw/erase cursor
2002 REM   ---------------
2003 :
2010         DRAW CRSR$,XX-XOF,YY,LUMN
2089 :
2090         RETURN
2091 :
2100 REM   ---------------
2101 REM   - scroll right
2102 REM   ---------------
2103 :
2120         FOR I=0 TO 2 : SYS 51578 : NEXT
2130         XOF = XOF-MVE
2189 :
2190         RETURN
2191 :
2200 REM   ---------------
2201 REM   - scroll left
2202 REM   ---------------
2203 :
2220         FOR I=0 TO 2 : SYS 51540 : NEXT
2230         XOF = XOF+MVE
2289 :
2290         RETURN
2291 :
2292 REM   ===============
2293 :
3000 REM   ===============
3001 REM   = setup screen
3002 REM   ===============
3003 :
3005         PRINT HOME$
3010         HIRES 0,15: ROT 0,1
3020         NUM=2:X=8:Y=40:XX=LFT:YY=70
3030         LUMN=1 :GOSUB 3200                    :REM draw staff
3035         LUMN=1 :GOSUB 3300                    :REM draw melody
3040         LUMN=1 :GOSUB 2000                    :REM draw cursor
3099 :
3100         TEXT 32,170,"Use Cursor Keys for:  U, D, L, R",1,1,8
3110         TEXT 16,180,"I: Inserts a note, D: deletes a note",1,1,8
3120         TEXT  4,190,"W:Whole,H:Half,Q:Quarter,+:Sharp,F:Flat",1,1,8
3189 :
3190         RETURN
```

```
3191 :
3200 REM       ----------------
3201 REM       - draw staff(s)
3202 REM       ----------------
3203 :
3205          FOR  J=1 TO NUM
3210            FOR  I=0 TO 24 STEP 6
3220              LINE X,Y+I,X+295,Y+I,1
3230            NEXT I
3240              IF J=1 THEN DRAW GC$,X+FX,Y+FY,1
3250              IF J=2 THEN DRAW FC$,X+FX,Y+FY,1
3260            Y=Y+36
3270          NEXT J
3289 :
3290          RETURN
3291 :
3300 REM       ----------------
3301 REM       - draw melody
3302 REM       ----------------
3303 :
3310          CRNT = NTE(0,RL)
3319 :
3320            IF NTE(CRNT,XPNT)>RHT OR CRNT=0 THEN 3380
3330          GOSUB 3500                          :REM draw note
3340          CRNT = NTE(CRNT,RL)
3350          GOTO 3320
3379 :
3380          CRNT = 0
3385            IF NTE(NTE(CRNT,RL),XPNTR) <= XX THEN CRNT = NTE(CRNT,RL)
3389 :
3390          RETURN
3391 :
3392 REM   ================
3393 :
3500 REM   ================
3501 REM   = draw note
3502 REM   ================
3503 :
3520          XDRW = NTE(CRNT,XPNTR)-XOF
3530          YDRW = 154 - 3*( 7*NTE(CRNT,OCT)+NTE(CRNT,LTTR) )
3540          DRAW NTE$( INT(NTE(CRNT,LNTH)/24)+1 ),XDRW,YDRW,LUMN
3550           IF YDRW = 70 THEN GOSUB 3700          :REM ledger lines
3560           IF NTE(CRNT,ACC) <> 0 THEN GOSUB 3600   :REM accidentals
3589 :
3590          RETURN
3591 :
3600 REM       ----------------
3601 REM       - draw accidentals
3602 REM       ----------------
3603 :
3610            ON NTE(CRNT,ACC)+2 GOSUB 3660, 3670, 3680
3639 :
3640          RETURN
3641 :
3660            DRAW F$ ,XDRW-12,YDRW,LUMN:RETURN
3670            RETURN
3680            DRAW S$ ,XDRW-12,YDRW,LUMN:RETURN
3691 :
3700 REM       ----------------
3701 REM       - ledger lines
3702 REM       ----------------
3703 :
3710            LINE XDRW-7,YDRW,XDRW+7,YDRW,LUMN
2789 :
3790          RETURN
3791 :
3790 REM   ================
```

```
3792 :
3793 REM****************
3794 :
3795 :
4000 REM****************
4001 REM* load a file
4002 REM****************
4003 :
4010     PRINT HOME$
4020     PRINT AT(2,23)   "FILE NAME ($ FOR DIR) ";
4025     INPUT FLNM$
4030      IF FLNM$<>"$" THEN 4050
4035        DIR"$
4040        PRINT:PRINT:PRINT:GOTO 4020
4049 :
4050     OPEN 2,8,2,"0:"+FLNM$+",S,R"
4060     CRNT = 0
4069 :
4080        INPUT#2, NTE(CRNT,LTTR)
4082        INPUT#2, NTE(CRNT,ACC)
4084        INPUT#2, NTE(CRNT,OCT)
4086        INPUT#2, NTE(CRNT,LNTH)
4088        INPUT#2, NTE(CRNT,LL)
4090        INPUT#2, NTE(CRNT,RL)
4092        INPUT#2, NTE(CRNT,XPNTR)
4100         IF NTE(CRNT,RL) = 0 THEN 4180
4110           CRNT = NTE(CRNT,RL)
4120     GOTO 4080
4179 :
4180     CLOSE 2
4189 :
4190     RETURN
4191 :
4200 REM****************
4201 REM* save a file
4202 REM****************
4203 :
4210     PRINT HOME$
4220     PRINT AT(2,23)   "FILE NAME ($ FOR DIR) ";
4225     INPUT FLNM$
4230      IF FLNM$<>"$" THEN 4250
4235        DIR"$
4240        PRINT:PRINT:PRINT:GOTO 4220
4249 :
4250     OPEN 2,8,2,"0:"+FLNM$+",S,W"
4270     PNTR = 0
4279 :
4280        PRINT#2, NTE(CRNT,LTTR)
4282        PRINT#2, NTE(CRNT,ACC)
4284        PRINT#2, NTE(CRNT,OCT)
4286        PRINT#2, NTE(CRNT,LNTH)
4288        PRINT#2, NTE(CRNT,LL)
4290        PRINT#2, NTE(CRNT,RL)
4292        PRINT#2, NTE(CRNT,XPNTR)
4300         IF NTE(CRNT,RL)=0 THEN 4380
4310           CRNT = NTE(CRNT,RL)
4320     GOTO 4280
4369 :
4380     CLOSE 2
4389 :
4390     RETURN
4391 :
5000 REM****************
5001 REM* title page
5002 REM****************
5003 :
5005     HOME$=CHR$(147)                          :REM clear screen
```

```
5010       PRINT HOME$
5020       PRINT AT(12,8)   "****************"
5030       PRINT AT(12,9)   "* MELODY MAKER *"
5040       PRINT AT(12,10)  "****************"
5050       GOSUB 9000                                      :REM initialize
5060       PRINT AT(6,23)   "<PRESS ANY KEY TO CONTINUE>"
5080       GET Q$:IF Q$="" THEN 5060
5089 :
5090       RETURN
5091 :
5100 REM****************
5101 REM* main index
5102 REM****************
5103 :
5110       PRINT HOME$
5120       PRINT AT(2,4)   "WHAT WOULD YOU LIKE TO DO..."
5130       PRINT AT(7,8)   "1. LOAD A MELODY"
5140       PRINT AT(7,10)  "2. EDIT A MELODY"
5150       PRINT AT(7,12)  "3. SAVE A MELODY"
5160       PRINT AT(7,16)  "9. EXIT"
5170       PRINT AT(2,21)  "CHOOSE A NUMBER...";
5175       INPUT NX$
5177        IF NX$<"1" OR (NX$>"3" AND NX$<>"9") THEN 5170
5189 :
5190       RETURN
5191 :
9000 REM****************
9001 REM* init variables
9002 REM****************
9003 :
9005       DR=48 :FX=10 :FY=24 :TP=37 :BTM=103 :LUMN=1
9010       LTTR=0 :ACC=1 :OCT=2 :LNTH=3 :LL=4 :RL=5 :XPNTR=6
9015       MAX=60 :LFT=71 :RHT=279 :MVE=24
9020       FCTR=(-1)
9034 :
9035       GOSUB 9100                                      :REM define shapes
9040       GOSUB 9500                                      :REM setup nte()
9045       GOSUB 9600                                      :REM load scroller
9049 :
9050 REM--- DEF FN ---
9055       DEF FN MD7(Z) = INT((Z/7-INT(Z/7))*7+.05)
9089 :
9090       RETURN
9091 :
9100 REM  ===============
9101 REM  = define shapes
9102 REM  ===============
9103 :
9105 REM   --- CLEFS ---
9110       GC$ =       "12222256868787575555565666666668668666686666"
9111       GC$ = GC$+"86668666686586666256625662566525665757575777"
9112       GC$ = GC$+"77787878787878887878787877878777777537575757575575"
9113       GC$ = GC$+"75555555565556565656566868068806886878687868786"
9114       GC$ = GC$+"27862786278757807757333111133866665656568056805"
9115       GC$ = GC$+"680568056566256565569"
9119 :
9120       FC$ =       "331155656565565656565656565656656000056873333666"
9121       FC$ = FC$+"6686000005786333338686888688888888887887878787777"
9122       FC$ = FC$+"757575555566256686568686877778666668777778666666"
9123       FC$ = FC$+"8777771868656806655656500000557555788807555578"
9124       FC$ = FC$+"8887555578888755557888875555788887555788887555578"
9125       FC$ = FC$+"871877878789"
9199 :
9200 REM   --- NOTES ---
9210       DIM NTE$(5)
9220       NTE$(3) =       "333375755555657565668688888"
9221       NTE$(3) = NTE$(3)+"78687879"                    :REM whole
```

```
9230        NTE$(2) =         "000068688888786878775755555"
9235        NTE$(2) = NTE$(2)+"657565666666666666666669"      :REM half
9240        NTE$(1) =         "000068688888786878775755555"
9245        NTE$(1) = NTE$(1)+"657565688887888680556555006"
9250        NTE$(1) = NTE$(1)+"66666666666669"               :REM quarter
9299 :
9300 REM   --- ACCIDENTALS ---
9310        F$  =     "78788666666666666622222225565756257879"
9350        S$  =     "22222223366668865566668865566666222225555"
9360        S$  = S$+"6666622225578878880007775578888875557779"
9399 :
9400 REM   --- CURSOR ---
9410        CRSR$ = "3333660005500572773388338619"
9489 :
9490        RETURN
9491 :
9500 REM   ===============
9501 REM   = setup nte()
9502 REM   ===============
9503 :
9510        DIM NTE(MAX,6)
9520        FOR  I=1 TO MAX
9530          NTE(I-1,RL)=I
9540        NEXT I
9545        NTE(MAX,RL)=0 :NTE(0,RL)=0
9550        CRNT=0 :NXT=1 :XOF=0
9589 :
9590        RETURN
9591 :
9600 REM   ================
9601 REM   = load scroller(ml)
9602 REM   ================
9603 :
9610        FOR  I=51456 TO 51649
9620          READ A :POKE I,A
9630        NEXT I
9689 :
9690        RETURN
9691 :
9700 REM   --- DATA ---
9705        DATA 173,14,220,41,254,141,14,220
9710        DATA 165,1,41,253,133,1,96,165
9715        DATA 1,9,2,133,1,173,14,220
9720        DATA 9,1,141,14,220,96,174,171
9725        DATA 201,189,172,201,133,253,24,105
9730        DATA 8,133,251,189,173,201,133,254
9735        DATA 133,252,238,171,201,238,171,201
9740        DATA 96,174,171,201,189,172,201,133
9745        DATA 253,56,233,8,133,251,189,173
9750        DATA 201,133,254,133,252,238,171,201
9755        DATA 238,171,201,96,169,0,141,171
9760        DATA 201,173,169,201,141,170,201,32
9765        DATA 0,201,160,0,32,30,201,177
9770        DATA 251,145,253,200,204,168,201,208
9775        DATA 246,206,170,201,208,236,32,15
9780        DATA 201,96,169,0,141,171,201,173
9785        DATA 169,201,141,170,201,32,0,201
9790        DATA 172,168,201,32,57,201,177,251
9795        DATA 145,253,136,192,0,208,247,177
9800        DATA 251,145,253,206,170,201,208,232
9805        DATA 32,15,201,96,0,0,0,0,239,11
9810        DATA 0,0,240,227,48,229,112,230,176
9815        DATA 231,240,232,48,234,112,235,176
9820        DATA 236,240,237,48,239,112,240
9889 :
9892 REM****************
```

```
 10 REM ************************
 15 REM *====================*
 20 REM *=                  =*
 25 REM *=    MELODY MAKER   =*
 30 REM *=                  =*
 35 REM *=      (APPLE)      =*
 40 REM *=                  =*
 45 REM *====================*
 50 REM ************************
100 :
120     GOSUB 5000                             :REM title page
140     GOSUB 5100                             :REM main index
160     IF NX$ = "1" THEN GOSUB 4000 :GOTO 140    :REM load
180     IF NX$ = "3" THEN GOSUB 4200 :GOTO 140    :REM save
200     IF NX$ = "9" THEN GOTO  490               :REM quit
220     GOSUB 3000                             :REM generate screen
240     GOSUB 500                              :REM editor
400     GOTO 140
489 :
490     END
491 :
492 :
500 REM ***************
501 REM * editor (calls)
502 REM ***************
503 :
550     GET NPT$
555 :
570     IF NPT$ = CHR$(8)  THEN GOSUB 1200 :GOTO 550      :REM left
590     IF NPT$ = CHR$(21) THEN GOSUB 1300 :GOTO 550      :REM right
610     IF NPT$ = "A" THEN GOSUB 1400 :GOTO 550      :REM up
630     IF NPT$ = "Z" THEN GOSUB 1500 :GOTO 550      :REM down
650     IF NPT$ = "I" THEN GOSUB 1000 :GOTO 550      :REM insert
670     IF NPT$ = "D" THEN GOSUB 1100 :GOTO 550      :REM delete
690     IF NPT$ = "W" THEN DR=48 :GOSUB 1900 :GOTO 550
700           :REM whole note
710     IF NPT$ = "H" THEN DR=24 :GOSUB 1900 :GOTO 550
720           :REM half note
730     IF NPT$ = "Q" THEN DR=12 :GOSUB 1900 :GOTO 550
740           :REM quarter note
750     IF NPT$ = "+" THEN GOSUB 1700 :GOTO 550      :REM sharp
770     IF NPT$ = "-" THEN GOSUB 1800 :GOTO 550      :REM flat
900     IF NPT$ <>"X" THEN 550
989 :
990     TEXT :RETURN
991 :
1000 REM ===============
1001 REM = insert (after)
1002 REM ===============
1003 :
1010     TEMP = NTE(NXT,RL)
1020     NTE(NXT,RL)  = NTE(CRNT,RL)
1030     NTE(CRNT,RL) = NXT
1040     NTE(NXT,LL)  = CRNT
1050     NTE(NTE(NXT,RL),LL) = NXT
1060     CRNT = NXT
1070     NXT  = TEMP
1080     GOSUB 1600                             :REM record/display note
1089 :
1090     RETURN
1091 :
1100 REM ===============
1101 REM = delete (after)
1102 REM ===============
1103 :
1110     IF CRNT = 0 THEN 1190
```

```
1115        LUMN=0 :GOSUB 3500 :LUMN=3            :REM erase note
1120        GOSUB 2000                           :REM draw cursor
1124 :
1125        NTE(NTE(CRNT,LL),RL) = NTE(CRNT,RL)
1130        NTE(NTE(CRNT,RL),LL) = NTE(CRNT,LL)
1140        NTE(CRNT,RL) = NXT
1150        NXT = CRNT
1160        CRNT = NTE(CRNT,LL)
1170        NTE(NXT,LTTR)=0:NTE(NXT,ACC)=0:NTE(NXT,OCT)=0:NTE(NXT,LNTH)=0
1189 :
1190        RETURN
1191 :
1200 REM  ===============
1201 REM  = move left
1202 REM  ===============
1203 :
1210        IF (XX=LFT) AND (XOF=0) THEN 1290
1220        LUMN=0 :GOSUB 2000                   :REM erase cursor
1225        IF NTE(CRNT,XPNTR)=XX THEN GOSUB 3500   :REM redraw note
1230        XX = XX-MVE
1240        IF XX < (LFT+XOF) THEN GOSUB 2100       :REM scroll right
1250        GOSUB 2000                           :REM draw cursor
1260        IF (NTE(CRNT,XPNTR)>XX) THEN CRNT = NTE(CRNT,LL)
1270        IF XX = NTE(CRNT,XPNTR) THEN GOSUB 3500 :REM draw note
1289 :
1290        RETURN
1291 :
1300 REM  ===============
1301 REM  = move right
1302 REM  ===============
1303 :
1310        IF CRNT = MAX THEN 1390
1320        LUMN=0 :GOSUB 2000 :LUMN=3            :REM erase cursor
1325        IF NTE(CRNT,XPNTR)=XX THEN GOSUB 3500   :REM redraw note
1330        XX = XX+MVE
1340        IF XX > (RHT+XOF) THEN GOSUB 2200       :REM scroll left
1350        GOSUB 2000                           :REM draw cursor
1360        IF XX>=NTE(NTE(CRNT,RL),XPNTR) AND NTE(CRNT,RL)<>0
                   THEN CRNT=NTE(CRNT,RL)
1370        IF XX = NTE(CRNT,XPNTR) THEN GOSUB 3500 :REM draw note
1389 :
1390        RETURN
1391 :
1400 REM  ===============
1401 REM  = move up
1402 REM  ===============
1403 :
1410        LUMN=0 :GOSUB 2000 :LUMN=3            :REM erase cursor
1420        IF NTE(CRNT,XPNTR)=XX THEN GOSUB 3500   :REM redraw note
1430        YY = YY-3
1435        IF YY<TP THEN YY=BTM
1440        GOSUB 2000                           :REM draw cursor
1489 :
1490        RETURN
1491 :
1500 REM  ===============
1501 REM  = move down
1502 REM  ===============
1503 :
1510        LUMN=0 :GOSUB 2000 :LUMN=3            :REM erase cursor
1520        IF NTE(CRNT,XPNTR)=XX THEN GOSUB 3500   :REM redraw note
1530        YY = YY+3
1535        IF YY>BTM THEN YY=TP
1540        GOSUB 2000                           :REM draw cursor
1589 :
1590        RETURN
1591 :
```

```
1600 REM    ===============
1601 REM    = record note
1602 REM    ===============
1603 :
1610          IF CRNT = 0 THEN 1690
1620          NTE(CRNT,LTTR)  = FN MD7((154-YY)/3)
1625          NTE(CRNT,OCT)   = INT((154-YY)/21)
1630          NTE(CRNT,ACC)   = 0
1635          NTE(CRNT,LNTH)  = DR
1640          NTE(CRNT,XPNTR) = XX
1650          GOSUB 3500                                :REM draw note
1689 :
1690          RETURN
1691 :
1700 REM    ===============
1701 REM    = add a sharp
1702 REM    ===============
1703 :
1710          IF CRNT = 0 THEN 1790
1720          NTE(CRNT,ACC) = 1
1730          GOSUB 3500                                :REM draw accidental
1789 :
1790          RETURN
1791 :
1800 REM    ===============
1801 REM    = add a flat
1802 REM    ===============
1803 :
1810          IF CRNT = 0 THEN 1890
1820          NTE(CRNT,ACC) = -1
1830          GOSUB 3500
1889 :
1890          RETURN
1891 :
1900 REM    ===============
1901 REM    = change note value
1902 REM    ===============
1903 :
1910          IF CRNT = 0 THEN 1990
1920          IF NTE(CRNT,XPNTR)-XOF < LFT THEN 1990
1930          LUMN=0 :GOSUB 3500 :LUMN=3
1940          NTE(CRNT,LNTH)=DR
1950          GOSUB 3500
1989 :
1990          RETURN
1991 :
2000 REM    ------------------
2001 REM    - draw/erase cursor
2002 REM    ------------------
2003 :
2010          HCOLOR=LUMN :DRAW CSR AT XX-XOF,YY
2089 :
2090          RETURN
2091 :
2100 REM    ------------------
2101 REM    - scroll right
2102 REM    ------------------
2103 :
2120          FOR I=0 TO 2 : CALL (ml scroller) : NEXT
2130          XOF = XOF-MVE
2189 :
2190          RETURN
2191 :
2200 REM    ------------------
2201 REM    - scroll left
2202 REM    ------------------
2203 :
```

```
2220            FOR I=0 TO 2 : CALL (ml scroller) : NEXT
2230            XOF = XOF+MVE
2289 :
2290            RETURN
2291 :
2292 REM    ===============
2293 :
3000 REM    ===============
3001 REM    = setup screen
3002 REM    ===============
3003 :
3005            HOME
3010            HGR :HCOLOR=3 :ROT=0 :SCALE=1
3020            NUM=2:X=8:Y=40:XX=LFT:YY=70
3030            LUMN=3 :GOSUB 3200                    :REM draw staff
3035            LUMN=3 :GOSUB 3300                    :REM draw melody
3040            LUMN=3 :GOSUB 2000                    :REM draw cursor
3099 :
3100            VTAB 21 :PRINT "CURSOR KEYS: <-, ->, A, Z      (L,R,U,D)"
3110            VTAB 22 :PRINT "I: INSERT, D: DELETE, +: SHARP, -: FLAT"
3120            VTAB 23 :PRINT "W: WHOLE  H: HALF  Q: QUARTER   X: EXIT"
3189 :
3190            RETURN
3191 :
3200 REM    ----------------
3201 REM    - draw staff(s)
3202 REM    ----------------
3203 :
3205            FOR  J=1 TO NUM
3210              FOR  I=0 TO 24 STEP 6
3220                HPLOT X,Y+I TO X+263,Y+I
3230              NEXT I
3240              DRAW CLF(J) AT X+FX,Y+FY
3250              Y=Y+36
3260            NEXT J
3289 :
3290            RETURN
3291 :
3300 REM    ----------------
3301 REM    - draw melody
3302 REM    ----------------
3303 :
3310            CRNT = NTE(0,RL)
3319 :
3320              IF CRNT=0 OR NTE(CRNT,XPNT)>RHT THEN 3390
3330            GOSUB 3500                            :REM draw note
3340            CRNT = NTE(CRNT,RL)
3350            GOTO 3320
3379 :
3380            CRNT = 0
3385              IF NTE(NTE(CRNT,RL),XPNTR) <= XX THEN CRNT = NTE(CRNT,RL)
3389 :
3390            RETURN
3391 :
3392 REM    ===============
3393 :
3500 REM    ===============
3501 REM    = draw note
3502 REM    ===============
3503 :
3520            XDRW = NTE(CRNT,XPNTR)-XOF
3530            YDRW = 154 - 3*( 7*NTE(CRNT,OCT)+NTE(CRNT,LTTR) )
3540            HCOLOR=LUMN :DRAW INT(NTE(CRNT,LNTH)/24)+3 AT XDRW,YDRW
3550             IF YDRW = 70 THEN GOSUB 3700          :REM ledger lines
3560             IF NTE(CRNT,ACC) <> 0 THEN GOSUB 3600   :REM accidentals
3589 :
```

```
3590        RETURN
3591 :
3600 REM     -----------------
3601 REM     - draw accidentals
3602 REM     -----------------
3603 :
3610          ON NTE(CRNT,ACC)+2 GOSUB 3660, 3670, 3680
3639 :
3640          RETURN
3641 :
3660          HCOLOR=LUMN :DRAW F AT XDRW-12,YDRW :RETURN
3670          RETURN
3680          HCOLOR=LUMN :DRAW S AT XDRW-12,YDRW :RETURN
3691 :
3700 REM     -----------------
3701 REM     - ledger lines
3702 REM     -----------------
3703 :
3710          HCOLOR=LUMN :HPLOT XDRW-7,YDRW TO XDRW+7,YDRW
2789 :
3790          RETURN
3791 :
3790 REM  ================
3792 :
3793 REM****************
3794 :
3795 :
4000 REM****************
4001 REM* load a file
4002 REM****************
4003 :
4010     CLS
4020     VTAB 23 :PRINT "FILE NAME: ";
4030     INPUT FLNM$
4049 :
4050     OPEN (FLNM$: insert code)
4060     CRNT = 0
4069 :
4080        INPUT NTE(CRNT,LTTR)
4082        INPUT NTE(CRNT,ACC)
4084        INPUT NTE(CRNT,OCT)
4086        INPUT NTE(CRNT,LNTH)
4088        INPUT NTE(CRNT,LL)
4090        INPUT NTE(CRNT,RL)
4092        INPUT NTE(CRNT,XPNTR)
4100         IF NTE(CRNT,RL) = 0 THEN 4180
4110           CRNT = NTE(CRNT,RL)
4120     GOTO 4080
4179 :
4180     PRINT CHR$(4);"CLOSE "+FLNM$
4189 :
4190     RETURN
4191 :
4200 REM****************
4201 REM* save a file
4202 REM****************
4203 :
4210     HOME
4220     VTAB 23 :PRINT "  FILE NAME: ";
4225     INPUT FLNM$
4249 :
4250     PRINT CHR$(4);"OPEN "+FLNM$
4255     PRINT CHR$(4);"WRITE "+FLNM$
4270     CRNT = 0
4279 :
4280        PRINT NTE(CRNT,LTTR)
```

```
4282        PRINT NTE(CRNT,ACC)
4284        PRINT NTE(CRNT,OCT)
4286        PRINT NTE(CRNT,LNTH)
4288        PRINT NTE(CRNT,LL)
4290        PRINT NTE(CRNT,RL)
4292        PRINT NTE(CRNT,XPNTR)
4300          IF NTE(CRNT,RL)=0 THEN 4380
4310            CRNT = NTE(CRNT,RL)
4320        GOTO 4280
4369 :
4380      PRINT CHR$(4);"CLOSE "+FLNM$
4389 :
4390      RETURN
4391 :
5000 REM***************
5001 REM* title page
5002 REM***************
5003 :
5010      HOME
5020      VTAB8  :HTAB12 :PRINT "***************"
5030      VTAB9  :HTAB12 :PRINT "* MELODY MAKER *"
5040      VTAB10 :HTAB12 :PRINT "***************"
5050      GOSUB 9000                                    :REM initialize
5060      VTAB23 :HTAB6  :PRINT  "<PRESS ANY KEY TO CONTINUE>"
5080      GET Q$
5089 :
5090      RETURN
5091 :
5100 REM****************
5101 REM* main index
5102 REM****************
5103 :
5110      HOME
5120      VTAB4  :HTAB2 :PRINT "WHAT WOULD YOU LIKE TO DO..."
5130      VTAB8  :HTAB7 :PRINT "1. LOAD A MELODY"
5140      VTAB10 :HTAB7 :PRINT "2. EDIT A MELODY"
5150      VTAB12 :HTAB7 :PRINT "3. SAVE A MELODY"
5160      VTAB16 :HTAB7 :PRINT "9. EXIT"
5170      VTAB21 :HTAB2 :PRINT "CHOOSE A NUMBER...";
5175      INPUT NX$
5177        IF NX$<"1" OR (NX$>"3" AND NX$<>"9") THEN 5170
5189 :
5190      RETURN
5191 :
9000 REM****************
9001 REM* init variables
9002 REM****************
9003 :
9005      DR=48 :FX=10 :FY=24 :TP=37 :BTM=103 :LUMN=3
9010      LTTR=0 :ACC=1 :OCT=2 :LNTH=3 :LL=4 :RL=5 :XPNTR=6
9015      MAX=60 :LFT=51 :RHT=254 :MVE=21
9020      F=6 :S=7 :CSR=8 :FCTR=(-1)
9025      CLF(1)=1 :CLF(2)=2
9034 :
9035      GOSUB 9100                                    :REM define shapes
9040      GOSUB 9500                                    :REM setup nte()
9045      GOSUB 9600                                    :REM load scroller
9049 :
9050 REM--- DEF FN ---
9055      DEF FN MD7(Z) = INT((Z/7-INT(Z/7))*7+.05)
9089 :
9090      RETURN
9091 :
9100 REM  ==============
9101 REM  = load shapes
9102 REM  ==============
```

```
9103 :
9110          PRINT CHR$(4)"BLOAD shape table, A$0C00"
9120          POKE 232,0 :POKE 233,12
9489 :
9490          RETURN
9491 :
9500 REM  ================
9501 REM  = setup nte()
9502 REM  ================
9503 :
9510          DIM NTE(MAX,6)
9520          FOR  I=1 TO MAX
9530            NTE(I-1,RL)=I
9540          NEXT I
9545          NTE(MAX,RL)=0 :NTE(0,RL)=0
9550          CRNT=0 :NXT=1 :XOF=0
9589 :
9590          RETURN
9591 :
9600 REM  ================
9601 REM  = load scroller(ml)
9602 REM  ================
9603 :
9610          FOR  I=4096 TO 4405
9620            READ ML :POKE I,ML
9630          NEXT I
9639 :
9640          RETURN
9649 :
9650 REM  --- ML data ---
9660          DATA 174,132,16,189,133,16,133,253
9662          DATA 24,105,1,133,251,189,134,16
9664          DATA 133,254,133,252,238,132,16,238
9666          DATA 132,16,96,174,132,16,189,133
9668          DATA 16,133,253,56,233,1,133,251
9670          DATA 189,134,16,133,254,133,252,238
9672          DATA 132,16,238,132,16,96,169,0
9674          DATA 141,132,16,173,130,16,141,131
9676          DATA 16,173,128,16,141,129,16,238
9678          DATA 129,16,160,0,32,0,16,177
9680          DATA 251,145,253,200,204,129,16,208
9682          DATA 246,206,131,16,208,236,96,169
9684          DATA 0,141,132,16,173,130,16,141
9686          DATA 131,16,172,128,16,32,27,16
9688          DATA 177,251,145,253,136,192,255,208
9690          DATA 247,206,131,16,208,236,96,0
9692          DATA 30,31,88,0,176,4,34,4
9694          DATA 38,4,42,4,46,4,50,4
9696          DATA 54,4,58,4,62,132,34,132
9698          DATA 38,132,42,132,46,132,50,132
9700          DATA 54,132,58,132,62,4,35,4
9702          DATA 39,4,43,4,47,4,51,4
9704          DATA 55,4,59,4,63,132,35,132
9706          DATA 39,132,43,132,47,132,51,132
9708          DATA 55,132,59,132,63,44,32,44
9710          DATA 36,44,40,44,44,44,48,44
9712          DATA 52,44,56,44,60,172,32,172
9714          DATA 36,172,40,172,44,172,48,172
9716          DATA 52,172,56,172,60,44,33,44
9718          DATA 37,44,41,44,45,44,49,44
9720          DATA 53,44,57,44,61,172,33,172
9722          DATA 37,172,41,172,45,172,49,172
9724          DATA 53,172,57,172,61,44,34,44
9726          DATA 38,44,42,44,46,44,50,44
9728          DATA 54,44,58,44,62,172,34,172
9730          DATA 38,172,42,172,46,172,50,172
```

```
9732        DATA 54,172,58,172,62,44,35,44
9734        DATA 39,44,43,44,47,44,51,44
9736        DATA 55,44,59,44,63,0,0,0
9989 :
9990 REM************************


10 REM************************
12 REM*====================*
14 REM*=                  =*
16 REM*=  melodic analysis  =*
18 REM*= program for IBM-PC =*
20 REM*=                  =*
22 REM*====================*
24 REM************************
99 :
100     WIDTH 40
120     GOSUB 8000                          :REM title/init
140     GOSUB 7000                          :REM main index
160      IF NX=9 THEN 400
180     ON NX GOSUB 4000,5000,6000,1000
300     GOTO 140
399 :
400     CLS
489 :
490     END
491 :
1000 REM************************
1001 REM* analysis index
1002 REM************************
1003 :
1010     CLS
1020     LOCATE  2,2 :PRINT "What would you like to do..."
1030     LOCATE  6,7 :PRINT "1. Interval succession"
1040     LOCATE  8,7 :PRINT "2. Melodic range (high/low)"
1050     LOCATE 10,7 :PRINT "3. Conjunctivity index"
1060     LOCATE 12,7 :PRINT "4. Pitch inventory"
1070     LOCATE 14,7 :PRINT "5. Imbrication search"
1080     LOCATE 18,7 :PRINT "9. <RETURN to main menu>"
1090     LOCATE 22,2 :PRINT "choose a number...";
1100     INPUT N2$
1110      IF N2$="9" THEN 1490
1120      IF N2$<"1" OR N2$>"5" THEN 1090
1130     N2 = VAL(N2$)
1199 :
1200     ON N2 GOSUB 1500,2000,2500,3000,3500,
1210     GOTO 1010
1489 :
1490     RETURN
1491 :
1500 REM  ======================
1501 REM  = interval succession
1502 REM  ======================
1503 :
1505     CLS :NTVL$=""
1510     CRNT = NTE(0,RL)
1520     NXT  = NTE(CRNT,RL)
1530     P2 = 12*NTE(CRNT,OCT) + LKUP(NTE(CRNT,LTTR)) + NTE(CRNT,ACC)
1549 :
1550      IF NXT=0 THEN 1900
1560     P1 = P2
1570     P2 = 12*NTE(NXT,OCT) + LKUP(NTE(NXT,LTTR)) + NTE(NXT,ACC)
1580     NTVL  = P2-P1
1590     NTVL$ = NTVL$+" "+STR$(NTVL)
1600     CRNT  = NXT
1610     NXT   = NTE(CRNT,RL)
1620     GOTO 1550
```

```
1899 :
1900         LOCATE  6,2 :PRINT "Melody: "
1910         LOCATE  8,2 :PRINT " ";MEL$
1920         LOCATE 14,2 :PRINT "Interval succession: "
1930         LOCATE 16,2 :PRINT " ";NTVL$
1980         GOSUB 9510
1989 :
1990         RETURN
1991 :
2000 REM  =========================
2001 REM  = melodic range (h/l)
2002 REM  =========================
2003 :
2005         CLS
2010          IF NTE(O,RL)=0 THEN PRINT "NO MELODY ERROR" :GOTO 2180
2020         HI=0 :LO=0
2029 :
2030         CRNT = NTE(O,RL)
2040         THI = 12*NTE(CRNT,OCT) + LKUP(NTE(CRNT,LTTR)) + NTE(CRNT,ACC)
2045         TLO = 12*NTE(CRNT,OCT) + LKUP(NTE(CRNT,LTTR)) + NTE(CRNT,ACC)
2049 :
2050         PNTR = 12*NTE(CRNT,OCT) + LKUP(NTE(CRNT,LTTR)) + NTE(CRNT,ACC)
2060          IF PNTR >= THI THEN HI=CRNT :THI=PNTR
2070          IF PNTR <= TLO THEN LO=CRNT :TLO=PNTR
2080         CRNT = NTE(CRNT,RL)
2090          IF CRNT <> O THEN 2050
2099 :
2100         TEMP = HI :GOSUB 2200 :HI$=TEMP$
2110         TEMP = LO :GOSUB 2200 :LO$=TEMP$
2120         LOCATE  6,2 :PRINT "Melodic range:"
2130         LOCATE  8,5 :PRINT "Highest pitch:      ";HI$
2140         LOCATE  9,5 :PRINT "Lowest pitch:       ";LO$
2150         LOCATE 11,5 :PRINT "Semi-tone spread: ";THI-TLO
2179 :
2180         GOSUB 9510
2189 :
2190         RETURN
2191 :
2200 REM    -------------------------
2201 REM    - convert to characters
2202 REM    -------------------------
2203 :
2205          TEMP$=""
2210           IF NTE(TEMP,LTTR) < 5 THEN TEMP$=CHR$(NTE(TEMP,LTTR)+67)
2220           IF NTE(TEMP,LTTR) >=5 THEN TEMP$=CHR$(NTE(TEMP,LTTR)+60)
2230           IF NTE(TEMP,ACC)=O THEN 2250
2240         TEMP$ = TEMP$+CHR$(44-NTE(TEMP,ACC))
2250         TEMP$ = TEMP$+RIGHT$(STR$(NTE(TEMP,OCT)),1)
2289 :
2290          RETURN
2291 :
2500 REM  =====================
2501 REM  = conjunctivity index
2502 REM  =====================
2503 :
2505         CLS :SUM=0 :CNT=0
2510         CRNT = NTE(O,RL)
2520         NXT = NTE(CRNT,RL)
2530         P2 = 12*NTE(CRNT,OCT) + LKUP(NTE(CRNT,LTTR)) + NTE(CRNT,ACC)
2549 :
2550          IF NXT=0 THEN 2700
2560         P1 = P2
2570         P2 = 12*NTE(NXT,OCT) + LKUP(NTE(NXT,LTTR)) + NTE(NXT,ACC)
2580         SUM = SUM + ABS(P2-P1)
2590         CNT = CNT+1
2600         CRNT = NXT
2610         NXT = NTE(CRNT,RL)
```

```
2620          GOTO 2550
2699 :
2700          LOCATE  6,2 :PRINT "Conjunctivity index:"
2710          LOCATE  8,5 :PRINT "Sum of intervals: ";SUM
2720          LOCATE  9,5 :PRINT "Total intervals:   ";CNT
2725           IF CNT=0 THEN PRINT "NO MELODY ERROR" :GOTO 2980
2730          LOCATE 11,5 :PRINT "Index:            ";SUM/CNT
2980          GOSUB 9510
2989 :
2990          RETURN
2991 :
3000 REM  ========================
3001 REM  = pitch inventory
3002 REM  ========================
3003 :
3005          CLS
3010          FOR Z=1 TO MAX :MTCH$(Z)="" :NEXTZ
3020          CRNT = NTE(0,RL)
3029 :
3030           IF CRNT=0 THEN 3100
3040          TEMP=CRNT :GOSUB 2200          :REM convert to chars
3050          FOR  Z=1 TO MAX
3060           IF TEMP$=MTCH$(Z) THEN 3090
3070           IF MTCH$(Z)="" THEN MTCH$(Z)=TEMP$ :GOTO 3090
3080          NEXT Z
3090          CRNT = NTE(CRNT,RL) :GOTO 3030
3099 :
3100          LOCATE  8,1 :PRINT "Melody contains the following pitches:"
3105          LOCATE 10,1 :PRINT "  ";
3110          FOR  Z=1 TO MAX
3120             IF MTCH$(Z)="" THEN 3150
3130           PRINT MTCH$(Z);" ";
3140          NEXT Z
3150          PRINT
3479 :
3480          GOSUB 9510
3489 :
3490          RETURN
3491 :
3500 REM  ========================
3501 REM  = imbrication search
3502 REM  ========================
3503 :
3510          CLS
3520          CRNT = NTE(0,RL)
3530          CNT  = 0
3539 :
3540           IF CRNT=0 THEN 3600
3545          CNT  = CNT+1
3550          TEMP = CRNT :GOSUB 2200 :MTCH$(CNT)=TEMP$
3560          CRNT = NTE(CRNT,RL) :GOTO 3540
3599 :
3600           IF CNT<3 THEN PRINT"MELODY TOO SHORT ERROR" :GOTO 3780
3610          LOCATE 8,2 :PRINT "Enter size of pattern (3 -";CNT;")";
3612          INPUT SZE
3615           IF SZE<3 OR SZE>CNT THEN 3610
3620          FOR  Z=1 TO SZE
3630           INPUT"    note";N$(Z)
3640          NEXT Z
3649 :
3650          GOSUB 3800                      :REM search for match
3780          GOSUB 9510
3789 :
3790          RETURN
3791 :
3800 REM     ------------------------
3801 REM     - search routine
3802 REM     ------------------------
```

```
3803 :
3810          FOR  OLP=1 TO CNT-(SZE-1)
3820            FOR  ILP=OLP TO OLP+(SZE-1)
3830              IF N$(ILP-(OLP-1))<>MTCH$(ILP) THEN 3860
3840            NEXT ILP
3850             PRINT "Match found at note #";OLP
3860          NEXT OLP
3989 :
3990          RETURN
3991 :
3992 REM************************
3993 :
4000 REM************************
4001 REM* input a melody
4002 REM************************
4003 :
4005      MEL$=""
4007      GOSUB 9300
4009 :
4010      CLS :PRINT "Melody:" :PRINT MEL$
4015      L$="" :A$="" :O$="" :IP$="" :ER=0
4020      LOCATE 10,2 :PRINT "Enter pitch ('Q' to quit)";
4025      INPUT IP$
4030       IF LEN(IP$)>3 THEN ER=1
4040      L$=LEFT$(IP$,1)
4041       IF L$<"A" OR L$>"G" THEN ER=1
4050      O$ = RIGHT$(IP$,1)
4051       IF O$<"1" OR O$>"8" THEN ER=1
4060       IF LEN(IP$)=3 THEN A$=MID$(IP$,2,1)
4061       IF A$<>"+" AND A$<>"-" AND A$<>"" THEN ER=1
4070       IF IP$="Q" THEN 4490
4075       IF ER=1 THEN 4010
4079 :
4080      GOSUB 4500                        :REM store in linked-list
4085      MEL$ = MEL$+" "+IP$
4090      GOTO 4010
4489 :
4490      RETURN
4491 :
4500 REM  =======================
4501 REM  = store in linked-list
4502 REM  =======================
4503 :
4510          NTE(NXT,LTTR) = FN M7(ASC(L$)-67)
4520          NTE(NXT,OCT)  = VAL(O$)
4530           IF A$<>"" THEN NTE(NXT,ACC) = 44-ASC(A$)
4599 :
4600 REM     --- insert in list ---
4609 :
4610          TEMP = NTE(NXT,RL)
4620          NTE(NXT,RL)   = NTE(CRNT,RL)
4630          NTE(CRNT,RL) = NXT
4640          NTE(NXT,LL)   = CRNT
4650          NTE(NTE(NXT,RL),LL) = NXT
4660          CRNT = NXT
4670          NXT  = TEMP
4689 :
4690          RETURN
4691 :
5000 REM************************
5001 REM* save a file
5002 REM************************
5003 :
5010      CLS
5020      LOCATE 10,5 :PRINT "File name: ";
5030      INPUT FLNM$
5049 :
5050      OPEN FLNM$ FOR OUTPUT AS #1
```

```
5060      PNTR=0
5069 :
5080      WRITE #1, NTE(PNTR,LTTR)
5082      WRITE #1, NTE(PNTR,ACC)
5084      WRITE #1, NTE(PNTR,OCT)
5086      WRITE #1, NTE(PNTR,LNTH)
5088      WRITE #1, NTE(PNTR,LL)
5090      WRITE #1, NTE(PNTR,RL)
5092      WRITE #1, NTE(PNTR,XPNTR)
5100       IF NTE(PNTR,RL) = 0 THEN 5170
5110        PNTR = NTE(PNTR,RL)
5120      GOTO 5080
5169 :
5170      WRITE #1,MEL$
5180      CLOSE #1
5489 :
5490      RETURN
5491 :
6000 REM************************
6001 REM* load a file
6002 REM************************
6003 :
6010      CLS
6020      LOCATE 10,5 :PRINT "File name: ";
6030      INPUT FLNM$
6049 :
6050      OPEN FLNM$ FOR INPUT AS #1
6060      PNTR=0
6069 :
6080      INPUT #1, NTE(PNTR,LTTR)
6082      INPUT #1, NTE(PNTR,ACC)
6084      INPUT #1, NTE(PNTR,OCT)
6086      INPUT #1, NTE(PNTR,LNTH)
6088      INPUT #1, NTE(PNTR,LL)
6090      INPUT #1, NTE(PNTR,RL)
6092      INPUT #1, NTE(PNTR,XPNTR)
6100       IF NTE(PNTR,RL) = 0 THEN 6170
6110        PNTR = NTE(PNTR,RL)
6120      GOTO 6080
6169 :
6170      MEL$="" :INPUT #1,MEL$
6180      CLOSE #1
6489 :
6490      RETURN
6491 :
7000 REM************************
7001 REM* main index
7002 REM************************
7003 :
7010      CLS
7020      LOCATE  2,2 :PRINT "What would you like to do..."
7030      LOCATE  6,7 :PRINT "1. Input a new melody"
7040      LOCATE  8,7 :PRINT "2. Store a melody on disk"
7050      LOCATE 10,7 :PRINT "3. Load a melody from disk"
7060      LOCATE 12,7 :PRINT "4. Analyse a melody"
7070      LOCATE 16,7 :PRINT "9. <QUIT>"
7080      LOCATE 22,2 :PRINT "Choose a number...";
7100      INPUT NX$
7110       IF (NX$<"1" OR NX$>"4") AND NX$<>"9" THEN 7080
7200      NX=VAL(NX$)
7489 :
7490      RETURN
7491 :
8000 REM************************
8001 REM* title page
8002 REM************************
8003 :
```

```
8010       CLS
8020       LOCATE 10,8 :PRINT "Melodic Analysis Program"
8300       GOSUB 9000                        :REM initialize
8400       GOSUB 9510
8489 :
8490       RETURN
8491 :
9000 REM**************************
9001 REM* initialize
9002 REM**************************
9003 :
9020       LTTR=0 :ACC=1 :OCT=2 :LNTH=3 :LL=4 :RL=5 :XPNTR=6
9030       MAX=60 :DIM MTCH$(MAX), N$(MAX)
9039 :
9040       DEF FN M7(Z) = INT((Z/7-INT(Z/7))*7+.05)
9099 :
9100       DIM NTE(MAX,6) :GOSUB 9300
9110       GOSUB 9400
9289 :
9290       RETURN
9291 :
9300 REM  --------------------------
9301 REM  - init linked-list
9302 REM  --------------------------
9303 :
9320       FOR  I=1 TO MAX
9330         NTE(I-1,RL) = I
9340       NEXT I
9350       NTE(0,RL)=0 :NTE(0,LL)=0 :NTE(MAX,RL)=0
9360       CRNT=0 :NXT=1
9389 :
9390       RETURN
9391 :
9400 REM  --------------------------
9401 REM  - init lookup table
9402 REM  --------------------------
9403 :
9405       DIM LKUP(6)
9410       FOR  I=0 TO 6
9420         READ LKUP(I)
9430       NEXT I
9440       DATA 0,2,4,5,7,9,11
9489 :
9490       RETURN
9491 :
9500 REM**** utilities ****
9509 :
9510       LOCATE 23,5 "<PRESS SPACE BAR TO CONTINUE>"
9515       Q$=INKEY$ :IF Q$="" THEN 9515
9520       RETURN
9989 :
9990 REM**************************
9991 REM*====================*
9992 REM**************************




10 REM**************************
12 REM*====================*
14 REM*=                  =*
16 REM*=  melodic analysis =*
18 REM*=  program for c-64 =*
20 REM*=                  =*
22 REM*====================*
24 REM**************************
99 :
100    GOSUB 8000                        :REM title/init
```

```
120      GOSUB 7000                          :REM main index
140       IF NX=9 THEN 400
160      ON NX GOSUB 4000,5000,6000,1000
300      GOTO 120
399 :
400      PRINT HOME$
489 :
490      END
491 :
1000 REM***********************
1001 REM* analysis index
1002 REM***********************
1003 :
1010     PRINT HOME$
1020     PRINTAT(2,2) "What would you like to do..."
1030     PRINTAT(7,6) "1. Interval succession"
1040     PRINTAT(7,8) "2. Melodic range (high/low)"
1050     PRINTAT(7,10)"3. Conjunctivity index"
1060     PRINTAT(7,12)"4. Pitch inventory"
1070     PRINTAT(7,14)"5. Imbrication search"
1080     PRINTAT(7,18)"9. <RETURN to main menu>"
1090     PRINTAT(2,22)"choose a number...";
1100     INPUT N2$
1110      IF N2$="9" THEN 1490
1120      IF N2$<"1" OR N2$>"5" THEN 1090
1130     N2 = VAL(N2$)
1199 :
1200     ON N2 GOSUB 1500,2000,2500,3000,3500,
1210     GOTO 1010
1489 :
1490     RETURN
1491 :
1500 REM  =======================
1501 REM  = interval succession
1502 REM  =======================
1503 :
1505     PRINT HOME$ :NTVL$=""
1510     CRNT = NTE(0,RL)
1520     NXT  = NTE(CRNT,RL)
1530     P2 = 12*NTE(CRNT,OCT) + LKUP(NTE(CRNT,LTTR)) + NTE(CRNT,ACC)
1549 :
1550      IF NXT=0 THEN 1900
1560     P1 = P2
1570     P2 = 12*NTE(NXT,OCT) + LKUP(NTE(NXT,LTTR)) + NTE(NXT,ACC)
1580     NTVL  = P2-P1
1590     NTVL$ = NTVL$+" "+STR$(NTVL)
1600     CRNT  = NXT
1610     NXT   = NTE(CRNT,RL)
1620     GOTO 1550
1899 :
1900     PRINTAT(2,6) "Melody: "
1910     PRINTAT(2,8) " ";MEL$
1920     PRINTAT(2,14)"Interval succession: "
1930     PRINTAT(2,16)" ";NTVL$
1980     GOSUB 9510
1989 :
1990     RETURN
1991 :
2000 REM  =======================
2001 REM  = melodic range (h/l)
2002 REM  =======================
2003 :
2005     PRINT HOME$
2010      IF NTE(0,RL)=0 THEN PRINT "NO MELODY ERROR" :GOTO 2180
2020     HI=0 :LO=0
2029 :
2030     CRNT = NTE(0,RL)
```

```
2040        THI = 12*NTE(CRNT,OCT) + LKUP(NTE(CRNT,LTTR)) + NTE(CRNT,ACC)
2045        TLO = 12*NTE(CRNT,OCT) + LKUP(NTE(CRNT,LTTR)) + NTE(CRNT,ACC)
2049 :
2050        PNTR = 12*NTE(CRNT,OCT) + LKUP(NTE(CRNT,LTTR)) + NTE(CRNT,ACC)
2060         IF PNTR >= THI THEN HI=CRNT :THI=PNTR
2070         IF PNTR <= TLO THEN LO=CRNT :TLO=PNTR
2080        CRNT = NTE(CRNT,RL)
2090         IF CRNT <> 0 THEN 2050
2099 :
2100        TEMP = HI :GOSUB 2200 :HI$=TEMP$
2110        TEMP = LO :GOSUB 2200 :LO$=TEMP$
2120        PRINTAT(2,6) "Melodic range:"
2130        PRINTAT(5,8) "Highest pitch:     ";HI$
2140        PRINTAT(5,9) "Lowest pitch:      ";LO$
2150        PRINTAT(5,11)"Semi-tone spread: ";THI-TLO
2179 :
2180        GOSUB 9510
2189 :
2190        RETURN
2191 :
2200 REM    ------------------------
2201 REM    - convert to characters
2202 REM    ------------------------
2203 :
2205        TEMP$=""
2210         IF NTE(TEMP,LTTR) < 5 THEN TEMP$=CHR$(NTE(TEMP,LTTR)+67)
2220         IF NTE(TEMP,LTTR) >=5 THEN TEMP$=CHR$(NTE(TEMP,LTTR)+60)
2230         IF NTE(TEMP,ACC)=0 THEN 2250
2240        TEMP$ = TEMP$+CHR$(44-NTE(TEMP,ACC))
2250        TEMP$ = TEMP$+RIGHT$(STR$(NTE(TEMP,OCT)),1)
2289 :
2290        RETURN
2291 :
2500 REM    =======================
2501 REM    = conjunctivity index
2502 REM    =======================
2503 :
2505        PRINT HOME$ :SUM=0 :CNT=0
2510        CRNT = NTE(0,RL)
2520        NXT  = NTE(CRNT,RL)
2530        P2 = 12*NTE(CRNT,OCT) + LKUP(NTE(CRNT,LTTR)) + NTE(CRNT,ACC)
2549 :
2550         IF NXT=0 THEN 2700
2560        P1 = P2
2570        P2 = 12*NTE(NXT,OCT) + LKUP(NTE(NXT,LTTR)) + NTE(NXT,ACC)
2580        SUM = SUM + ABS(P2-P1)
2590        CNT = CNT+1
2600        CRNT = NXT
2610        NXT  = NTE(CRNT,RL)
2620        GOTO 2550
2699 :
2700        PRINTAT(2,6) "Conjunctivity index:"
2710        PRINTAT(5,8) "Sum of intervals: ";SUM
2720        PRINTAT(5,9) "Total intervals:  ";CNT
2725         IF CNT=0 THEN PRINTAT(5,11)"NO MELODY ERROR" :GOTO 2980
2730        PRINTAT(5,11)"Index:            ";SUM/CNT
2980        GOSUB 9510
2989 :
2990        RETURN
2991 :
3000 REM    =======================
3001 REM    = pitch inventory
3002 REM    =======================
3003 :
3005        PRINT HOME$
3010        FOR Z=1 TO MAX :MTCH$(Z)="" :NEXTZ
3020        CRNT = NTE(0,RL)
```

```
3029 :
3030        IF CRNT=0 THEN 3100
3040        TEMP=CRNT :GOSUB 2200
3050        FOR  Z=1 TO MAX
3060          IF TEMP$=MTCH$(Z) THEN 3090
3070          IF MTCH$(Z)="" THEN MTCH$(Z)=TEMP$ :GOTO 3090
3080        NEXT Z
3090        CRNT = NTE(CRNT,RL) :GOTO 3030
3099 :
3100        PRINTAT(1,8) "Melody contains the following pitches:"
3105        PRINTAT(1,10)"  ";
3110        FOR  Z=1 TO MAX
3120          IF MTCH$(Z)="" THEN 3150
3130          PRINT MTCH$(Z);" ";
3140        NEXT Z
3150        PRINT
3479 :
3480        GOSUB 9510
3489 :
3490        RETURN
3491 :
3500 REM   =====================
3501 REM   = imbrication search
3502 REM   =====================
3503 :
3510        PRINT HOME$
3520        CRNT = NTE(0,RL)
3530        CNT  = 0
3539 :
3540         IF CRNT=0 THEN 3600
3545        CNT  = CNT+1
3550        TEMP = CRNT :GOSUB 2200 :MTCH$(CNT)=TEMP$
3560        CRNT = NTE(CRNT,RL) :GOTO 3540
3599 :
3600         IF CNT<3 THEN PRINT"MELODY TOO SHORT ERROR" :GOTO 3780
3610        PRINTAT(2,8) "Enter size of pattern (3 -";CNT;")";
3612        INPUT SZE
3615         IF SZE<3 OR SZE>CNT THEN 3610
3620        FOR  Z=1 TO SZE
3630         INPUT"   note";N$(Z)
3640        NEXT Z
3649 :
3650        GOSUB 3800                    :REM search for match
3780        GOSUB 9510
3789 :
3790        RETURN
3791 :
3800 REM   ----------------------
3801 REM   - search routine
3802 REM   ----------------------
3803 :
3810         FOR  OLP=1 TO CNT-(SZE-1)
3820           FOR  ILP=OLP TO OLP+(SZE-1)
3830             IF N$(ILP-(OLP-1))<>MTCH$(ILP) THEN 3860
3840           NEXT ILP
3850            PRINT"Match found at note #";OLP
3860         NEXT OLP
3989 :
3990        RETURN
3991 :
3992 REM************************
3993 :
4000 REM************************
4001 REM* input a melody
4002 REM************************
4003 :
4005     MEL$=""
```

```
4007        GOSUB 9300
4009  :
4010        PRINT HOME$ :PRINT "Melody:" :PRINT MEL$
4015        L$="" :A$="" :O$="" :IP$="" :ER=0
4020        PRINTAT(2,10) "Enter pitch ('Q' to quit)";
4025        INPUT IP$
4030         IF LEN(IP$)>3 THEN ER=1
4040        L$=LEFT$(IP$,1)
4041         IF L$<"A" OR L$>"G" THEN ER=1
4050        O$ = RIGHT$(IP$,1)
4051         IF O$<"1" OR O$>"8" THEN ER=1
4060         IF LEN(IP$)=3 THEN A$=MID$(IP$,2,1)
4061         IF A$<>"+" AND A$<>"-" AND A$<>"" THEN ER=1
4070         IF IP$="Q" THEN 4490
4075         IF ER=1 THEN 4010
4079  :
4080        GOSUB 4500                        :REM store in linked-list
4085        MEL$ = MEL$+" "+IP$
4090        GOTO 4010
4489  :
4490        RETURN
4491  :
4500 REM   =======================
4501 REM   = store in linked-list
4502 REM   =======================
4503  :
4510        NTE(NXT,LTTR) = FN M7(ASC(L$)-67)
4520        NTE(NXT,OCT)  = VAL(O$)
4530         IF A$<>"" THEN NTE(NXT,ACC) = 44-ASC(A$)
4599  :
4600 REM      --- insert in list ---
4609  :
4610        TEMP = NTE(NXT,RL)
4620        NTE(NXT,RL)   = NTE(CRNT,RL)
4630        NTE(CRNT,RL) = NXT
4640        NTE(NXT,LL)   = CRNT
4650        NTE(NTE(NXT,RL),LL) = NXT
4660        CRNT = NXT
4670        NXT  = TEMP
4689  :
4690        RETURN
4691  :
5000 REM************************
5001 REM* save a file
5002 REM************************
5003  :
5010        PRINT HOME$
5020        PRINTAT(5,10) "File name: ";
5030        INPUT FLNM$
5049  :
5050        OPEN 2,8,2,"@0:"+FLNM$+",S,W"
5060        PNTR=0
5069  :
5080        PRINT#2, NTE(PNTR,LTTR)
5082        PRINT#2, NTE(PNTR,ACC)
5084        PRINT#2, NTE(PNTR,OCT)
5086        PRINT#2, NTE(PNTR,LNTH)
5088        PRINT#2, NTE(PNTR,LL)
5090        PRINT#2, NTE(PNTR,RL)
5092        PRINT#2, NTE(PNTR,XPNTR)
5100         IF NTE(PNTR,RL) = 0 THEN 5170
5110         PNTR = NTE(PNTR,RL)
5120        GOTO 5080
5169  :
5170        PRINT#2,MEL$
5180        CLOSE 2
5489  :
```

```
5490        RETURN
5491 :
6000 REM*************************
6001 REM* load a file
6002 REM*************************
6003 :
6010        PRINT HOME$
6020        PRINTAT(5,10) "File name: ";
6030        INPUT FLNM$
6049 :
6050        OPEN 2,8,2,"0:"+FLNM$+",S,R"
6060        PNTR=0
6069 :
6080        INPUT#2, NTE(PNTR,LTTR)
6082        INPUT#2, NTE(PNTR,ACC)
6084        INPUT#2, NTE(PNTR,OCT)
6086        INPUT#2, NTE(PNTR,LNTH)
6088        INPUT#2, NTE(PNTR,LL)
6090        INPUT#2, NTE(PNTR,RL)
6092        INPUT#2, NTE(PNTR,XPNTR)
6100         IF NTE(PNTR,RL) = 0 THEN 6170
6110          PNTR = NTE(PNTR,RL)
6120        GOTO 6080
6169 :
6170        MEL$="" :INPUT#2,MEL$
6180        CLOSE 2
6489 :
6490        RETURN
6491 :
7000 REM*************************
7001 REM* main index
7002 REM*************************
7003 :
7010        PRINT HOME$
7020        PRINTAT(2,2) "What would you like to do..."
7030        PRINTAT(7,6) "1. Input a new melody"
7040        PRINTAT(7,8) "2. Store a melody on disk"
7050        PRINTAT(7,10)"3. Load a melody from disk"
7060        PRINTAT(7,12)"4. Analyse a melody"
7070        PRINTAT(7,16)"9. <QUIT>"
7080        PRINTAT(2,22)"Choose a number...";
7100        INPUT NX$
7110         IF (NX$<"1" OR NX$>"4") AND NX$<>"9" THEN 7080
7200        NX=VAL(NX$)
7489 :
7490        RETURN
7491 :
8000 REM*************************
8001 REM* title page
8002 REM*************************
8003 :
8010        PRINT CHR$(147)
8020        PRINTAT(8,10) "Melodic Analysis Program"
8300        GOSUB 9000                          :REM initialize
8400        GOSUB 9510
8489 :
8490        RETURN
8491 :
9000 REM*************************
9001 REM* initialize
9002 REM*************************
9003 :
9010        HOME$=CHR$(147)
9020        LTTR=0 :ACC=1 :OCT=2 :LNTH=3 :LL=4 :RL=5 :XPNTR=6
9030        MAX=60 :DIM MTCH$(MAX), N$(MAX)
9039 :
9040        DEF FN M7(Z) = INT((Z/7-INT(Z/7))*7+.05)
```

```
9099 :
9100      DIM NTE(MAX,6) :GOSUB 9300
9110      GOSUB 9400
9289 :
9290      RETURN
9291 :
9300 REM  ------------------------
9301 REM  - init linked-list
9302 REM  ------------------------
9303 :
9320      FOR  I=1 TO MAX
9330        NTE(I-1,RL) = I
9340      NEXT I
9350      NTE(0,RL)=0 :NTE(0,LL)=0 :NTE(MAX,RL)=0
9360      CRNT=0 :NXT=1
9389 :
9390      RETURN
9391 :
9400 REM  ------------------------
9401 REM  - init lookup table
9402 REM  ------------------------
9403 :
9405      DIM LKUP(6)
9410      FOR  I=0 TO 6
9420        READ LKUP(I)
9430      NEXT I
9440       DATA 0,2,4,5,7,9,11
9489 :
9490      RETURN
9491 :
9500 REM**** utilities ****
9509 :
9510      PRINTAT(5,23) "<PRESS SPACE BAR TO CONTINUE>"
9515      GET Q$:IF Q$="" THEN 9515
9520      RETURN
9989 :
9990 REM***********************
9991 REM*=====================*
9992 REM***********************


10 REM***********************
12 REM*=====================*
14 REM*=                   =*
16 REM*=   melodic analysis =*
18 REM*=   program for APPLE =*
20 REM*=                   =*
22 REM*=====================*
24 REM***********************
99 :
100    GOSUB 8000                    :REM title/init
120    GOSUB 7000                    :REM main index
140     IF NX=9 THEN 400
160    ON NX GOSUB 4000,5000,6000,1000
300    GOTO 120
399 :
400    HOME
489 :
490    END
491 :
1000 REM***********************
1001 REM* analysis index
1002 REM***********************
1003 :
1010      HOME
1020      VTAB  2 :PRINT TAB(2)"WHAT WOULD YOU LIKE TO DO..."
1030      VTAB  6 :PRINT TAB(7)"1. INTERVAL SUCCESSION"
```

```
1040        VTAB  8 :PRINT TAB(7)"2. MELODIC RANGE (HIGH/LOW)"
1050        VTAB 10 :PRINT TAB(7)"3. CONJUNCTIVITY INDEX"
1060        VTAB 12 :PRINT TAB(7)"4. PITCH INVENTORY"
1070        VTAB 14 :PRINT TAB(7)"5. IMBRICATION SEARCH"
1080        VTAB 18 :PRINT TAB(7)"9. <RETURN TO MAIN MENU>"
1090        VTAB 22 :PRINT TAB(2)"CHOOSE A NUMBER...";
1100        INPUT N2$
1110         IF N2$="9" THEN 1490
1120         IF N2$<"1" OR N2$>"5" THEN 1090
1130        N2 = VAL(N2$)
1199 :
1200        ON N2 GOSUB 1500,2000,2500,3000,3500,
1210        GOTO 1010
1489 :
1490        RETURN
1491 :
1500 REM   =======================
1501 REM   = interval succession
1502 REM   =======================
1503 :
1505        HOME :NTVL$=""
1510        CRNT = NTE(O,RL)
1520        NXT  = NTE(CRNT,RL)
1530        P2 = 12*NTE(CRNT,OCT) + LKUP(NTE(CRNT,LTTR)) + NTE(CRNT,ACC)
1549 :
1550         IF NXT=0 THEN 1900
1560        P1 = P2
1570        P2 = 12*NTE(NXT,OCT) + LKUP(NTE(NXT,LTTR)) + NTE(NXT,ACC)
1580        NTVL  = P2-P1
1590        NTVL$ = NTVL$+" "+STR$(NTVL)
1600        CRNT  = NXT
1610        NXT   = NTE(CRNT,RL)
1620        GOTO 1550
1899 :
1900        VTAB  6 :PRINT TAB(2)"MELODY: "
1910        VTAB  8 :PRINT TAB(2)" ";MEL$
1920        VTAB 14 :PRINT TAB(2)"INTERVAL SUCCESSION: "
1930        VTAB 16 :PRINT TAB(2)" ";NTVL$
1980        GOSUB 9510
1989 :
1990        RETURN
1991 :
2000 REM   =======================
2001 REM   = melodic range (h/l)
2002 REM   =======================
2003 :
2005        HOME
2010         IF NTE(O,RL)=0 THEN PRINT "NO MELODY ERROR" :GOTO 2180
2020        HI=0 :LO=0
2029 :
2030        CRNT = NTE(O,RL)
2040        THI = 12*NTE(CRNT,OCT) + LKUP(NTE(CRNT,LTTR)) + NTE(CRNT,ACC)
2045        TLO = 12*NTE(CRNT,OCT) + LKUP(NTE(CRNT,LTTR)) + NTE(CRNT,ACC)
2049 :
2050        PNTR = 12*NTE(CRNT,OCT) + LKUP(NTE(CRNT,LTTR)) + NTE(CRNT,ACC)
2060         IF PNTR >= THI THEN HI=CRNT :THI=PNTR
2070         IF PNTR <= TLO THEN LO=CRNT :TLO=PNTR
2080        CRNT = NTE(CRNT,RL)
2090         IF CRNT <> 0 THEN 2050
2099 :
2100        TEMP = HI :GOSUB 2200 :HI$=TEMP$
2110        TEMP = LO :GOSUB 2200 :LO$=TEMP$
2120        VTAB  6 :PRINT TAB(2)"MELODIC RANGE:"
2130        VTAB  8 :PRINT TAB(5)"HIGHEST PITCH:    ";HI$
2140        VTAB  9 :PRINT TAB(5)"LOWEST PITCH:     ";LO$
2150        VTAB 11 :PRINT TAB(5)"SEMI-TONE SPREAD: ";THI-TLO
2179 :
```

```
2180          GOSUB 9510
2189 :
2190          RETURN
2191 :
2200 REM      ---------------------------
2201 REM      - convert to characters
2202 REM      ---------------------------
2203 :
2205           TEMP$=""
2210            IF NTE(TEMP,LTTR) < 5 THEN TEMP$=CHR$(NTE(TEMP,LTTR)+67)
2220            IF NTE(TEMP,LTTR) >=5 THEN TEMP$=CHR$(NTE(TEMP,LTTR)+60)
2230            IF NTE(TEMP,ACC)=0 THEN 2250
2240           TEMP$ = TEMP$+CHR$(44-NTE(TEMP,ACC))
2250           TEMP$ = TEMP$+RIGHT$(STR$(NTE(TEMP,OCT)),1)
2289 :
2290          RETURN
2291 :
2500 REM      =======================
2501 REM      = conjunctivity index
2502 REM      =======================
2503 :
2505          HOME :SUM=0 :CNT=0
2510          CRNT = NTE(0,RL)
2520          NXT  = NTE(CRNT,RL)
2530          P2 = 12*NTE(CRNT,OCT) + LKUP(NTE(CRNT,LTTR)) + NTE(CRNT,ACC)
2549 :
2550           IF NXT=0 THEN 2700
2560          P1 = P2
2570          P2 = 12*NTE(NXT,OCT) + LKUP(NTE(NXT,LTTR)) + NTE(NXT,ACC)
2580          SUM = SUM + ABS(P2-P1)
2590          CNT = CNT+1
2600          CRNT = NXT
2610          NXT  = NTE(CRNT,RL)
2620          GOTO 2550
2699 :
2700          VTAB  6 :PRINT TAB(2)"CONJUNCTIVITY INDEX:"
2710          VTAB  8 :PRINT TAB(5)"SUM OF INTERVALS: ";SUM
2720          VTAB  9 :PRINT TAB(5)"TOTAL INTERVALS:  ";CNT
2725           IF CNT=0 THEN PRINT "NO MELODY ERROR" :GOTO 2980
2730          VTAB 11 :PRINT TAB(5)"INDEX:            ";SUM/CNT
2980          GOSUB 9510
2989 :
2990          RETURN
2991 :
3000 REM      =======================
3001 REM      = pitch inventory
3002 REM      =======================
3003 :
3005          HOME
3010          FOR Z=1 TO MAX :MTCH$(Z)="" :NEXTZ
3020          CRNT = NTE(0,RL)
3029 :
3030           IF CRNT=0 THEN 3100
3040          TEMP=CRNT :GOSUB 2200          :REM convert to chars
3050          FOR  Z=1 TO MAX
3060            IF TEMP$=MTCH$(Z) THEN 3090
3070            IF MTCH$(Z)="" THEN MTCH$(Z)=TEMP$ :GOTO 3090
3080          NEXT Z
3090          CRNT = NTE(CRNT,RL) :GOTO 3030
3099 :
3100          VTAB  8 :PRINT " MELODY CONTAINS THE FOLLOWING PITCHES:"
3105          VTAB 10 :PRINT "   ";
3110          FOR  Z=1 TO MAX
3120            IF MTCH$(Z)="" THEN 3150
3130           PRINT MTCH$(Z);" ";
3140          NEXT Z
3150          PRINT
```

```
3479 :
3480         GOSUB 9510
3489 :
3490         RETURN
3491 :
3500 REM   ========================
3501 REM   = imbrication search
3502 REM   ========================
3503 :
3510         HOME
3520         CRNT = NTE(0,RL)
3530         CNT  = 0
3539 :
3540          IF CRNT=0 THEN 3600
3545         CNT  = CNT+1
3550         TEMP = CRNT :GOSUB 2200 :MTCH$(CNT)=TEMP$
3560         CRNT = NTE(CRNT,RL) :GOTO 3540
3599 :
3600          IF CNT<3 THEN PRINT "MELODY TOO SHORT ERROR" :GOTO 3780
3610         VTAB 8 :PRINT TAB(2)"ENTER SIZE OF PATTERN (3 -";CNT;")";
3612         INPUT SZE
3615          IF SZE<3 OR SZE>CNT THEN 3610
3620         FOR  Z=1 TO SZE
3630           INPUT"   NOTE";N$(Z)
3640         NEXT Z
3649 :
3650         GOSUB 3800                      :REM search for match
3780         GOSUB 9510
3789 :
3790         RETURN
3791 :
3800 REM      ----------------------
3801 REM      - search routine
3802 REM      ----------------------
3803 :
3810          FOR  OLP=1 TO CNT-(SZE-1)
3820            FOR  ILP=OLP TO OLP+(SZE-1)
3830              IF N$(ILP-(OLP-1))<>MTCH$(ILP) THEN 3860
3840            NEXT ILP
3850             PRINT "MATCH FOUND AT NOTE #";OLP
3860          NEXT OLP
3989 :
3990         RETURN
3991 :
3992 REM************************
3993 :
4000 REM************************
4001 REM* input a melody
4002 REM************************
4003 :
4005      MEL$=""
4007      GOSUB 9300
4009 :
4010      HOME :PRINT "MELODY:" :PRINT MEL$
4015      L$="" :A$="" :O$="" :IP$="" :ER=0
4020      VTAB 10 :PRINT TAB(2)"ENTER PITCH ('Q' TO QUIT)";
4025      INPUT IP$
4030       IF LEN(IP$)>3 THEN ER=1
4040      L$=LEFT$(IP$,1)
4041       IF L$<"A" OR L$>"G" THEN ER=1
4050      O$ = RIGHT$(IP$,1)
4051       IF O$<"1" OR O$>"8" THEN ER=1
4060       IF LEN(IP$)=3 THEN A$=MID$(IP$,2,1)
4061       IF A$<>"+" AND A$<>"-" AND A$<>"" THEN ER=1
4070       IF IP$="Q" THEN 4490
4075       IF ER=1 THEN 4010
4079 :
```

```
4080        GOSUB 4500                          :REM store in linked-list
4085        MEL$ = MEL$+" "+IP$
4090        GOTO 4010
4489 :
4490        RETURN
4491 :
4500 REM    ========================
4501 REM    = store in linked-list
4502 REM    ========================
4503 :
4510        NTE(NXT,LTTR) = FN M7(ASC(L$)-67)
4520        NTE(NXT,OCT)  = VAL(O$)
4530         IF A$<>"" THEN NTE(NXT,ACC) = 44-ASC(A$)
4599 :
4600 REM      --- insert in list ---
4609 :
4610        TEMP = NTE(NXT,RL)
4620        NTE(NXT,RL)  = NTE(CRNT,RL)
4630        NTE(CRNT,RL) = NXT
4640        NTE(NXT,LL)  = CRNT
4650        NTE(NTE(NXT,RL),LL) = NXT
4660        CRNT = NXT
4670        NXT  = TEMP
4689 :
4690        RETURN
4691 :
5000 REM************************
5001 REM* save a file
5002 REM************************
5003 :
5010        HOME
5020        VTAB 10 :PRINT TAB(5)"FILE NAME: ";
5030        INPUT FLNM$
5049 :
5050        PRINT CHR$(4);"OPEN ";FLNM$ :PRINT CHR$(4);"WRITE ";FLNM$
5060        PNTR=0
5069 :
5080        PRINT NTE(PNTR,LTTR)
5082        PRINT NTE(PNTR,ACC)
5084        PRINT NTE(PNTR,OCT)
5086        PRINT NTE(PNTR,LNTH)
5088        PRINT NTE(PNTR,LL)
5090        PRINT NTE(PNTR,RL)
5092        PRINT NTE(PNTR,XPNTR)
5100         IF NTE(PNTR,RL) = 0 THEN 5170
5110          PNTR = NTE(PNTR,RL)
5120        GOTO 5080
5169 :
5170        PRINT MEL$
5180        PRINT CHR$(4);"CLOSE ";FLNM$
5489 :
5490        RETURN
5491 :
6000 REM************************
6001 REM* load a file
6002 REM************************
6003 :
6010        HOME
6020        VTAB 10 :PRINT TAB(5)"FILE NAME: ";
6030        INPUT FLNM$
6049 :
6050        PRINT CHR$(4);"OPEN ";FLNM$ :PRINT CHR$(4);"READ ";FLNM$
6060        PNTR=0
6069 :
6080        INPUT NTE(PNTR,LTTR)
6082        INPUT NTE(PNTR,ACC)
6084        INPUT NTE(PNTR,OCT)
```

```
6086        INPUT NTE(PNTR,LNTH)
6088        INPUT NTE(PNTR,LL)
6090        INPUT NTE(PNTR,RL)
6092        INPUT NTE(PNTR,XPNTR)
6100         IF NTE(PNTR,RL) = 0 THEN 6170
6110          PNTR = NTE(PNTR,RL)
6120        GOTO 6080
6169 :
6170        MEL$="" :INPUT MEL$
6180        PRINT CHR$(4);"CLOSE ";FLNM$
6489 :
6490        RETURN
6491 :
7000 REM************************
7001 REM* main index
7002 REM************************
7003 :
7010        HOME
7020        VTAB   2 :PRINT TAB(2)"WHAT WOULD YOU LIKE TO DO..."
7030        VTAB   6 :PRINT TAB(7)"1. INPUT A NEW MELODY"
7040        VTAB   8 :PRINT TAB(7)"2. STORE A MELODY ON DISK"
7050        VTAB  10 :PRINT TAB(7)"3. LOAD A MELODY FROM DISK"
7060        VTAB  12 :PRINT TAB(7)"4. ANALYSE A MELODY"
7070        VTAB  16 :PRINT TAB(7)"9. <QUIT>"
7080        VTAB  22 :PRINT TAB(2)"CHOOSE A NUMBER...";
7100        INPUT NX$
7110         IF (NX$<"1" OR NX$>"4") AND NX$<>"9" THEN 7080
7200        NX=VAL(NX$)
7489 :
7490        RETURN
7491 :
8000 REM************************
8001 REM* title page
8002 REM************************
8003 :
8010        HOME
8020        VTAB 10 :PRINT TAB(8)"MELODIC ANALYSIS PROGRAM"
8300        GOSUB 9000                      :REM initialize
8400        GOSUB 9510
8489 :
8490        RETURN
8491 :
9000 REM************************
9001 REM* initialize
9002 REM************************
9003 :
9020        LTTR=0 :ACC=1 :OCT=2 :LNTH=3 :LL=4 :RL=5 :XPNTR=6
9030        MAX=60 :DIM MTCH$(MAX), N$(MAX)
9039 :
9040        DEF FN M7(Z) = INT((Z/7-INT(Z/7))*7+.05)
9099 :
9100        DIM NTE(MAX,6) :GOSUB 9300
9110        GOSUB 9400
9289 :
9290        RETURN
9291 :
9300 REM  ----------------------
9301 REM  - init linked-list
9302 REM  ----------------------
9303 :
9320          FOR  I=1 TO MAX
9330            NTE(I-1,RL) = I
9340          NEXT I
9350          NTE(0,RL)=0 :NTE(0,LL)=0 :NTE(MAX,RL)=0
9360          CRNT=0 :NXT=1
9389 :
9390          RETURN
```

```
9391 :
9400 REM   ------------------------
9401 REM   - init lookup table
9402 REM   ------------------------
9403 :
9405       DIM LKUP(6)
9410       FOR  I=0 TO 6
9420        READ LKUP(I)
9430       NEXT I
9440        DATA 0,2,4,5,7,9,11
9489 :
9490       RETURN
9491 :
9500 REM**** utilities ****
9509 :
9510      VTAB 23 :PRINT TAB(5)"<PRESS SPACE BAR TO CONTINUE>"
9515      GET Q$
9520      RETURN
9989 :
9990 REM*************************
9991 REM*===================*
9992 REM*************************
```

APPENDIX A
GUIDE TO BASIC

The following guide presents summary descriptions and the syntax of the most commonly used BASIC commands for the IBM-PC, the Apple II, and the Commodore 64. It is not exhaustive, either in the commands covered or in the amount of detail given for each, although most commands are listed and most of the detail is covered. This guide is instead intended as a thumbnail guide. Consult any one of the excellent reference guides for the different machines for complete details. The following conventions are followed in describing the commands:

UPPER CASE is used to indicate what must be entered literally.
Lower case indicates items which you customize with your own relevant information ("varname" for places variable names go, etc.).
. (periods) are used in lower case in order to make names more intelligible.
[] (brackets) are used to indicate optional items.
// (slashes) are used to indicate a list of items from which you choose one; the items are separated by |.
... indicates that the immediately preceding item may be repeated any number of times.

The commands, expressions, modifiers, and functions are grouped according to general categories.

LINE NUMBERS AND REMARKS

A BASIC program is a sequence of commands placed on numbered lines (statements). These numbers generally determine the order of execution of the statements. More than one command may be included on a line if separated by colons (":"). The allowable range for line numbers is 0-65529 (IBM) or 0-63999 (Apple and Commodore). Remarks may be indicated by the remark command REM. Everything on the line following REM (including colons) will be ignored during execution. IBM BASIC also allows remarks to follow the single quote (').

Examples

```
999 END
999 PRINT : REM IGNORE THIS
999 STOP  'THIS IS A COMMENT
```

CONSTANTS

A constant is a data value which does not change. BASIC allows two types of constants. A character string constant is any sequence of characters enclosed by quotation marks. A numeric constant is any number. BASIC allows numbers to be specified any of three ways. Integers have no decimal point, while real numbers do. Numbers in scientific notation have the form n...nEe...e, where n...n is a real number and e...e is a power of 10 (see example below). They are used to express very small or very large numbers.

string constant	"J. S. BACH"
numeric constants	
integer	4
real	8.27
scientific notation	4.243E-06
	($= 4.243 \times 10 \uparrow -6 = .000004243$)

VARIABLES

A variable is a label given to a memory location (or locations) used to store data values. The value contained in a variable may be changed, hence the name. The mailbox provides a good analogy. The variable is like the mailbox itself (identified by a variable name as the mailbox is identified by the resident's name), and the data value stored in the variable is like a single letter placed in a mailbox.

BASIC features three types of variables. The type is determined by the form of the variable name and determines what type of data may be stored in that variable. Real variable names have no special ending, while integer variable names end with "%" and string variable names end with "$". (IBM BASIC also allows other types.) Variable names must begin with a letter and may then be completed with any number of letters or numerals (or periods on the IBM). However, in Applesoft BASIC and Commodore BASIC only the first two characters of the name are significant. In other words, VR1 and VR2 are indistinguishable variable names. IBM BASIC considers the first forty characters of the variable name significant. Variable names may not be keywords (generally the upper case words in this guide); in addition, on the Apple and the Commodore, variable names may not contain embedded keywords.

```
Examples:   X, AMOUNT, Z12, TAX
Incorrect:  END     (is a keyword)
            ATOM    (contains the keyword TO)
```

Several variables may be grouped together by using the same name with subscripts, as in COMPOSER$(14) or ROW(6,3). The following commands are used for these subscripted variables or arrays, as they are also called.

DIM   dimensions an array to be a certain size, that is, allocates a certain number of locations for it. This number is the number in the DIM statement plus one (for the zero subscript element). An array that is used without having been DIMensioned is assigned 11 subscripts (0–10) per dimension by default.

```
Syntax:     DIM varname(largest.subscript1[,largest.subscript2...])
                [,varname(largest.subscript1[,largest.subscript2...])...]
Examples:   DIM A$(4,5)
            DIM NTE(10,7), ROW(12,12)
```

OPTION BASE (IBM only)   allows the smallest subscript to be specified as zero or one. By default, it is zero. Setting it to one saves space if the programmer prefers (as many do) not to use the zero subscript.

```
Syntax:   OPTION BASE /0 | 1/
```

ERASE (IBM only)   undoes the DIM statement (deallocates the space for the given arrays).

```
Syntax:   ERASE varname[,varname]...
```

ASSIGNMENT

There is one assignment command. It is used to store data values (either specified directly as constants or indirectly as variable names or other expressions) into variables.

LET   Syntax: [LET] varname = expression

OPERATORS AND EXPRESSIONS

An operator is used to effect an action on some item or items. An example is "+", which adds together the items on either side of it, as in "A + B". Operators have precedence; that is, as an expression is being evaluated, higher precedence operations are performed before lower precedence ones. Operations of equal precedence are performed left to right. Each line of the list below represents a level of precedence.

arithmetic:	(highest)	functions
		parentheses
		↑ (exponentiation)
		− (negation or unary minus)
		* (mult.), / (div.), \ (div. truncated-IBM only) . . .
		. . .MOD (modulo arithmetic-IBM only)
	(lowest)	+ (addtn.), − (subtrctn.)
logical:	(highest)	NOT
		AND
		OR
		XOR (IBM only)
		EQV (IBM only)
	(lowest)	IMP (IBM only)
string:		+ (concatenation):

An expression is a combination of variable names or constants and operators. It may be assigned to a variable, used in a relational command (such as IF..THEN..ELSE), or used as a function argument.

FUNCTIONS

Functions take arguments enclosed in parentheses following the function name and use them as input for some operation. Then they return a value which may be used as an expression or part of an expression. The list below is arranged according to the following function types: general mathematical, trigonometric, management, print, string, and user-defined. Two commands which are not functions are included because they are very closely associated with particular functions.

General Mathematical Functions

INT   takes a number and returns the truncated value of that number (i.e. with the fractional portion dropped).

Syntax: INT(number)
Examples: INT(4.777)   (equals 4)
           INT(A)

ABS   takes a number and returns its absolute value.

Syntax: ABS(number)
Examples: ABS(−17.4)   (equals 17.4)
           ABS(X24)

SGN   takes a number and returns 1 if it is positive, 0 if it is 0, or −1 if it is negative.

Syntax: SGN(number)

SQR   takes a number and returns its square root. Negative square roots are not allowed.

Syntax: SQR(number)

LOG   takes a number and returns its natural base logarithm.

Syntax: LOG(number)

Helpful hint: To use the LOG function to calculate a logarithm in any base, use the following formula: LOG(number) / LOG(base)

EXP   takes a number and raises it to that power. The inverse of LOG.

Syntax: EXP(number)

RND   takes a dummy numeric argument (i.e. it doesn't matter what is used) and returns a random real number between 0 and 1.

Syntax: RND(dummy.number)

RANDOMIZE (not a function - IBM only)   takes an integer number and uses it to generate a set of random numbers from which the RND function will choose. Each integer produces a different set.

Syntax: RANDOMIZE number

Trigonometric Functions

SIN   returns the sine of an angular value specified in radians.

Syntax: SIN(angle)

COS   returns the cosine of an angular value specified in radians.

Syntax: COS(angle)

TAN   returns the tangent of an angular value specified in radians.

Syntax: TAN(angle)

ATN   given a value, returns the arctangent (in radians) of that value.

Syntax: ATN(number)

Management Functions

FRE   takes a dummy integer argument and returns the number of bytes of free memory.

Syntax: FRE(dummy.number)

PEEK   takes a memory location number and returns the value currently stored in that location.

Syntax: PEEK(location.number)

POKE (not a function)   stores the given integer value (must be in the range 0–255) in the given memory location (must be in the range appropriate for each machine). POKE is the inverse of PEEK.

Syntax: POKE location.number,value

POS   takes a dummy argument and returns the number of the column where the cursor is currently located.

Syntax: POS(dummy.number)

CSRLIN (IBM only)   this function has no argument and therefore no parentheses. It returns the number of the line where the cursor is currently located.

Syntax: CSRLIN

Print Functions

These functions may be used only within PRINT statements.

TAB moves the cursor to the column indicated by the argument.

Syntax: TAB(integer.number)
Example: PRINT X; TAB(30); Y

SPC inserts the given number of spaces into the printed information.

Syntax: SPC(integer.number)
Example: PRINT X; SPC(4); Y

String Functions

ASC given a character string, returns the number associated with the first character of that string in the ASCII code system.

Syntax: ASC(character.string)
Example: N = ASC("A")   (assigns 65 to N)

VAL given a character string, returns the numeric portion of the first part of the string (up to the first non-number). If the first character of the string is nonnumeric, returns 0.

Syntax: VAL(character.string)
Example: N = VAL("123 OAK STREET")   (assigns 123 to N)

LEN returns the length (in characters) of the given string.

Syntax: LEN(character.string)

INSTR (IBM only) given a character string to search for, a character string to search in, and a character position to start the search at, returns the character position at which the string was found. If the string was not found, 0 is returned.

Syntax: INSTR(start.position, search.in.string,search.for.string)

*CHR$* given an integer number, returns the character associated with that number in the ASCII code system. CHR$ is the inverse of ASC.

Syntax: CHR$(number)
Example: X$ = CHR$(65)   (assigns "A" to X$)

*STR$* given a number, returns the string which contains that number. STR$ is the inverse of VAL.

Syntax: STR$(number)
Example: STR$(24334)   (returns the string "24334")

LEFT$ given a string and an integer number n, returns the n leftmost characters of the string.

Syntax: LEFT$(character.string,number)
Example: LEFT$("BAZOOKA",5)   (returns "BAZOO")

MID$ given a string, a starting position, and a number of characters, returns the substring of the given length beginning at the given position.

Syntax: MID$(character.string,start.position,number)
Example: MID$("BAZOOKA",3,4)   (returns "ZOOK")

RIGHT$ given a string and an integer number n, returns the n rightmost characters of the string.

Syntax: RIGHT$(character.string,number)
Example: RIGHT$("BAZOOKA",2)   (returns "KA")

SPACE$ (IBM only)   takes an integer number and returns a string consisting of that number of blank spaces.

Syntax: SPACE$(number)

User-Defined Functions

DEF FN   any one statement can be incorporated into a user-defined function. The function is defined with the DEF FN command; it is invoked by naming it in an expression, and when it is invoked the actual arguments in the name reference are substituted for all occurrences of the dummy arguments in the definition. Only IBM BASIC allows more than one argument.

Syntax: (definition) DEF FNname(dummy.arg[,dummy.arg]...)=expression
           (invocation) FNname(actual.arg[,actual.arg]...)
Example: DEF FN TEMPCVER(F) = (F − 32) / 1.8
           CENTIGRADE = FN TEMPCVER(212)   (assigns 100 to variable)

OUTPUT AND INPUT

Output

PRINT   prints information on the current output device (generally the video screen).

Syntax: PRINT [expression][separator [expression]]...

Expressions can be single constants or variables as well as more complex expressions. Different separators have different effects on the resulting output. Semicolons or blanks separate items with a single space. Commas tab to the beginning of the next screen field (these positions vary from machine to machine). PRINT by itself creates a blank line.

Examples

```
PRINT  "A";B$;TAB(24);C%
PRINT  ASC(X$)
PRINT  X,SQR(X),X*X,X*X+SIN(X*PI/180)
PRINT "FORM LETTER FOR" YOU$ "TO READ"
```

Input

INPUT   causes the program to pause and wait for input from the user, which is stored in the given variable(s). If a string is included, it is printed before the program pauses.

> Syntax: INPUT [string;] varname[,varname]...
> Example: INPUT "Enter your name:"; YOU$

READ   obtains data from a DATA statement and assigns data values to specified variables. Each time a data item is READ, the system moves a pointer in the DATA to the next item in the DATA statements (whether the next item is in the same DATA statement or the next DATA statement).

> Syntax: READ varname[,varname]...
> Example: READ A,B$,C%

DATA   contains the data which is to be input into variables by the READ command. DATA statements are usually gathered together in one place so that they can easily be replaced or modified.

> Syntax: DATA data.item[,data.item]...
> Example: DATA 4.23,PENGUIN,27,2.33,GOOSE,45

Note: If the types (integer,string,etc.) of the READ commands don't agree with the appropriate DATA commands, errors may occur.

RESTORE   resets the DATA pointer back to the first item of the first DATA statement of the program.

> Syntax: RESTORE

GET (Apple and Commodore only)   allows capture of a single item of data and storage into a variable. The Apple pauses until the user enters the data;

the Commodore captures the data immediately, requiring a construction like that shown in the example.

> Syntax: GET string.variable
> Example: 10 GET IN$: IF IN$ ="" THEN 10

INKEY$ (IBM only)   IBM's equivalent of GET. It is a function which returns the key just pressed on the keyboard. Like Commodore's GET, it executes immediately. Therefore if you want to pause until the user enters something, use a construction like the example.

> Syntax: INKEY$
> Example: 10 IN$ = INKEY$: IF IN$="" THEN 10

FLOW OF CONTROL COMMANDS

It has just been noted that, generally, BASIC executes statements in numerical order, ending after executing the statement with the largest line number. The following commands alter execution sequence, adding the flexibility of branching and looping to the language.

END   marks the END of program execution. The program stops after executing an END statement, even if higher numbered statements follow it.

> Syntax: END

STOP   has the same effect as the END command, but with the possibility of resumption of execution (see below). Very useful for debugging.

> Syntax: STOP

CONT   restarts program execution after a STOP at the line following the STOP statement. END, STOP, and CONT do not erase variable values (RUN does). This command is entered at the BASIC system level rather than being included in a program.

> Syntax: CONT

GOTO   unconditionally transfers the program to the given line number. The statement at that line will be executed next. Any line numbers between the one that contains the GOTO and the one named in the statement are skipped and not executed (unless control is transferred to one of them later by some other statement). GOTO may branch in a backward direction as well as forward.

> Syntax: GOTO line.number

GOSUB calls (begins execution of) the subroutine that begins at the given line number. Somewhere after that line number there should be a RETURN statement to return control to the statement following the line containing the GOSUB. The lines between the first line of the subroutine and the RETURN statement comprise the body of the subroutine. Subroutine calls may be nested. Subroutines improve the modularity and readability of the program and should be used liberally.

Syntax: GOSUB line.number

RETURN transfers control back to the line following the last GOSUB statement executed. If no GOSUB statement has been executed or if all GO-SUBs have encountered their RETURNs, an error occurs.

Syntax: RETURN

CALL (IBM and Apple only) begins execution of the machine language program located at the given memory location. If that program does not end with the appropriate machine language return command, the program will probably end up dying somewhere in the bowels of your computer. Otherwise control will eventually be returned to the statement following the CALL statement.

Syntax: CALL memory.location.address

USR like CALL, except USR allows one variable to be passed to the machine language routine. (IBM's CALL allows multiple variables to be placed on the stack.) On the IBM, USR specifies the routine by number (relationships between numbers and addresses are established by the DEF USR statement). On the Apple and the Commodore the address is obtained from certain constant memory locations.

Syntax: (IBM) USR [number] (varname)
(others) USR (varname)

DEF USR (IBM only) associates the given memory location with the given number for use in the USR command. The number must be an integer between 0 and 9.

Syntax: DEF USR number=memory.location.address

FOR..TO..STEP marks the beginning of a FOR/NEXT loop. The first time this statement is executed the control variable is initialized to the initial value. Each time the statement is executed the control variable is checked to see whether it has reached or exceeded the final value. If it has, control is transferred to the statement following the associated NEXT statement. If it has not, the control variable is incremented (or decremented) by the amount of the STEP (1 if omitted) and the statements following the FOR statement are executed. All values must be numeric. FOR/NEXT loops may be nested.

> Syntax: FOR control.variable = initial.value TO final.value [STEP step.value]
> Example: FOR I = 23 TO 16 STEP −0.7

NEXT   marks the end of a FOR/NEXT loop. When this statement is executed, control passes back to the associated FOR statement (see above for FOR's method of execution).

> Syntax: NEXT [control.variable]

ON..GOTO   unconditionally transfers control to the statement in the list of line numbers which corresponds to the integer value of the variable. For example, if the variable equals 4, this statement will GOTO the line number fourth in the list. If the number is 0, is not positive, or if it is larger than the number of line numbers in the list, control passes to the statement following the ON..GOTO (as usual).

> Syntax: ON varname GOTO list.of.line.numbers
> Example: ON X GOTO 100,200,300,400,500

ON..GOSUB   is the same as ON..GOTO, except that one of a number of subroutines will be called based on the value of the variable. See the restrictions on subroutines listed above under GOSUB.

> Syntax: ON varname GOSUB list.of.line.numbers

IF..THEN   If the conditional expression is true, the consequent statement is executed. If it is false, the consequent statement is not executed. A line number may be used as a consequent statement. The effect is the same as IF..THEN GOTO.

> Syntax: IF conditional.expression THEN consequent.expression
> Examples: IF X > 14 THEN PRINT "THAT'S OVER TWO WEEKS!"
>   IF NIGHT = DAY THEN 3524

IF..THEN..ELSE (IBM only)   is the same as IF..THEN, except that if the conditional expression is false, the else expression will be executed.

> Syntax: IF conditional.expression THEN consequent.expression ELSE else.expression
> Example: IF ANS$ = CORRECT$ THEN PRINT "WOW!" ELSE PRINT "OW!"

WHILE (IBM only)   marks the beginning of a WHILE/WEND loop. Each time this statement is executed, the conditional expression is evaluated. If it is true, control passes to the next statement. If it is false, control passes to the statement following the corresponding WEND statement. WHILE/WEND loops may be nested.

Syntax: WHILE conditional.expression

WEND (IBM only)   marks the end of a WHILE/WEND loop. Whenever the WEND statement is executed, control is passed back to the corresponding WHILE statement, where the conditional expression is tested again.

Syntax: WEND

GRAPHICS COMMANDS

The major BASIC graphics commands are simply listed here with their syntactical form. For more information on their effects see Chapter 5 and/or a reference book.

IBM

SCREEN /0 | 1/
COLOR background.and.border.color,foreground.palette
PSET (xcoord,ycoord)[,hue.number]
LINE [(xcoord1,ycoord1)]-(xcoord2,ycoord2)[,[hue.number][,B[F]]]
CIRCLE (xcoord,ycoord),radius[,[hue.number][,[start.ang,end.ang][,aspect.ratio]]]
PAINT (xcoord,ycoord)[,fill.hue[,boundary.hue]]
DRAW draw.string
GET (xcoord1,ycoord1)-(xcoord2,ycoord2),array.name
PUT (xcoord,ycoord),array.name[,/AND | OR | XOR | PSET | PRESET/]

Apple

TEXT
GR
COLOR= /0 | 1 | 2 | 3 | 4 | 5 | 6 | 7 | 8 | 9 | 10 | 11 | 12 | 13 | 14 | 15/
SCRN(xcoord,ycoord)   [function]
HLIN start.column,end.column AT row
VLIN start.row,end.row AT column
PLOT xcoord,ycoord
HGR
HGR2
HCOLOR= /0 | 1 | 2 | 3 | 4 | 5 | 6 | 7/
HPLOT xcoord1,ycoord1 [TO xcoord2,ycoord2]...
DRAW shape.number AT xcoord,ycoord

XDRAW shape.number AT xcoord,ycoord
ROT= rotation.number
SCALE= scale.number

Commodore

Commodore graphics is done primarily with POKE, PEEK, and logical operators (AND, OR, etc.). For this reason it is quite complex. No attempt will be made here to describe its workings. See Chapter 5.

SOUND COMMANDS

Like graphics, the sound commands are simply listed. See Chapter 6 and/or a reference book.

IBM

BEEP
SOUND frequency.number,duration.number
PLAY play.string

Apple

Applesoft BASIC has no sound commands. See Chapter 6.

Commodore

Commodore BASIC uses PEEK, POKE, etc. to control the 64's very sophisticated synthesizer. See Chapter 6.

CURSOR POSITIONING AND SCREEN CLEARING

IBM

CLS clears the screen and sends the cursor to the upper left corner.
  Syntax: CLS
LOCATE moves the cursor to the specified location on the screen.
Visibility is either 0 (invisible) or 1 (visible).
  Syntax: LOCATE [row][,[column][,visibility]]

Apple

HOME clears the screen and sends the cursor to the upper left corner column.
  Syntax: HOME
HTAB moves the cursor to the specified column.
  Syntax: HTAB column
VTAB moves the cursor to the specified row.
  Syntax: VTAB row

Commodore

The Commodore has the ability to do the functions described above for the other machines (as well as some others such as changing text color) by embedding special keyboard-accessible characters in strings and then PRINTing those strings.

OTHER

CLEAR (IBM and Apple) or **CLR** (Commodore) zeroes out all variables and arrays.

Syntax: CLEAR
CLR

APPENDIX B
AN APPLE SHAPE MAKER

USING THE SHAPE MAKER PROGRAM

There are many excellent shape maker programs commercially available for the
Apple II family of computers. It is our feeling, however, that for simple educational purposes the often complex nature of these programs, as well as the
expense involved in obtaining sufficient copies, makes them somewhat impractical. It is for these reasons that the code for a simple shape maker utility has
been included with this book.

To use the program, simply type in the code and SAVE it on a disk
(make a back-up copy while you're at it). When you run the program you will see
the following menu:

```
WHAT WOULD YOU LIKE TO DO...

        1. INITIALIZE A NEW TABLE
        2. LOAD AN OLD TABLE
        3. QUIT

CHOOSE A NUMBER...?
```

Choosing the first option will allow you to start a new shape table. The first question you are asked is how many shapes you want in the table. Any number from 1 to the maximum number of shapes, 255, is allowed.

Choosing the second option will allow you to load in an old shape table in order to add shapes to it, assuming of course that space remains in that table for the addition of more shapes. When the old table is loaded into memory from the disk, the program will determine the number of shapes currently in the table and what shape number you may begin to work on.

Once in the editor portion of the program, you will have the following choices:

U = move up one pixel
R = move right one pixel
D = move down one pixel
L = move left one pixel
P = toggles PLOT to allow move with or without plotting
E = erase the last pixel plotted
X = redo (start the entire shape over)
F = finished with the shape

When you have finished creating a shape, the program will ask you whether you want to keep it or start over. It will also ask you whether you want to quit or add another shape to the table. When you choose to quit, the program will allow you to save the shape table on your disk.

```
10 REM ************************
11 REM *========================*
12 REM *=                      =*
13 REM *= Shape Maker Utility  =*
14 REM *=    for Apple II+/e   =*
15 REM *=                      =*
16 REM *========================*
17 REM ************************
19 :
20        GOSUB 1000              :REM initialize
30        GOSUB 2000              :REM index
40         ON NX GOSUB 3000, 4000 :REM new/old table
50        GOSUB 500               :REM edit mode
60        GOSUB 8000              :REM done/save table
70        GOTO 30
89 :
90        END
91 :
500 REM ***********************
501 REM * editor
502 REM ***********************
503 :
510        HOME :GOSUB 5000       :REM set-up screen
549 :
550        GET N$
559 :
```

```
560        IF N$="U" THEN GOSUB 5200 :GOTO 650
570        IF N$="R" THEN GOSUB 5400 :GOTO 650
580        IF N$="D" THEN GOSUB 5600 :GOTO 650
590        IF N$="L" THEN GOSUB 5800 :GOTO 650
600        IF N$="P" THEN GOSUB 6000 :GOTO 650
610        IF N$="E" THEN GOSUB 6200 :GOTO 650
620        IF N$="X" THEN GOSUB 6400 :GOTO 650
630        IF N$="F" THEN GOTO  700
640      PRINT CHR$(7)
650      GOTO 550
699 :
700      HOME :VTAB21 :PRINT "WOULD YOU LIKE TO SAVE THIS SHAPE (Y/N)";:
              GET Q$ :PRINT
710      IF Q$="N" THEN VCTPNT=TBLEPNT + ( PEEK(TBLEPNT+1)*256 +
              PEEK(TBLPNT) ) :GOTO 510
720      IF CRNT<NUM THEN PRINT"WOULD YOU LIKE TO DO ANOTHER SHAPE(Y/N)";
              :GET Q$ :IF Q$="Y" THEN GOSUB 7000 :GOTO 510
789 :
790      RETURN
791 :
1000 REM =====================
1001 REM = setup variables
1002 REM =====================
1003 :
1010      HOME
1020      NUM=0 :CRNT=1 :TBLPNT=32768 :STRT=32768 :UP=0 :PP=1 :CNT=1
1030      HIMEM: 32767
1040      PLT$="ON" :NPLT$="OFF"
1089 :
1090      RETURN
1091 :
2000 REM =====================
2001 REM = index
2002 REM =====================
2003 :
2010      HOME :VTAB 5
2020      PRINT "WHAT WOULD YOU LIKE..."
2030      VTAB10 :PRINT "    1. START A NEW TABLE"
2040      VTAB12 :PRINT "    2. ADD TO AN OLD TABLE"
2050      VTAB14 :PRINT "    3. ";: INVERSE :PRINT "QUIT" :NORMAL
2060      VTAB21 :INPUT "CHOOSE A NUMBER...";NX$
2070        IF NX$<"1" OR NX$>"3" THEN 2060
2080      NX = VAL(NX$)
2089 :
2090      RETURN
2091 :
3000 REM =====================
3001 REM = start a new table
3002 REM =====================
3003 :
3010      HOME
3020      VTAB10 :INPUT "HOW MANY SHAPES...(1-255) ";NUM
3030        IF NUM <1 OR NUM>255 THEN 3020
3039 :
3040      POKE STRT,NUM :POKE STRT+1,CRNT :TBLPNT=STRT+2
3050      FOR I=TBLPNT TO TBLPNT+(2*NUM) :POKE I,0 :NEXT
3060      VCTPNT = TBLPNT+(2*NUM)
3070      HEX = VCTPNT-STRT :GOSUB 9000 :POKE TBLPNT,LO :POKE TBLPNT+1,HI
3089 :
3090      RETURN
3091 :
4000 REM =====================
4001 REM = load & init old table
4002 REM =====================
4003 :
4010      HOME
4020      VTAB10 :PRINT "WHAT IS THE TABLE NAME..."
```

```
4030        INPUT NM$
4040        PRINT CHR$(4) "BLOAD ";NM$;", A$8000"
4050        NUM = PEEK(STRT) :CRNT = PEEK(STRT+1) :TBLPNT = STRT+(2*CRNT) :
                 VCTPNT = PEEK(TBLPNT+1)*256 + PEEK(TBLPNT)+STRT
4060        PRINT  :PRINT "STARTING WITH SHAPE #";CRNT;" OF ";NUM
4070        VTAB23 :PRINT "<PRESS ANY KEY TO CONTINUE...>"; :GET Q$
4089 :
4090        RETURN
4091 :
5000 REM =======================
5001 REM = set-up screen
5002 REM =======================
5003 :
5010        HOME :HGR :HCOLOR=3 :X=140 :Y=80
5020        VTAB21 :PRINT "U=UP     D=DOWN      R=RIGHT      L=LEFT"
5030        VTAB22 :PRINT "P=" :INVERSE :PRINT PLT$; :NORMAL :PRINT "/";
                 NPLT$;" E=ERASE      X=RE-DO      F=DONE"
5040        PFLG=4 :                    :REM 4=on (0=off)
5050        VTAB 1
5089 :
5090        RETURN
5091 :
5200 REM =======================
5201 REM = "U" = up
5202 REM =======================
5203 :
5210         IF UP=1 AND PFLG=0 THEN FOR I=1 TO 4 :PRINT CHR$(7); :NEXT :
                 GOTO 5390
5220        Y = Y-1 :IF PFLG=0 THEN UP=1
5230         IF PFLG=4 THEN UP=0 :HPLOT X,Y
5240        DIR=0 :GOSUB 9200
5289 :
5290        RETURN
5291 :
5400 REM =======================
5401 REM = "R" = right
5402 REM =======================
5403 :
5410        X = X+1 :UP=0
5420         IF PFLG=4 THEN HPLOT X,Y
5430        DIR=1 :GOSUB 9020
5489 :
5490        RETURN
5491 :
5600 REM =======================
5601 REM = "D" = down
5602 REM =======================
5603 :
5610        Y = Y+1 :UP=0
5620         IF PFLG=4 THEN HPLOT X,Y
5630        DIR=2 :GOSUB 9020
5689 :
5690        RETURN
5691 :
5800 REM =======================
5801 REM = "L" = left
5802 REM =======================
5803 :
5810        X = X-1 :UP=0
5820         IF PFLG=4 THEN HPLOT X,Y
5830        DIR=3 :GOSUB 9020
5889 :
5890        RETURN
5891 :
6000 REM =======================
6001 REM = "P" = plot/no plot
6002 REM =======================
```

```
6003 :
6010        IF PFLG=4 THEN PFLG=0 :VTAB22 : HTAB3 :NORMAL :PRINT PLT$;"/";
                :INVERSE :PRINT NPLT$ :NORMAL :VTAB1 :GOTO 6090
6020        IF PFLG=0 THEN PFLG=4 :VTAB22 : HTAB3 :INVERSE :PRINT PLT$;
                :NORMAL :PRINT "/";NPLT$ :VTAB1 :GOTO 6090
6089 :
6090        RETURN
6091 :
6200 REM ========================
6201 REM = "E" = erase
6202 REM ========================
6203 :
6205        IF CNT<2 THEN 6290
6210        PP = PP-1 :IF PP<1 THEN PP=3 :VCTPNT=VCTPNT-1 :CNT=CNT-1 :
                GOSUB 6350
6220        IF PP=3 THEN POKE VCTPNT+1,0 :FCTR=P(3)
6230        IF PP=3 AND P(3)=0 THEN PP=2
6240        IF PP=2 THEN FCTR=P(2) :GOTO 6260
6250        IF PP=1 THEN FCTR=P(1)
6260        IF FCTR>3 THEN HCOLOR=0 :HPLOT X,Y :HCOLOR=3 :FCTR=FCTR-4
6270        ON FCTR+1 GOSUB 6300, 6310, 6320, 6330
6289 :
6290        RETURN
6291 :
6300        Y=Y+1 :RETURN
6310        X=X-1 :RETURN
6320        Y=Y-1 :RETURN
6330        X=X+1 :RETURN
6399 :
6400 REM ========================
6401 REM = "X" = re-do
6402 REM ========================
6403 :
6410        HOME :VTAB21 :PRINT "ARE YOU SURE (Y/N)?"; :GET Q$ :PRINT
6420        IF Q$<>"Y" THEN GOSUB 5020 :GOTO 6490
6430          VCTPNT = TBLPNT + ( PEEK(TBLPNT+1)*256 + PEEK(TBLPNT) )
6440          GOSUB 5000
6489 :
6490        RETURN
6491 :
7000 REM ========================
7001 REM = process for next shape
7002 REM ========================
7003 :
7010        GOSUB 7000               :REM finish off current byte
7020        POKE VCTPNT+1,0 :VCTPNT=VCTPNT+2
7030        CRNT=CRNT+1 :POKE STRT+1,CRNT
7040        TBLPNT=TBLPNT+2
7050        HEX=VCTPNT-STRT :GOSUB 9000 :POKE TBLPNT,LO :POKE TBLPNT+1,HI
7060        PP=1 :CNT=1
7089 :
7090        RETURN
7091 :
7200 REM   -----------------------
7201 REM   - finish off last byte
7202 REM   -----------------------
7203 :
7210        IF PP=1 THEN POKE VCTPNT,0
7220        IF PP=2 THEN POKE VCTPNT,P(1)
7230        IF PP=3 THEN POKE VCTPNT,P(1)+(8*P(2))
7289 :
7290        RETURN
7291 :
7292 REM ========================
7293 :
8000 REM ========================
8001 REM = save a table
```

```
8002 REM ========================
8003 :
8010       HOME :HGR :TEXT :VTAB 10
8020       PRINT "DO YOU WANT TO SAVE THE TABLE(Y/N)"; :GET Q$ :PRINT
8030       IF Q$="N" THEN 8090
8040       IF CRNT<NUM THEN GOSUB 7000
8045       IF CRNT=NUM THEN GOSUB 7200 :POKE VCTPNT+1,0
8050       INPUT "TABLE NAME: ";TBLE$
8060       PRINT CHR$(4);"BSAVE ";TBLE$", A$8000, L";VCTPNT+2-STRT
8089 :
8090       RETURN
8091 :
9000 REM  ------------------------
9001 REM  - convert DEC to HEX
9002 REM  ------------------------
9003 :
9010       HI = INT(HEX/256) :LO = HEX-(HI*256)
9014 :
9015       RETURN
9016 :
9020 REM  ------------------------
9021 REM  - update last byte
9022 REM  ------------------------
9023 :
9030       IF PP=1 OR PP=2 THEN P(PP)=DIR+PFLG :GOTO 9080
9040       IF PP=3 AND DIR>0 AND PFLG=0 THEN P(PP)=DIR :
                 GOSUB 9100 :GOTO 9030
9050       P(3)=0 :GOSUB 9100 :PP=1 :CNT=CNT+1 :GOTO 9030
9080       PP=PP+1 :IF PP>3 THEN PP=1 :CNT=CNT+1
9089 :
9090       RETURN
9091 :
9100 REM  ----------------
9109 :
9110       POKE VCTPNT,P(1) + (P(2)*8) + (P(3)*64)
9120       VCTPNT=VCTPNT+1
9189 :
9190       RETURN
9191 :
9192 REM  ************************
```

LOADING AND INITIALIZING THE SHAPE TABLE

Now that we have learned how to create a shape table, we must examine how to load and initialize it within a program. Two steps are required:

1. We must locate a safe place within the computer's memory and load our shape table into it, and
2. We need to tell the computer (and our program) where the shape table can be found.

For the moment we will load the shape table into the higher part of BASIC memory starting at location 32768. In order to protect it from being overwritten by our BASIC program, we must lower the top end of the BASIC memory to 32767, that is, one byte lower than the beginning of our shape table. To do this, we use the HIMEM: command as in the program segment that follows.

Once we have determined a starting address, we must then convert the address into a form understandable by the computer and POKE the new values into the appropriate memory location. The following equations are needed to compute a HIgh address and a LOw address from the actual starting ADDRess:

```
HI = INT(ADDR/256)
LO = ADDR - (HI * 256)
```

The reason for two addresses is that a single byte cannot store a number greater than 255. Most computers utilize two bytes to enable addresses ranging in size up to 65536. In a typical scheme, the second of the two bytes (the one with the higher address) is called the HI byte and represents multiples of the number 256. Thus, if this number contains 128 (as in the example), it represents the value 32768, that is, 128 * 256. To arrive at the HI byte value (128), we divide our desired address by 256 and disregard the remainder. However, the remainder of our division must be saved. Since its value is always less than 256, we store it as the LO byte value. The computer is able to determine any address by multiplying the HI byte by 256 and adding the LO byte value to it. Thus in our example, for ADDRess 32768, LO = 0 and HI = 128. The following program segment will load and initialize the shape table.

```
30 REM ***************
31 REM * LOAD AND INITIALIZE SHAPE TABLE
32 REM ***************
33 :
34     HIMEM: 32767
35     PRINT CHR$(4) "BLOAD shape table filename,A32768"
36     POKE 232,LO : POKE 233,HI
```

The HIMEM: (HIghest MEMory) command in line 34 sets the highest usable memory available to BASIC to the address specified after the colon. Note that the colon in this case is part of the command.

Line 35 embeds the DOS command BLOAD (Binary LOAD) in the print statement and includes the address at which to load the filename of the shape table, A32768. The command PRINT CHR$(4) is important to note: it sends ("prints") a command to the Disk Operating System instead of to the screen as is the normal case with a PRINT command. Also note carefully the form of the embedded BLOAD command: "BLOAD fn, A32768". Finally, line 36 places the converted address into two consecutive bytes of memory. After once BLOADing the shape table, any reference within the program to that shape table will cause the computer to go to these two locations (addresses 232 and 233) to find the address of the beginning of the shape table.

APPENDIX C
MEMORY PROBLEMS
ON THE APPLE II

Memory organization presents us with a special problem when it comes to developing programs of significant length that utilize hi-res graphics on the Apple II. The earliest Apples were predominantly 16K machines. As hi-res graphics required 8K, the simplest solution was to allocate the fist 8K of memory to BASIC programs and the remaining 8K to graphics. As the memory of the Apple grew to 48K and beyond, the graphics memory still needed to remain in the second 8K block of memory in order for the expanded machines to retain their compatibility with programs written for the smaller machine. Unfortunately, Applesoft BASIC in its normal configuration is unable to utilize any of this extra memory for BASIC code because it can only access consecutive memory locations. In other words, BASIC cannot use the first 8K of memory, jump around the graphics memory, and then begin accessing more memory beginning with the third 8K block. This situation therefore keeps the maximum program size under 8K, which is a severe limitation (see Figure C.1).

There is a solution to the problem, namely fool BASIC into ignoring the first 16K (2048 to 16383) of memory and, instead, using the larger block of memory located above graphics (from 16384 to about 40000). The trick is to move the required pointers in order to make the Applesoft interpreter think that the BASIC program begins at 16384. This creates another problem, for Applesoft BASIC can only move these pointers prior to loading and running a program.

In order to make possible the relocation of the BASIC code, we have

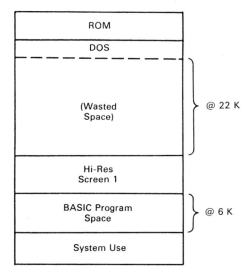

BASIC Program
space

Figure C.1

written the following short "EXEC CREATOR" program that will create an
EXEC file. When run, this file will reset the required pointers and run the
interval drill (or any other) program. Having been relocated, our drill program
can then utilize the lower block of memory to store shape tables and other
machine language programs. To make this EXEC CREATOR program work,
simply replace the word "filename" in the listing with the actual name of the
program you wish to run, type in the code of the EXEC CREATOR program,
and then RUN it (which will create an EXEC file on your disk identified by a "T"
prefix on the CATALOG listing). When you wish to run the lesson, simply type
"EXEC filename LOADER" and it will take care of the memory problem and
run the lesson for you. Here is the code.

```
10 REM ***************
11 REM * EXEC CREATOR
12 REM ***************
13 :
15     D$ = CHR$(4)
20     PRINT D$ "OPEN filename LOADER"
25     PRINT D$ "WRITE filename LOADER"
26 :
30       PRINT "POKE 50,128"
40       PRINT "POKE 103,01"
```

```
50          PRINT "POKE 104,64"
60          PRINT "POKE 16384,0"
70          PRINT "CALL 54514"
80          PRINT "POKE 50,255"
85          PRINT "RUN filename"
86 :
90      PRINT D$ "CLOSE"
94 :
95      END
96 :
99 REM ***************
```

With this done, we can then use the newly freed 6K of low-end memory for the storage of our shape tables.

APPENDIX D
MACHINE CODES
FOR SCREEN SCROLLER
PORTION
OF MELODY MAKER
PROGRAMS

In order to make the melody maker program presented in Chapter 7 more effective and interesting, we included Apple and Commodore machine language routines to scroll the graphics screen left and right. (The IBM-PC does not require an equivalent machine language routine.) Due to the technical nature of these routines, we simply presented them as DATA statements to be loaded with a "BASIC loader." For the convenience of those who understand Assembly language and may wish to alter these routines in some way, we are including copies of the original assembly listings.

Listing I: C-64

```
SCROLL2......PAGE 0001

LINE# LOC    CODE         LINE


00001  0000                     *=$C9A8
00002  C9A8              ;
00003  C9A8              ; LOOKUP TABLE HOLDS STARTING
00004  C9A8              ; ADDRESSES OF EACH LINE OF
00005  C9A8              ; 8-BYTE CHARACTERS
00006  C9A8              ; WITH A MAX OF TWO ADDRS.
00007  C9A8              ;
00008  C9A8              IO      =$DC0E         ; DISABLES I/O
00009  C9A8              BANK    =$01           ; RAM/ROM SWITCH
00010  C9A8              TBLE    =$FB           ; INDIRECT INDEX POINTERS
00011  C9A8              ;
00012  C9A8   EF         LNTH    .BYTE $EF      ; CHAR COLUMNS X'S 8
00013  C9A9   0B         HGTH    .BYTE $0B      ; CHAR ROWS X'S 8
```

```
00014   C9AA    00           HGTH2   .BYTE $00        ; WORK SPACE
00015   C9AB                 ;
00016   C9AB    00           PNTR    .BYTE $00        ; OFFSET INTO LOOKUP TABLE
00017   C9AC                 ;
00018   C9AC    F0 E3        LKUP    .WORD $E3F0,$E530,$E670,$E7B0
00018   C9AE    30 E5
00018   C9B0    70 E6
00018   C9B2    B0 E7
00019   C9B4    F0 E8                .WORD $E8F0,$EA30,$EB70,$ECB0
00019   C9B6    30 EA
00019   C9B8    70 EB
00019   C9BA    B0 EC
00020   C9BC    F0 ED                .WORD $EDF0,$EF30,$F070
00020   C9BE    30 EF
00020   C9C0    70 F0
00021   C9C2                         *=$C900
00022   C900                 ;
00023   C900                 ; SUBROUTINE:
00024   C900                 ;
00025   C900                 ; DISABLE I/O INTERRUPTS AND
00026   C900                 ; SWITCH OUT KERNAL ROM
00027   C900                 ;
00028   C900    AD 0E DC     DSABL   LDA IO
00029   C903    29 FE                AND #$FE
00030   C905    8D 0E DC             STA IO
00031   C908    A5 01                LDA BANK
00032   C90A    29 FD                AND #$FD
00033   C90C    85 01                STA BANK
00034   C90E    60                   RTS
00035   C90F                 ;
00036   C90F                 ; SUBROUTINE:
00037   C90F                 ;
00038   C90F                 ; ENABLE I/O INTERRUPTS AND
00039   C90F                 ; SWITCH IN KERNAL ROM
00040   C90F                 ;
00041   C90F    A5 01        ENABL   LDA BANK
00042   C911    09 02                ORA #$02
00043   C913    85 01                STA BANK
00044   C915    AD 0E DC             LDA IO
00045   C918    09 01                ORA #$01
00046   C91A    8D 0E DC             STA IO
00047   C91D    60                   RTS
00048   C91E                 ;
00049   C91E                 ; SUBROUTINE:
00050   C91E                 ;
00051   C91E                 ; PLACE SCREEN LOCATIONS INTO
00052   C91E                 ; LOOKUP TABLE IN ZERO PAGE
00053   C91E                 ;
00054   C91E    AE AB C9     UPDTE   LDX PNTR
00055   C921    BD AC C9             LDA LKUP,X
00056   C924    85 FD                STA TBLE+2       ; STARTING ADDR OF CHAR ROW
00057   C926    18                   CLC
00058   C927    69 08                ADC #$08
00059   C929    85 FB                STA TBLE
00060   C92B    BD AD C9             LDA LKUP+1,X
00061   C92E    85 FE                STA TBLE+3
00062   C930    85 FC                STA TBLE+1
00063   C932                 ;
00064   C932    EE AB C9             INC PNTR
00065   C935    EE AB C9             INC PNTR
00066   C938    60                   RTS
00067   C939                 ;
00068   C939                 ; SUBROUTINE:
00069   C939                 ;
00070   C939                 ; PLACE SCREEN LOCATIONS INTO
00071   C939                 ; LOOKUP TABLE IN ZERO PAGE
00072   C939                 ;
00073   C939    AE AB C9     UPDT2   LDX PNTR
```

```
00074   C93C   BD AC C9        LDA LKUP,X
00075   C93F   85 FD           STA TBLE+2
00076   C941   38              SEC
00077   C942   E9 08           SBC #$08
00078   C944   85 FB           STA TBLE
00079   C946   BD AD C9        LDA LKUP+1,X
00080   C949   85 FE           STA TBLE+3
00081   C94B   85 FC           STA TBLE+1
00082   C94D                ;
00083   C94D   EE AB C9        INC PNTR
00084   C950   EE AB C9        INC PNTR
00085   C953   60              RTS
00086   C954              ;
00087   C954              ; MAIN PROGRAM:
00088   C954              ;
00089   C954              ; START OF MAIN LOOP. SCROLLS
00090   C954              ; 'HGTH' LINE(S) OF 'LNTH'
00091   C954              ; (X'S 8) CHARS.
00092   C954              ;
00093   C954              ; LEFT SHIFT
00094   C954              ;
00095   C954   A9 00    LEFT   LDA #$00
00096   C956   8D AB C9        STA PNTR         ; CLEAR TABLE OFFSET POINTER
00097   C959   AD A9 C9        LDA HGTH
00098   C95C   8D AA C9        STA HGTH2        ; MOVE VALUE TO TEMP WORK SPACE
00099   C95F   20 00 C9        JSR DSABL
00100   C962              ;
00101   C962   A0 00    START  LDY #$00         ; OFFSET INTO THE ROW
00102   C964   20 1E C9        JSR UPDTE
00103   C967   B1 FB    LP1    LDA (TBLE),Y
00104   C969   91 FD           STA (TBLE+2),Y   ; SHIFT 1 BYTE TO THE LEFT
00105   C96B   C8              INY              ; INCREMENT THE OFFSET
00106   C96C   CC A8 C9        CPY LNTH
00107   C96F   D0 F6           BNE LP1          ; CONTINUE UNTIL THE END OF ROW
00108   C971   CE AA C9        DEC HGTH2
00109   C974   D0 EC           BNE START        ; CONTINUE UNTIL COLUMN END
00110   C976              ;
00111   C976   20 0F C9        JSR ENABL
00112   C979   60              RTS
00113   C97A              ;
00114   C97A              ; RIGHT SHIFT
00115   C97A              ;
00116   C97A   A9 00    RIGHT  LDA #$00
00117   C97C   8D AB C9        STA PNTR         ; CLEAR TABLE OFFSET POINTER
00118   C97F   AD A9 C9        LDA HGTH
00119   C982   8D AA C9        STA HGTH2        ; MOVE VALUE TO TEMP WORK SPACE
00120   C985   20 00 C9        JSR DSABL
00121   C988              ;
00122   C988   AC A8 C9  STRT2  LDY LNTH        ; OFFSET INTO THE ROW
00123   C98B   20 39 C9        JSR UPDT2
00124   C98E   B1 FB    LP2    LDA (TBLE),Y
00125   C990   91 FD           STA (TBLE+2),Y   ; SHIFT 1 BYTE TO THE RIGHT
00126   C992   88              DEY              ; DECREMENT THE OFFSET
00127   C993   C0 00           CPY #$00
00128   C995   D0 F7           BNE LP2          ; CONTINUE UNTIL THE END OF ROW
00129   C997   B1 FB           LDA (TBLE),Y
00130   C999   91 FD           STA (TBLE+2),Y
00131   C99B   CE AA C9        DEC HGTH2
00132   C99E   D0 E8           BNE STRT2        ; CONTINUE UNTIL COLUMN END
00133   C9A0              ;
00134   C9A0   20 0F C9        JSR ENABL
00135   C9A3   60              RTS
00136   C9A4              ;
00137   C9A4                   .END
```

ERRORS = 00000

SYMBOL TABLE

SYMBOL VALUE

BANK	0001	DSABL	C900	ENABL	C90F	HGTH	C9A9
HGTH2	C9AA	IO	DC0E	LEFT	C954	LKUP	C9AC
LNTH	C9A8	LP1	C967	LP2	C98E	PNTR	C9AB
RIGHT	C97A	START	C962	STRT2	C988	TBLE	00FB
UPDT2	C939	UPDTE	C91E				

END OF ASSEMBLY

Listing II: Apple II Family

```
1080                    1            ORG $1080
1080                    2   ; LOOKUP TABLE AND SYSTEM VARSPROGRAM VARS.
1080                    3   ;
00FB                    4   TBLE      EPZ $FB
1080 1E                 5   LNTH      HEX 1E
1081 00                 6   LNTH2     HEX 00
1082 58                 7   HGTH      HEX 58
1083 00                 8   HGTH2     HEX 00
1084                    9   ;
1084 00                10   PNTR      HEX 00
1085                   11   ;
1085 04 22 04          12   LKUP      ADR $2204,$2604,$2A04,$2E04
1088 26 04 2A
108B 04 2E
108D 04 32 04          13             ADR $3204,$3604,$3A04,$3E04
1090 36 04 3A
1093 04 3E
1095 84 22 84          14             ADR $2284,$2684,$2A84,$2E84
1098 26 84 2A
109B 84 2E
109D 84 32 84          15             ADR $3284,$3684,$3A84,$3E84
10A0 36 84 3A
10A3 84 3E
10A5 04 23 04          16             ADR $2304,$2704,$2B04,$2F04
10A8 27 04 2B
10AB 04 2F
10AD 04 33 04          17             ADR $3304,$3704,$3B04,$3F04
10B0 37 04 3B
10B3 04 3F
10B5 84 23 84          18             ADR $2384,$2784,$2B84,$2F84
10B8 27 84 2B
10BB 84 2F
10BD 84 33 84          19             ADR $3384,$3784,$3B84,$3F84
10C0 37 84 3B
10C3 84 3F
10C5 2C 20 2C          20             ADR $202C,$242C,$282C,$2C2C
10C8 24 2C 28
10CB 2C 2C
10CD 2C 30 2C          21             ADR $302C,$342C,$382C,$3C2C
10D0 34 2C 38
10D3 2C 3C
10D5 AC 20 AC          22             ADR $20AC,$24AC,$28AC,$2CAC
10D8 24 AC 28
10DB AC 2C
10DD AC 30 AC          23             ADR $30AC,$34AC,$38AC,$3CAC
10E0 34 AC 38
10E3 AC 3C
10E5 2C 21 2C          24             ADR $212C,$252C,$292C,$2D2C
10E8 25 2C 29
10EB 2C 2D
10ED 2C 31 2C          25             ADR $312C,$352C,$392C,$3D2C
10F0 35 2C 39
```

```
10F3 2C 3D
10F5 AC 21 AC    26              ADR $21AC,$25AC,$29AC,$2DAC
10F8 25 AC 29
10FB AC 2D
10FD AC 31 AC    27              ADR $31AC,$35AC,$39AC,$3DAC
1100 35 AC 39
1103 AC 3D
1105 2C 22 2C    28              ADR $222C,$262C,$2A2C,$2E2C
1108 26 2C 2A
110B 2C 2E
110D 2C 32 2C    29              ADR $322C,$362C,$3A2C,$3E2C
1110 36 2C 3A
1113 2C 3E
1115 AC 22 AC    30              ADR $22AC,$26AC,$2AAC,$2EAC
1118 26 AC 2A
111B AC 2E
111D AC 32 AC    31              ADR $32AC,$36AC,$3AAC,$3EAC
1120 36 AC 3A
1123 AC 3E
1125 2C 23 2C    32              ADR $232C,$272C,$2B2C,$2F2C
1128 27 2C 2B
112B 2C 2F
112D 2C 33 2C    33              ADR $332C,$372C,$3B2C,$3F2C
1130 37 2C 3B
1133 2C 3F
1135            34  ;
1000            35              ORG $1000
1000            36  ;
1000            37  ; SUBROUTINE
1000            38  ;
1000            39  ;   LOADS EACH STARTING ADDRESS INTO
1000            40  ;   THE OFFSET LOCATION IN PAGE ZERO
1000            41  ;
1000 AE 84 10   42  LUPDTE    LDX PNTR
1003 BD 85 10   43            LDA LKUP,X
1006 85 FD      44            STA TBLE+2
1008 18         45            CLC
1009 69 01      46            ADC #$01
100B 85 FB      47            STA TBLE
100D BD 86 10   48            LDA LKUP+1,X
1010 85 FE      49            STA TBLE+3
1012 85 FC      50            STA TBLE+1
1014           51  ;
1014 EE 84 10   52            INC PNTR
1017 EE 84 10   53            INC PNTR
101A 60        54            RTS
101B           55  ;
101B           56  ; SUBROUTINE
101B           57  ;
101B           58  ;   (SAME AS ABOVE)
101B           59  ;
101B AE 84 10   60  RUPDTE    LDX PNTR
101E BD 85 10   61            LDA LKUP,X
1021 85 FD      62            STA TBLE+2
1023 38         63            SEC
1024 E9 01      64            SBC #$01
1026 85 FB      65            STA TBLE
1028 BD 86 10   66            LDA LKUP+1,X
102B 85 FE      67            STA TBLE+3
102D 85 FC      68            STA TBLE+1
102F           69  ;
102F EE 84 10   70            INC PNTR
1032 EE 84 10   71            INC PNTR
1035 60        72            RTS
1036           73  ;
1036           74  ; MAIN PROGRAM
1036           75  ;
```

```
1036                76  ;    START OF MAIN LOOP. SCROLLS 'HGTH'
1036                77  ;    LINES OF 'LNTH' CHARACTERS (8-BITS).
1036                78  ;
1036 A9 00          79  LEFT     LDA #$00
1038 8D 84 10       80           STA PNTR            ; CLEAR TABLE OFFSET POINTER
103B AD 82 10       81           LDA HGTH
103E 8D 83 10       82           STA HGTH2           ; MOVE VAL TO TEMP WORK SPACE
1041 AD 80 10       83           LDA LNTH
1044 8D 81 10       84           STA LNTH2
1047 EE 81 10       85           INC LNTH2
104A                86  ;
104A A0 00          87  START    LDY #$00
104C 20 00 10       88           JSR LUPDTE
104F B1 FB          89  LP1      LDA (TBLE),Y
1051 91 FD          90           STA (TBLE+2),Y      ; SHIFT ONE BYTE TO THE LEFT
1053 C8             91           INY
1054 CC 81 10       92           CPY LNTH2
1057 D0 F6          93           BNE LP1             ; CONTINUE UNTIL END OF ROW
1059                94  ;
1059 CE 83 10       95           DEC HGTH2
105C D0 EC          96           BNE START           ; CONTINUE UNTIL END OF COLUMN
105E                97  ;
105E 60             98           RTS                    •
105F                99  ;
105F               100  ;
105F               101  ; SCROLL RIGHT
105F               102  ;
105F               103  ;
105F A9 00         104  RIGHT    LDA #$00
1061 8D 84 10      105           STA PNTR
1064 AD 82 10      106           LDA HGTH
1067 8D 83 10      107           STA HGTH2
106A               108  ;
106A AC 80 10      109  STRT2    LDY LNTH            ; OFFSET INTO THE ROW
106D 20 1B 10      110           JSR RUPDTE
1070 B1 FB         111  LP2      LDA (TBLE),Y
1072 91 FD         112           STA (TBLE+2),Y
1074 88            113           DEY                 ; DECREMENT THE OFFSET
1075 C0 FF         114           CPY #$FF
1077 D0 F7         115           BNE LP2             ; CONTINUE UNTIL START OF LINE
1079 CE 83 10      116           DEC HGTH2
107C D0 EC         117           BNE STRT2
107E               118  ;
107E 60            119           RTS
107F               120  ;
107F               121           END
```

***** END OF ASSEMBLY

APPENDIX E
SOLUTIONS TO EXERCISES

Exercises 2.1

1. This exercise can be accomplished with the following addition:

```
100 REM ***********************
101 REM * EXERCISE 2.1:1
102 REM ***********************
103 :
110 REM SUPPOSE AN$="C++4"
119 :
2085    A$ = MID$(AN$,2,LEN(AN$)-2)
```

By using the expression LEN(AN$)−2, we, in effect, take the entire string minus the first and last characters.

2. Error messages can be printed in one of two manners: either as (1) part of the code line in which the error flag is set; or (2) in a separate subroutine. The solution given here is of the second type. It has the definite advantage of clearer structure and style.

```
2100 REM ***********************
2101 REM * EXERCISE 2.1:2
```

```
2102 REM *************************
2103 :
2110      ON ER GOTO 2120, 2130, 2140, 2150
2119 :
2120      PRINT "ILLEGAL STRING LENGTH"      :GOTO 2190
2130      PRINT "ILLEGAL NOTE NAME"          :GOTO 2190
2140      PRINT "ILLEGAL OCTAVE NUMBER"      :GOTO 2190
2150      PRINT "ILLEGAL ACCIDENTAL(S)"      :GOTO 2190
2189 :
2190      RETURN
```

Exercises 2.2

1. In order to retrograde a string of variable length substrings (e.g. C+4,D3, etc.), we must first build a routine to parse each substring and then rebuild them one at a time in reverse order. In the following code, lines 120 to 135 and 150 to 160 build the substring (B$) one character at a time. Whenever a space is encountered, the process stops, the value of B$ is added to the front of the string A2$ (line 140) and cleared (line 150), and the process begins again with the next substring.

```
100 REM **********************
101 REM * EXERCISE 2.2:1
102 REM **********************
103 :
110      A1$+"C+4 D+4 E4 G-4 F4 "
115      B$=""
120      FOR  I=1 TO LEN(A1$)
130        C$=MID$(A1$,I,1)
135         IF C$<>" " THEN B$=B$+C$ :GOTO 160
140          A2$=B$+" "+A2$
150          B$=""
160      NEXT I
170      PRINT A1$
180      PRINT A2$
```

2. To use the MID$() command within a loop we can use the loop counter as an index to the starting character

```
100 REM **********************
101 REM * EXERCISE 2.2:2
```

```
102 REM *********************
103 :
110 REM -- with a loop --
120        A1$ = "CDEFGABCBAGFEDC"
130        FOR  I=5 TO 8
140          B$ = B$+MID$(A1$,I,1)
150        NEXT I
160        PRINT A1$
170        PRINT B$
```

or you can simply assign the length of the substring to the final index of the command.

```
100 REM **********************
101 REM * EXERCISE 2.2:2
102 REM **********************
103 :
110 REM -- without a loop --
120        A1$ ="CDEFGABCBAGFEDC"
130        B$ = MID$(A1$,5,4)
160        PRINT A1$
170        PRINT B$
```

3. To replace a portion of a string, we must first save the preceding substring (line 120) and the ensuing substring (line 130). We can then reassemble the finished string with a new substring added.

```
100   REM **********************
101   REM * EXERCISE 2.2:3
102   REM **********************
103   :
110        A1$ = "C+4 D+4 E4 G-4 F4 "
115        A2$ = "A+4 "
119   :
120        B$ = LEFT$(A1$,4)          :REM take left 4
130        C$ = MID$(A1$,9)           :REM take 9 to end
140        A3$ = B$+A2$+C$
159   :
160        PRINT A1$
170        PRINT A3$
```

4. The solution to this problem is similar to that of exercise number 1 (i.e., use the loop counter as an index value).

```
100 REM **********************
101 REM * EXERCISE 2.2:4
102 REM **********************
103 :
110     A1$ = "C+4 D+4 E4 G-4 F4 "
119 :
120     FOR  I=1 TO LEN (A1$)
130        PRINT MID$(A1$,I,1)
140     NEXT I
```

5. As in exercise 1, we begin by building substrings and, in this case, only printing those with a LENgth of more than 2, thus indicating the presence of an accidental.

```
100 REM **********************
101 REM * EXERCISE 2.2:5
102 REM **********************
103 :
110     A1$ = "C+4 D+4 E4 G-4 F4 "
120     A2$ = ""
129 :
130     FOR  I=1 TO LEN (A1$)
140        B$ = MID$(A1$,I,1)
145         IF B$<>" " THEN A2$ = A2$+B$ :GOTO 170
150           IF LEN(A2$)>2 THEN PRINT A2$
160           A2$ = ""
170     NEXT I
```

6. This solution is similar to others discussed previously. In this case line 150 checks each parsed character to see if it is a legitimate octave value and, if it is, stores it in the string A$.

```
100 REM **********************
101 REM * EXERCISE 2.2:6
102 REM **********************
```

```
103 :
110       A1$ = "C+4 D+4 E4 G-4 F4 "
120       A2$ = ""
129 :
130       FOR  I=1 TO LEN(A1$)
140         B$ = MID$(A1$,I,1)
150           IF B$>="0" AND B$<="9" THEN A2$ = A2$+B$
160       NEXT I
169 :
170       PRINT A1$
180       PRINT A2$
```

7. In this solution, as the loop counter moves progressively through the string, each character and the one that follows it are stored in the two variables A$ and B$. Be careful to stop the main loop one shy of the string length or line 145 will cause an error.

```
100 REM ***********************
101 REM * EXERCISE 2.2:7
102 REM ***********************
103 :
110       A1$ = "CDEAGFEGB"
129 :
130       FOR  I=1 TO LEN (A1$)-1
140         B$ = MID$(A1$,I,1)
145         C$ = MID$(A1$,I+1,1)
150           IF B$ > C$ THEN PRINT "FIRST"
160           IF B$ < C$ THEN PRINT "SECOND"
170           IF B$ = C$ THEN PRINT "EQUAL"
180       NEXT I
```

8. In this solution line 130 assigns the ASCII value of each character in the string to the variable A. Line 140 checks whether the value in A is a legal character (A–G) and, if it is, prints it.

```
100 REM ***********************
101 REM * EXERCISE 2.2:8
102 REM ***********************
103 :
```

```
110        Al$ = "C+ D+ E G- F "
119  :
120        FOR I=1 TO LEN(Al$)
130          A = ASC( MID$(Al$,I,1) )
140            IF A >=65 AND A<=71 THEN PRINT A
150        NEXT I
```

Exercises 2.3

1. This assignment first requires DEFining a mod7 function. The rest of the solution should be self-explanatory.

```
100 REM ***********************
101 REM * EXERCISE 2.3:1
102 REM ***********************
103 :
110        SCLE$ = "CDEFGABC"
120        DEF FN M7(Z) = INT((Z/7 - INT(Z/7))*7+.05)
129 :
130        FOR  I=1 TO LEN(SCLE$)
140          B$ = MID$(SCLE$,I,1)
150            PRINT B$,  FN M7( ASC(B$)-67 )
160        NEXT I
```

2. This exercise can be accomplished by simply moving sequentially through the string, checking each character to see if it represents a letter name (lc), and, if it is, acting upon it.

```
100 REM ***********************
101 REM * EXERCISE 2.3:2
102 REM ***********************
103 :
110        Al$ = "C+ D+ E G- F "
115        A2$ = ""
120        DEF FN M7(Z) = INT((Z/7 - INT(Z/7))*7+.05)
129 :
130        FOR  I=1 TO LEN(Al$)
140          B$ = MID$(Al$,I,1)
145            IF B$<"A" OR B$>"G" THEN 170
```

```
150            B = FN M7(ASC(B$)-67)
160            A2$ = A2$+SPACE$+STR$(B)
170         NEXT I
179 :
180         PRINT A1$
190         PRINT A2$
```

3-4. The following program represents one of many possible ways of programming these problems. Pay particular attention to the way that the code in the revised lines 2000 to 2090 in exercise 4 handles the problem of allowing for one incorrect response.

```
100 REM **************************
101 REM * EXERCISE 2.3:3
102 REM **************************
103 :
110         DEF FN M12(Z) = INT((Z/12-INT(Z/12))*12+.05)
119 :
120         GOSUB 1000              :REM instructions
140         GOSUB 2000              :REM drill
160         GOSUB 3000              :REM more?
165          IF FLG=1 THEN 140
179 :
180         PRINT "Goodbye!"
190         END
191 :
1000 REM    =======================
1001 REM    = instructions
1002 REM    =======================
1003 :
1010         PRINT "I'll show you a number, and you guess"
1020 :       PRINT "what MOD12 (simple) interval it is."
1029 :
1030         PRINT "<PRESS ANY KEY TO CONTINUE>..."
1040         GET Q$ :IF Q$="" THEN 1040
1089 :
1090         RETURN
1091 :
2000 REM    =======================
2001 REM    = drill
2002 REM    =======================
2003 :
2010         NUM = INT(RND(1)*(100-12))+12
2019 :
2020         PRINT "Your number is: ";NUM
2025         INPUT "What's your guess?";G
2030          IF G=FN M12(NUM) THEN PRINT "Correct!" :GOTO 2090
2040           PRINT "Try again"
2050           GOTO 2020
2089 :
2090         RETURN
2091 :
3000 REM    =======================
3001 REM    = more?
3002 REM    =======================
3003 :
3010         FLG=0
3020         PRINT "Want another number (Y/N)?"
3030         GET Q$ :IF Q$="" THEN 3030
3040          IF Q$="Y" THEN FLG=1
```

```
3089 :
3090        RETURN
3091 :
3092 REM **************************
```

Exercises 2.4

1. In order to accomplish the conversion required for this exercise, an algorithm must be designed that requires more information than we have available to us. In other words, letter-class codes cannot easily be converted to pitch-class values. One way of accomplishing this is with the use of a look-up table. Each member of the table will be accessed by the letter-class number (0–6). The information contained in the look-up table will be the pitch-class value corresponding to each letter class. In this way the lc sequence 0,1,2,3,4,5,6 can be converted to 0,2,4,5,7,9,11. Once the conversion is complete, the final value is derived by adding the accidental value.

```
100 REM **************************
101 REM * EXERCISE 2.4:1
102 REM **************************
103 :
110        DEF FN MD7(Z) = INT((Z/7-INT(Z/7))*7+.05)
119 :
120        DIM LT(6)
130        FOR  I=0 TO 6
140          READ LT(I)
150        NEXT I
160        DATA 0,2,4,5,7,9,11
199 :
200 REM -- conversion --
209 :
210        DATA C+,D+,E,G-,F,99
219 :
220        READ NTE$
222         IF NTE$="99" THEN 300
224 :
225        L$ = LEFT$(NTE$,1)
230        LC = FN MD7( ASC(L$)-67 )
240        A$ = RIGHT$(NTE$,1)
250         IF A$="+" THEN ACC = 1 :GOTO 260
255         IF A$="-" THEN ACC =-1 :GOTO 260
257          ACC=0
260        PC = LT(LC) + ACC
269 :
270        PRINT NTE$,"<";PC;",";LC;">"
280        GOTO 220
299 :
300        END
```

2. This exercise utilizes the same look-up table approach used in question 1. The code should be relatively self-explanatory. Of importance to note is the way in which the value of the second variable (B$) is moved into the first (A$) and a new second value is read after each interval is determined.

```
100 REM **************************
101 REM * EXERCISE 2.4:2
102 REM **************************
103 :
110        DEF FN MD7(Z) = INT((Z/7-INT(Z/7))*7+.05)
115        DEF FN M12(Z) = INT((Z/12-INT(Z/12))*12+.05)
```

```
119 :
120       DIM LT(6)
130       FOR  I=0 TO 6
140         READ LT(I)
150       NEXT I
160        DATA 0,2,4,5,7,9,11
199 :
200 REM -- conversion --
209 :
210       DATA C+,D+,E,G-,F,99
219 :
220       READ A$
230       READ B$ :IF B$="99" THEN 400
239 :
240 REM -- convert to BR code --
241 :
245       TEMP$ = A$ :GOSUB 1000 :P1=PC :L1=:C
250       TEMP$ = B$ :GOSUB 1000 :P2=PC :L2=:C
259 :
260 REM -- compute interval succession --
261 :
265       B1 = (10 * P1) + L1
270       B2 = (10 * P2) + L2
280       NTVL  = FN M12( ABS(P2-P1) )
290       NTVL$ = NTVL$+" "+STR$(NTVL)
299 :
300 REM -- swap values & continue --
301 :
310       A$ = B$
320       GOTO 230
399 :
400 REM -- print results --
401 :
410       PRINT NTVL$
489 :
490       END
491 :
1000 REM  =======================
1001 REM  = convert to BR code
1002 REM  =======================
1003 :
1010      LC = FN MD7( ASC(LEFT$(TEMP$,1))-67 )
1020      A$ = RIGHT$(TEMP$,1)
1030       IF A$="+" THEN ACC = 1 :GOTO 1040
1035       IF A$="-" THEN ACC =-1 :GOTO 1040
1040       ACC=0
1050      PC = LT(LC) + ACC
1089 :
1090 RETURN
1091 :
1092 REM************************

100 REM ************************
101 REM * EXERCISE 2.4:3
102 REM ************************
103 :
110      DEF FN M1000(Z) = INT((Z/1000-(INT(Z/1000))*1000+.05)
115      DEF FN MD7(Z) = INT((Z/7-INT(Z/7))*7+.05)
119 :
120      DIM LT(6)
130      FOR  I=0 TO 6
140        READ LT(I)
150      NEXT I
160       DATA 0,2,4,5,7,9,11
199 :
200 REM -- conversion --
209 :
```

```
210        DATA C+4,D+4,E3,G-3,F3,99
219 :
220        READ NTE$
222         IF NTE$="99" THEN 400
224 :
225        L$ = LEFT$(NTE$,1)
230        O$ = RIGHT$(NTE$,1)
235         IF LEN(NTE$) <=2 THEN 240
237          A$ = MID$(NTE$,2,1)
239 :
240 REM -- determine BR & CBR codes --
241 :
245        LC = FN MD7( ASC(L$)-67 )
250         IF A$=""THEN ACC=0 :GOTO 260
252          IF A$="+" THEN ACC = 1 :GOTO 260
254          IF A$="-" THEN ACC =-1 :GOTO 260
260        PC = LT(LC) + ACC
261 :
262        BR  = (10 * PC) + LC
265        CBR = (1000 * VAL(O$)) + BR
269 :
270 REM -- decode BR & OCT --
271 :
275        BR  = FN M1000(CBR)
280        OCT = INT(CBR/1000)
299 :
300 REM -- print results --
301 :
310        PRINT NTE$;" ";CBR;" ";BR;" ";OCT
320        GOTO 220
399 :
400        END
```

Exercises 3.1

1. The solution to this problem is actually quite simple. Instead of defining a constant value for MAX$ (as in the old line 410), use the value of CNT (length of the string) to define a dynamic value for MAX$.

```
100 REM ***********************
101 REM * EXERCISE 3.1:1
102 REM ***********************
103 :
110 REM -- change line 410 to:
409 :
410        DIM NTE$(50) :MIN$="2" :BLNK$=" "
489 :
490 REM -- then add line 555:
491 :
555        MAX$ = STR$(CNT)
```

2. To begin, a new method for encoding the DATA must be devised. In this case an "X" is placed at the end of each phrase and a "99" at the end of the total string. By redoing the main calling routine of the program (lines 1–99) we can set up a loop that will read the first phrase, manipulate it, and continue back to the top in order to repeat the process until the entire melody has been evaluated (or until the user chooses to "Q"uit).

```
1 REM ************************
2 REM * EXERCISE 3.1:2
3 REM ************************
4 :
5 REM -- redo the main routine as follows: --
10        GOSUB 400
15        READ CNT$ :CNT = VAL(CNT$)
17         IF CNT = 99 THEN 90
20        GOSUB 500
30        GOSUB 100
40        GOSUB 200
50        GOSUB 300
60         IF QFLG=1 THEN 90
70          GOTO 15
89 :
90        END
91 :
500 REM   ========================
501 REM   = read data into NTE$()
502 REM   ========================
503 :
505 REM -- redo this routine as follows: --
510        FLG$ = "X"
520        FOR  I=1 TO CNT
530          READ NTE$(CNT)
540           IF NTE$(CNT)=FLG$ THEN 590
550        NEXT I
560 :
570        DATA 5,F+4,C+4,D+4,E4,F4,X
572        DATA 6,C4,C+4,D4,F4,B3,C4,X
574        DATA (etc.)
578        DATA 99
589 :
590        RETURN
```

Exercises 3.2

1. Here is a simple solution to this exercise.

```
100 REM *********************
101 REM * EXERCISE 3.2:1
102 REM *********************
103 :
105     DEF FN M7(Z) = INT((Z/7-INT(Z/7))*7+0.05)
110     INPUT "TYPE A LETTER CLASS (0-6): ";LC
115      IF LC < 5 THEN NN = LC + 67 : GOTO 130
120      NN = LC + 60
130     PRINT LC;" CONVERTS TO THE LETTER NAME ";CHR$(NN)
```

```
139 :
140      INPUT "MORE (Y/N)?  ";Q$
150       IF Q$ = "Y" THEN 110
189 :
190 END
```

2. In this program the conversion to a pitch class number appears in line 140, and the accidental is found in line 150.

```
100 REM ***********************
101 REM * EXERCISE 3.2:2
102 REM ***********************
103 :
105      DEF FN M7(Z) = INT((Z/7-INT(Z/7))*7+0.05)
110      INPUT "ENTER A LETTER CLASS (0-6): ";LC
120      INPUT "ENTER A PITCH CLASS (0-11): ";PC
129 :
130 REM -- convert lc to pc --
139 :
140      CPC = INT((LC*1.8)+.5)
150      ACC = PC-CPC
159 :
160 REM -- print results --
161 :
170      PRINT CHR$(FN M7(LC+2)+65);
180       IF ACC<>0 THEN PRINT CHR$(ABS(ACC-44))
189 :
190      END
```

Exercises 3.3

1–2. The following code shows the modifications necessary to solve problems 1 and 2.

```
500 REM *********************
501 REM * EXERCISE 3.3:1-3.3:2
502 REM *********************
503 :
```

```
505        PRINT "TOTAL NUMBER OF PITCHES INCLUDING"
507        PRINT "TRAILER CHARACTERS:"; :INPUT NUM
510        DIM N$(NUM)
520        CMA$="," :X$="X"
524 :
529 :
530        FOR  I=1 TO NUM
540          INPUT "TYPE NOTE:";N$(NUM)
560        NEXT I
589 :
590        RETURN
```

Exercises 3.4

1–3. The following code will solve the problems presented. First, the duration value is converted to a number and stored in the array NTE() in line 2410. In subroutine 2000, the duration value will be placed in the variable L\$. It is assumed that 1 = whole note, 2 = half, 4 = quarter, 8 = eighth, and 16 = sixteenth, and that the duration values are placed on the right end of the input note string, e.g. C+48 = C-sharp, octave 4, eighth note. We have not provided for dotted values here.

```
2000 REM ************************
2001 REM * EXERCISE 3.4:1-3
2002 REM ************************
2003 :
2004 REM -- CHANGE OR ADD LINES AS FOLLOWS
2005 :
2030       IF LEN(ANS$)>6 THEN ER=1
2045       FOR  J = 1 TO LEN(ANS$)
2050         IF MID(ANS$,J,1)="+" OR MID(ANS$,J,1)="-"
                   THEN A$ = A$+ MID$ (ANS$,J,1) : GOTO 2070
2055       O$ = MID$(ANS$(J,1) : IF O$<"1" OR O$>"8" THEN ER=1
2060       L$ = RIGHT$(ANS$,LEN(ANS$)-J)
2065        IF L$<>"1" AND L$<>"2" AND L$<>"4" AND L$<>"8"
                   AND L$<>"16" THEN ER=1: GOTO 2080
2070       NEXT J
2089 :
2090       RETURN
2399 :
```

```
2400 REM ========================
2401 REM = COMPUTE DURATION
2402 REM ========================
2043 :
2410      NTE(n,LNTH) = 48/VAL(L$)
2489 :
2490      RETURN
```

4. The same style of input routine can be used for intervals also. Below is an example of such a routine.

```
2000 REM **********************
2001 REM * EXERCISE 3.4:4
2002 REM **********************
2003 :
2010      ER=0 :QUAL$="" :SZE$=""
2020      INPUT AN$ :IF AN$="" THEN 2020
2030       IF LEN(AN$)>3 THEN ER=1
2040      QUAL$ = LEFT$(AN$,LEN(AN$)-1)
2050       IF QUAL$="P" OR QUAL$="MA" OR QUAL$="MI" THEN 2060
2055       IF QUAL$="D" OR QUAL$="A" THEN 2060
2057         ER = 1
2060      SZE$ = RIGHT$(AN$,1)
2065       IF SZE$<"1" OR SZE$>"8" THEN ER=1
2089 :
2090      RETURN
```

Exercises 3.5

1. Using the statement supplied with question 1, code lines 200 to 299 will print a matrix by means of two nested loops. Using strings can also work effectively for formatting, although the code becomes much less readable, as in lines 300 to 380.

```
100 REM **********************
101 REM * EXERCISE 3.5:1
102 REM **********************
103 :
110 REM -- add the following: --
111 :
```

```
220 REM - - - - - - - - - - - - - - - - - - - - - -
221 REM - PRINT MATRIX
222 REM - - - - - - - - - - - - - - - - - - - - - -
223 :
230       FOR  I=1 TO 12
240         FOR  J=1 TO 12
250           PRINT TAB(3*J);ROW(I,J);
260         NEXT J
270         PRINT
280       NEXT I
299 :
300 REM - - or - -
323 :
330       FOR  I=1 TO 12
335         A$= ""
340         FOR  J=1 TO 12
345           TEMP$ = STR$(ROW(I,J))
350           A$ = A$ + TEMP$
355            IF LEN(TEMP$)=1 THEN A$ = A$+" "
360           PRINT A$;
370         NEXT J
375         PRINT
380       NEXT I
```

2. In this solution two arrays are used. The first (LT$) stores the character strings
   for each note, and the second (LT) stores the pc number that corresponds to its
   LT$ counterpart. Given a user-supplied LTTR/ACC code (e.g. C+), lines 200 to
   290 will find it in LT$ and then print the pc value as found in the parallel array
   LT.

```
100 REM ***********************
101 REM * EXERCISE 3.5:2
102 REM ***********************
103 :
110 REM - - LOAD ARRAYS - -
115       DIM LT$(1), LT(21)
119 :
120       FOR  I=1 TO 2
130         FOR  J=1 TO 21
```

```
140            IF I=1 THEN READ LT$(J)
145            IF I=2 THEN READ LT(J)
150          NEXT J
160        NEXT I
169 :
170        DATA C-,C,C+,D-,D,D+,E-,E,E+,F-,F,F+
175        DATA G-,G,G+,A-,A,A+,B-,B,B+
180        DATA 11,0,1,1,2,3,3,4,5,4,5
185        DATA 6,6,7,8,8,9,10,10,11,0
199 :
200 REM -- CONVERT LTTR/ACC TO PC --
201 :
210        INPUT NPT$
219 :
220        FOR  I=1 TO 21
230          IF NPT$ = LT$(I) THEN 260
240        NEXT I
250        PRINT "ILLEGAL CODE" :GOTO 210
259 :
260        PC = LT(I)
270        PRINT PC
289 :
290        END
```

3. Using the basic imbrication techniques discussed in Chapter 3, the following four routines will search the matrix for matches. Each routine uses a pair of nested loops, one representing rows and the other columns. If the search moves from left to right or from top to bottom (array indices will increase), then a simple loop structure will suffice. On the other hand, if the search moves from right to left or bottom to top then a decreasing loop counter is necessary (with a STEP −1 command).

```
100 REM ************************
101 REM * EXERCISE  3.5:3
102 REM ************************
103 :
300 REM -- input pattern --
301 :
310     INPUT "Input pattern: ";PTTRN$
399 :
400 REM -- search left to right --
401 :
410     FOR  R=1 TO 12
420       FOR  C1=1 TO 12-(LEN(PTTRN$)-1)
425         TEMP$ = ""
```

```
430                FOR  C2=C1 TO C1+(LEN(PTTRN$)-1)
440                   TEMP$ = TEMP$+STR$(ROW(R,C2))
450                NEXT C2
460                  IF TEMP$=PTTRN$ THEN PRINT "Found at P:";R;C1
470             NEXT C1
480          NEXT R
499 :
500 REM -- search right to left --
501 :
510          FOR  R=1 TO 12
520            FOR  C1=12 TO 1+(LEN(PTTRN$)-1) STEP-1
525              TEMP$ = ""
530              FOR  C2=C1 TO C1-(LEN(PTTRN$)-1) STEP-1
540                TEMP$ = TEMP$+STR$(ROW(R,C2))
550              NEXT C2
560                IF TEMP$=PTTRN$ THEN PRINT "Found at R:";R;C1
570            NEXT C1
580          NEXT R
599 :
600 REM -- search top to bottom --
601 :
610          FOR  C=1 TO 12
620            FOR  R1=1 TO 12-(LEN(PTTRN$)-1)
625              TEMP$ = ""
630              FOR  R2=R1 TO R1+(LEN(PTTRN$)-1)
640                TEMP$ = TEMP$+STR$(ROW(R2,C))
650              NEXT R2
660                IF TEMP$=PTTRN$ THEN PRINT "Found at R:";R2;C
670            NEXT R1
680          NEXT C
699 :
700 REM -- search bottom to top --
701 :
710          FOR  C=1 TO 12
720            FOR  R1=12 TO 1+(LEN(PTTRN$)-1) STEP-1
725              TEMP$ = ""
730              FOR  R2=R1 TO R1-(LEN(PTTRN$)-1) STEP-1
740                TEMP$ = TEMP$+STR$(ROW(R2,C))
750              NEXT R2
760                IF TEMP$=PTTRN$ THEN PRINT "Found at RI:";R2;C
770            NEXT R1
780          NEXT C
```

Exercises 3.6

1-3. Once a linked-list structure is created, moving around in it is actually quite simple. The code lines 500 to 690 will move the CRNT pointer forward or backwards in the list. If the Insert and Delete routines are used, they will simply operate on the list at CRNT.

```
500 REM ************************
501 REM * EXERCISES 3.6:1-3
502 REM ************************
503 :
510 REM -- delete/insert? --
511 :
515       ID$="" :NB$="" :ID=0 :NB=0
520       INPUT "Print the melody (N)ormal or (B)ackwards?";NB$
525         IF NB$="N" THEN NB=1 :GOTO 540
530         IF NB$="B" THEN NB=2 :GOTO 540
535         GOTO 515
539 :
540       INPUT "(I)nsert of (D)elete a note?";ID$
545         IF ID$="I" THEN ID=1
```

```
550        IF ID$="D" THEN ID=2
555        IF ID = 0  THEN 570
560         INPUT "Which note ?";NTE
569 :
570        ON NB GOSUB 600, 700
591 :
600 REM    -----------------------
601 REM    - print list (N)ormally
602 REM    -----------------------
603 :
610         CRNT = NTE(CRNT,RL)
620          IF NTE(CRNT,RL)=0 THEN 690
630           PRINT NTE(CRNT,LTTR)...etc.
680          IF CRNT=NTE THEN ON ID GOSUB (insert), (delete)
689 :
690         RETURN
691 :
700 REM    -----------------------
701 REM    - print list (B)ackwards
702 REM    -----------------------
703 :
710         CRNT = NTE(CRNT,LL)
720          IF NTE(CRNT,LL)=0 THEN 790
730           PRINT NTE(CRNT,LTTR)...etc.
780          IF CRNT=NTE THEN ON ID GOSUB (insert), (delete)
789 :
790         RETURN
791 :
792 REM ************************
```

Exercises 4.1

1. This problem can be easily solved by moving the default value for a natural from 1 to 2, a flat from 0 to 1, and a sharp from 2 to 3. This process now leaves the values zero for double flat and 4 for double sharp. The revised code would look like this:

E--	B--	F-	C-	G-	D-	A-	E-	B-	F	C	etc.
20	60	31	01	41	11	51	21	61	32	02	etc.

2. There are numerous ways in which this program can be accomplished. While we will not make any attempt to give actual code, we do suggest that you follow the basic design procedures presented in Chapter 1 and style your program after the other program examples presented throughout this book.

Exercises 4.2

1. Numerous solutions are possible for this exercise. The following pseudo-code may be used as a guide for implementing an actual program.

```
** main program ********
   -initialize all variables
   -GOSUB routine to enter data
```

*Code for these subroutines can be taken from Ex. 3.23 in Chapter 3 (p. 99).

```
   -GOSUB routine to edit data
   -GOSUB routine to save data
   -quit
== enter data ==
   -choose between new data or existing file
   -based on choice gosub NEW,OLD
   -exit
   - - NEW - -
       -initialize size of class
       -enter data for student #1
       -if not QUIT then continue
       -exit
   - - OLD - -
        -input file name
        -open disk file
        -read file
        -close file
        -exit
== edit data ==
   -choose student by name or number
   -retrieve data for student
   -gosub EDIT
   -more? if YES then continue
   -exit
   - - EDIT - -
       -reenter student data
       -check data
       -if wrong then repeat
       -exit
== save file ==
   -open disk file
   -write student data
   -verify
   -close file
   -exit
* * * * * * * * * * * * * * * * * * * * * * *
```

2. Once a disk file is open the following program can be used to write it to a disk.

```
100 REM ************************
101 REM * SAVE LINKED-LIST
102 REM ************************
103 :
110     CRNT = 0
114 :
115     CRNT = NTE(CRNT,RL)
120      IF CRNT = 0 THEN 190
129 :
130     write NTE(CRNT,LTTR)
140     write NTE(CRNT,ACC)
150     write NTE(CRNT,OCT)
160     write NTE(CRNT,LNTH)
170     write NTE(CRNT,XPNTR)
175     write NTE(CRNT,RL)
179 :
180     GOTO 115
189 :
190     RETURN
```

The next subroutine will read in a linked-list melody. It could be asked why the .RL was saved in the above routine. When reading the file in the next routine there is no way to determine when the end of the melody has been reached unless we have some marker. In this case, the .RL values are read back in. When a zero (0) is encountered the melody is complete.

```
100 REM ************************
101 REM * READ LINKED-LIST
102 REM ************************
103 :
110     CRNT = 0 :NXT = 1
119 :
120     read NTE(NXT,LTTR)
130     read NTE(NXT,ACC)
140     read NTE(NXT,OCT)
150     read NTE(NXT,LNTH)
160     read NTE(NXT,XPNTR)
165     read NTE(NXT,RL)
```

```
169 :
170        GOSUB insert routine
180          IF RL = 0 THEN 190
185        GOTO 120
189 :
190        RETURN
```

Exercises 5.1

1. This is a relatively simple task once the concept of the line command is learned. (Lower case commands are pseudo-commands and will have to be replaced with machine specific code.)

```
100 REM *********************
101 REM * EXERCISE 5.1:1
102 REM *********************
103 :
500 REM -- single border --
509 :
510        X=1 :Y=1
520        line (X,Y) to (X+318,Y) to (X+318,Y+197) to (X,Y+197)
              to (X,Y)
529 :
530 REM -- double border --
539 :
540        line (X+2,Y+2) to (X+316,Y+2) to (X+316,Y+195)
              to (X+2,Y+195) to (X+2,Y+2)
559 :
560 REM *********************
```

2. In this exercise use the line command to draw your name. Try to connect as many points as you can to avoid excessive code. For example, the letter "M" could be plotted as:

```
100   line (X,Y) to (X,Y-20) to (X+10,Y-10)
           to (X+20,Y-20) to (X+20,Y)
```

3. The following routine will add a vertical line at the left edge of each staff and two vertical lines (one single width and the other double) at the right edge of each

staff. Note that offsets are used so that the same X,Y values used to draw the
staff will suffice for the bar lines.

```
100 REM ***********************
101 REM * EXERCISE 5.1:3
102 REM ***********************
103 :
110 REM -- modify the following subroutine: --
1300 REM ========================
1301 REM = draw staff lines
1302 REM ========================
1303 :
1310     FOR J=1 TO NUM
1320       FOR I=0 TO 24 STEP 6
1330         line (X,Y+I) to (X+200,Y+I)
1340       NEXT I
1345       GOSUB 1400          :REM draw bar lines
1350       Y = Y + 36
1360     NEXT J
1389 :
1390     RETURN
1391 :
1392 REM -- add this subroutine: --
1393 :
1400 REM   ------------------------
1401 REM   - draw bar lines
1402 REM   ------------------------
1403 :
1410       line (X,Y) to (X,Y+24)
1419 :
1420       line (X+200,Y) to (X+200,Y+24)
1430       line (X+199,Y) to (X+199,Y+24)
1440       line (X+197,Y) to (X+197,Y+24)
1489 :
1490       RETURN
1491 :
1492 REM ========================
```

Exercises 5.2

1. All a user would have to do is input the following information: (1) NUM: number of staffs; and (2) CLF(n): clef numbers for each staff.

```
100 REM ***********************
101 REM * input staff/clef info
102 REM ***********************
103 :
110       INPUT "number of staves:";NUM
119 :
120       FOR  I=1 TO NUM
130         INPUT "clef:";CLF(I)
140       NEXT I
189 :
190       RETURN
```

Exercises 5.3

1. This should be an easy problem, as most of the necessary code is already present. Simply change line 2530 to read

```
2530 IF NTE(n,ACC) <> 0 THEN GOSUB 2600 :REM draw accidental
```

Then add this subroutine:

```
2600 REM ======================
2601 REM = draw accidentals
2602 REM ======================
2603 :
2610       ON NTE(n,ACC)+2 GOTO 2630,2690,2640
2619 :
2630       draw FLAT at (X-FCTR,Y) :GOTO 2690
2640       draw SHARP at (X-FCTR,Y) :GOTO 2690
2689 :
2690       RETURN
```

It is important to note that the accidental shapes should be drawn so that one factor (FCTR) value will work for all. Also notice that, for the formula to be universal, it needs to supply a jump address for the natural note. Even though line 2530 will keep a natural note from entering this routine, we need a "dummy" address so that the values for flats and sharps will match the appropriate jump addresses.

2. The secret to this problem is to read more than one note value and store them for later use. In the following example the user can input NUM notes to be stored one at a time in the array TEMP$(). From within a second loop, the values are pulled out one at a time, computed, and drawn.

```
100   REM *********************
101   REM * EXERCISE 5.3:2
102   REM *********************
103   :
110   REM -- change the following subroutine: --
111   :
500   REM =========================
501   REM = enter & compute note values
502   REM =========================
503   :
510        FOR  I=1 TO NUM
520           GOSUB 2000                       :REM get input
525           TEMP$(I) = AN$
530        NEXT I
539   :
540        FOR  I=1 TO NUM
545          AN$ = TEMP$(I)
550           GOSUB 2100                       :REM compute LTTR
555           GOSUB 2200                       :REM compute ACC
560           GOSUB 2300                       :REM compute OCT
565           GOSUB 2500                       :REM draw notes
570        NEXT I
589   :
590        END
```

3. This problem takes the previous example and adds line 590, which calls a new evaluation subroutine based on the triad algorithm defined earlier. In the new subroutine a loop is used to concatenate the user's input strings, followed by the building of a second string pulled from a circle-of-fifths look-up table (LT$). The two strings are then compared.

```
100 REM *************************
101 REM * EXERCISE 5.3:3
102 REM *************************
103 :
110 REM -- change the following subroutine: --
111 :
500 REM =======================
501 REM = enter & compute note values
502 REM =======================
503 :
510       FOR  I=1 TO NUM
520         GOSUB 2000          :REM get input
525         TEMP$(I) = AN$
530       NEXT I
539 :
540       FOR  I=1 TO NUM
545         AN$ = TEMP$(I)
550         GOSUB 2100          :REM compute LTTR
555         GOSUB 2200          :REM compute ACC
560         GOSUB 2300          :REM compute OCT
565         GOSUB 2500          :REM draw notes
570       NEXT I
590       GOSUB 2600            :REM evaluate
594 :
595       END
599 :
600 REM -- change this subroutine also: --
601 :
2600 REM   -----------------------
2601 REM   - evaluate triad
2602 REM   -----------------------
2603 :
2610       R=0 :T=4 :F=1         :REM major triad offsets
2620       FOR I=1 TO NUM
2625         A2$ = A2$+TEMP$(I)
2630       NEXT I
2639 :
2640       AN$ = LT$(STRT+R) + LT$(STRT+T) + LT$(STRT+F)
2650       IF AN$=A2$ THEN PRINT "Correct!" :GOTO 2660
2655         PRINT "Wrong! The answer is: ";AN$
2659 :
2660       RETURN
```

Exercises 5.4

1. The formula for this one is actually quite simple: result = INT(X/24).
   Try it with all five values and see if it doesn't work!
2. The solution to this problem lies in the use of a look-up table array(LT) which
   will contain the X value for each move. The following code is a modification of
   the routine given in the chapter.

```
1400 REM *********************
1401 REM * arrow right
1402 REM *********************
1403 :
1410       XOLD = XPNTR :YOLD = YPNTR
```

```
1415        PNTR = PNTR + 1
1420        XPNTR = LT(PNTR)
1430         IF XPNTR < RHT THEN 1490
1440           PNTR = 1
1450           XPNTR = LT(PNTR)
1489 :
1490        RETURN
```

In this subroutine two pointers are kept. The first, XPNTR, holds the actual plot coordinate for the arrow. The second, PNTR, keeps track of which subscript of the array LT() keeps the current XPNTR value.

Exercises 5.5

1. This problem is very similar to that of question 1 in Exercises 5.3.

```
100 REM ***********************
101 REM * EXERCISE 5.5:1
102 REM ***********************
103 :
110 REM -- change the following: --
111 :
3600 REM   -----------------------
3601 REM   - draw accidentals
3602 REM   -----------------------
3603 :
3610        ON NTE(CRNT,ACC)+3 GOSUB 3650,3660,3670,3680,3690
3639 :
3640        RETURN
3641 :
3650          draw DF$ at (XDRW-12,YDRW)  :RETURN
3660          draw F$  at (XDRW-12,YDRW)  :RETURN
3670          draw N$  at (XDRW-12,YDRW)  :RETURN
3680          draw S$  at (XDRW-12,YDRW)  :RETURN
3690          draw DS$ at (XDRW-12,YDRW)  :RETURN
```

2. To implement a play function the following should be done:
   a. Insert a line of code in the GET routine that will recognize the "P" key and call the appropriate subroutine.
   b. Write a conversion routine that will take all the notes of the melody from the

linked-list, convert them one at a time to values useable for the sound routine, and store them.

c. Take the stored values and send them to an actual play routine.

d. If graphic display is required then the melody must be redrawn so that the beginning is showing on the screen, and a routine must be devised to scroll the melody to the next note as each pitch is played.

Exercises 6.1

2. The overall structure of the program should be:

Initialization/Title page
Translate entire melody
Play entire melody

The only initialization necessary is to set a counter (e.g. CNT) to -1, and the title page is a simple matter. Following is the subroutine for playing the translated melody, which is stored in an array SND.

```
7000 REM ================
7001 REM = Play melody
7002 REM ================
7003 :
7010     FOR  I = 1 TO (CNT + 1) / 2
7020         SOUND SND(2 * I - 1), SND(2 * I)
7030     NEXT I
7035 :
7090     RETURN
7091 :
```

The translation step is the most difficult. Basically, it involves removing (parsing) characters from the PLAY string and branching to different subroutines to process the string information. Here is the translation routine pseudo-code:

Begin loop

    FCH\$ = LEFT\$(M\$,1): REM first character of remaining string
      If FCH\$ = "" then exit loop (string processed)
      If FCH\$ = " " then ignore : M\$ = RIGHT\$(M\$,LEN(M\$)−1):
          Goto End loop
      If FCH\$ = "O" then remove first two characters from string:
          Extract octave number (second character):

Gosub octave subroutine with O$ = octave number
string:
Goto End loop

If FCH$ = ">" or "<" then remove first character from string:
Gosub octave subroutine with O$ = ">" or "<":
Goto End loop

If FCH$ = "A","B",...,"G" then remove two to four characters
from the string (up to the next " ","O",">","<",
pitch letter name, or the end of string):
Gosub Translate/Store subroutine:
Goto End loop

else error (string too complex to translate)

End loop

Two local subroutines are needed, one to change the octave number, the other
to translate and store pitches and durations.

```
5500 REM ----------------
5501 REM - Change octave number
5502 REM ----------------
5503 :
5510        IF O$ = ">" OR O$ = "<" THEN OCT = OCT + (ASC(O$)-61):
                  GOTO 5590
5515 :
5520        OCT = VAL(O$)
5589 :
5590        RETURN
5591 :
6000 REM ----------------
6001 REM - Translate and store pitches and durations
6002 REM ----------------
6003 :
6010        CNT = CNT + 2                 :REM increment counter
6020 :
6030        L$ = LEFT$(N$,1)
6040        LC = FN M7(ASC(L$) - 67)      :REM Letter Class (0-7)
6050        PC = INT(1.8 * LC + .05)      :REM Pitch Class (0-11)
6060        N$ = RIGHT$(N$,LEN(N$)-1)
6065 :
6070         IF ASC(LEFT$(N$),1)  > 48 THEN 6120
6080        A$ = LEFT(N$,1)               :REM process accidental
6090         IF A$ = "-" THEN PC = PC - 1 : GOTO 6110
6100        PC = PC + 1
6110        N$ = RIGHT$(N$,LEN(N$)-1)
6115 :
6120 REM--Convert and store pitch
6125 :
6130        HS = PC + 12 * (OCT -1)        :REM half steps
6135 :
6136 REM--C1 = 32.703192 Hz
6137 REM--12th root of 2 = 1.0594631
6138 :
6140        FRQ = 32.703192 * HS ∧ 1.0594631 :REM equal tempered
6150        SNC(CNT) = FRQ
6155 :
6160 REM--Convert and store duration
6161 REM--M.M. quarter = 60
6165 :
6170        D = VAL(N$)
6175        DRTN = 4/D * 18.2             :REM ticks
6180        SND(CNT+1) = DRTN
6189 :
6190        RETURN
6191 :
```

Exercises 6.2

Bach Invention BWV 779

3. M$ = "(CLR) 1 b5(F2) g5(F4) Z(F2) e5(F2) c6(F4) Z(F2)
                 a5(F2) F5(F4) Z(F2) D5(F2) b̶5(F4) Z(F2)
                 e6(F2) e5(F4) Z(F2) g5(F2) b5(F4) Z(F2)
                 d6(F2) d5(F4) Z(F2) f5(F2) a5(F4)

   (CLR)G"

4. ENVELOPE 1,4,4,5,15
    WAVE   1,01000000
5. ENVELOPE 3,6,1,8,12
    WAVE   3,00010000

Exercises 6.3

1. A4 (440 Hz) ; 2 seconds
2. POKE 0,132 : POKE 1,1   (From Table 6.2)
    POKE 2,17 : POKE 3,3*

* 1♪ * $\dfrac{1\text{♩}}{2\text{♪}}$ * $\dfrac{1 \text{ minute}}{84 \text{ ♩}}$ * $\dfrac{60 \text{ seconds}}{1 \text{ minute}}$ * $\dfrac{1480 \text{ (from Table 6.2)}}{1 \text{ second}}$ =

   528.57 + 256 (offset) = 784.57
   round to 785 and apply lines 1020–1025
3. POKE 0,202 : POKE 1,2   (From Table 6.2)
    POKE 2,144 : POKE 3,2*

* 1♩ * $\dfrac{2\text{♩}}{1\text{♩}}$ * $\dfrac{1 \text{ minute}}{132\text{♩}}$ * $\dfrac{60 \text{ seconds}}{1 \text{ minute}}$ * $\dfrac{440 \text{ (from Table 6.2)}}{1 \text{ second}}$ =

   400 + 256 (offset) = 656
   apply lines 1020–1025

Exercises 6.4

1. It reduces the octave number by 1, because ASA octave 4 is IBM octave 3.
2. **7710:** ensures that LF is from 65 (ASC of "a") to 71 (ASC of "g"), whether lower case or upper case (whose ASC values are 128 higher) is entered; change to upper case occurs only if an accidental warrants it.

   7715: no adjustment is needed if no accidental is present.

   7720: if a sharp is present, change the LF character code from lower case to upper case (remember that for the C-64, "a" = A natural and "A" = A sharp).

   7730: a flat is present; most characters will be changed to one letter back in the alphabet and to upper case; therefore add 127 to the LF character code, for example, E flat (ASC 69 = "e") becomes D sharp (69 + 127 = 196 = "D").

7740: there are some exceptions:

A flat ("a" = 65 + 127 = 192) must become

G sharp ("G" = 197)

7750: and the other exceptions are:

C flat ("c" = 67 + 127 = 194) becomes B natural
("b" = 194 − 128 = 66), and

F flat ("f" = 70 + 127 = 197) becomes E natural
("e" = 197 − 128 = 69).

3. SND(23) will be assigned the data for G sharp 3 / A flat 3; therefore, SND(23,PHIGH) will be 2.

4. *LETTER CLASS = NTE$(n,LTTR)* * *1.8 +* *0.5 INT of (= PITCH CLASS)*

C	0	0	0.5	0
D	1	1.8	2.3	2
E	2	3.6	4.1	4
F	3	5.4	5.9	5
G	4	7.2	7.7	7
A	5	9.0	9.5	9
B	6	10.8	11.3	11

INDEX

A

Accidental sign to accidental number conversion, 35, 57

Acoustics, musical, 148–52

Action block, 8–9

Alphanumeric music representation codes. *See* DARMS code; LTTR/ACC/OCT/ LNTH code; MUSTRAN code

Animation, 119–20

Arrays, 40
    one-dimensional, 40–42
    rules for use, 41–42
    two-dimensional, 54–55

ASA octave numbers, 152

ASC(), 26, 260

ASCII character codes, 26

Attack, 151, 161

B

Bach, Johann Sebastian (1685–1750)
    Fugue in C minor, 157
    Two Part Invention in F major, 167

BASIC computer programming language, ix, 254–68

BASIC string functions, 24–27, 260–61

Bauer-Mengelberg, Stefan, 20

Beethoven, Ludwig von (1770–1827)
    Symphony No. 9, Ode to Joy, 155

Blocks, nested, 8

Brahms, Johannes (1833–1897)
    Symphony No. 4 in E minor, 167

Branch block, 9

Brinkman's Binomial Representation (BR) code, 36–38

C

CAI (computer-assisted instruction)
    design principles, 76
    drill and practice, 75
    games, 75–76
    simulation, 76
    steps for designing a lesson, 77–82
    tutorial, 76

Calling program portion. *See* main program portion